T5-AFU-280

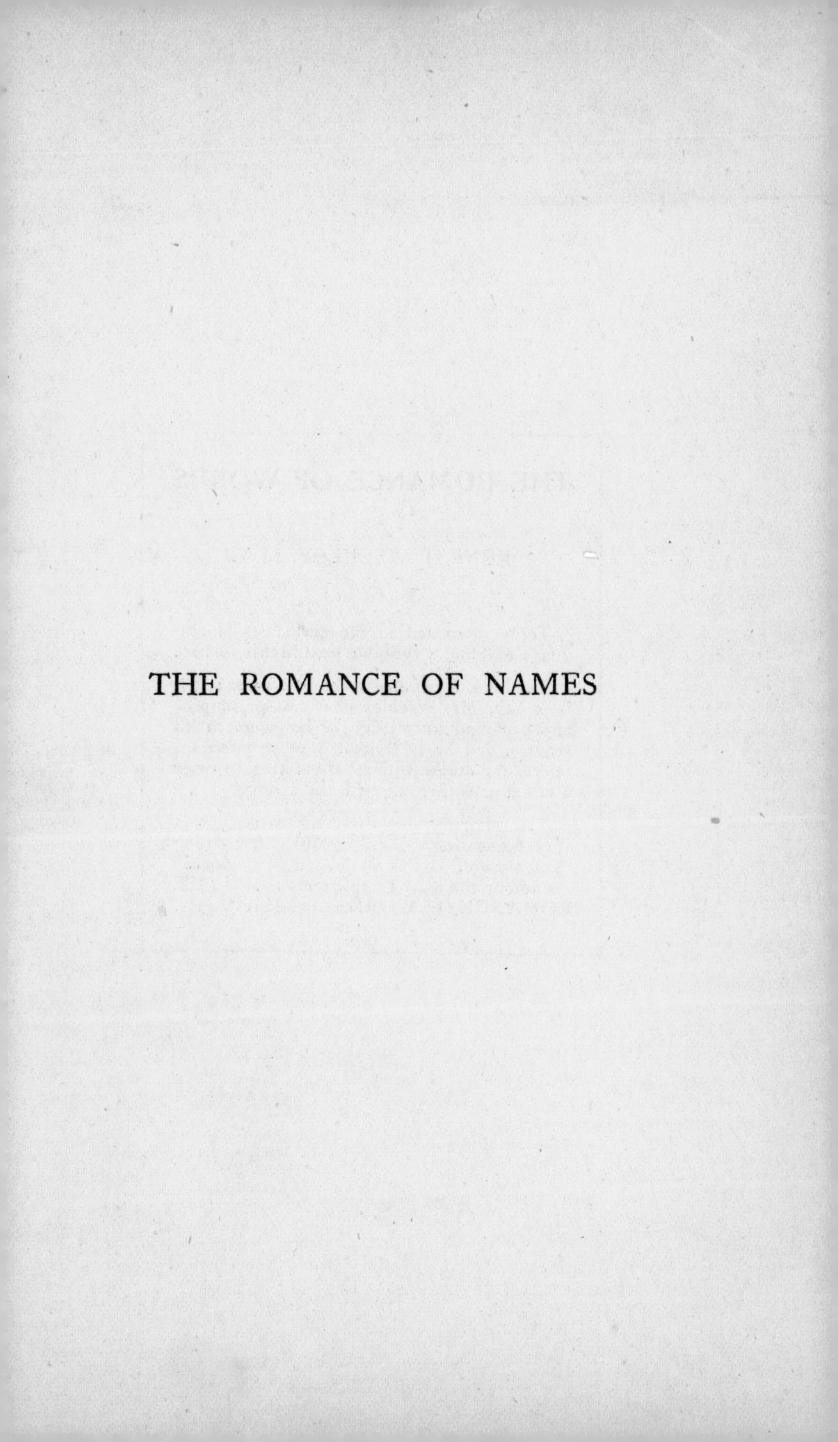

THE ROMANCE OF NAMES

THE ROMANCE OF NAMES

BY

ERNEST WEEKLEY, M.A.

PROFESSOR OF FRENCH AND HEAD OF THE MODERN LANGUAGE DEPARTMENT AT UNIVERSITY COLLEGE, NOTTINGHAM; SOMETIME SCHOLAR OF TRINITY COLLEGE, CAMBRIDGE

"I conceive, I say, that my descent from that great restorer of learning is more creditable to me as a man of letters than if I had numbered in my genealogy all the brawling, bullet-headed, iron-fisted old Gothic barons since the days of Crentheminachcryme—not one of whom, I suppose, could write his own name."

(SCOTT, *The Antiquary*, ch. vi.)

LONDON

JOHN MURRAY, ALBEMARLE STREET, W.

1914

PREFACE

THE interpretation of personal names has always had an attraction for the learned and others, but the first attempts to classify and explain our English surnames date, so far as my knowledge goes, from 1605. In that year Verstegan published his *Restitution of Decayed Intelligence,* which contains chapters on both font-names and surnames, and about the same time appeared Camden's *Remains Concerning Britain,* in which the same subjects are treated much more fully. Both of these learned antiquaries make excellent reading, and much curious information may be gleaned from their pages, especially those of Camden, whose position as Clarencieux King-at-Arms gave him exceptional opportunities for genealogical research. From the philological point of view they are of course untrustworthy, though less so than most modern writers on the same subject.

About the middle of the nineteenth century, the period of Archbishop Trench and Canon Taylor, began a kind of boom in works of this kind, and books on surnames are now numerous. But of all these industrious compilers one only, Bardsley, can be taken seriously. His *Dictionary of English Surnames,* published (Oxford Press, 1901) from his notes some years after his death, is invaluable to students. It represents the results of twenty years' conscientious research among early rolls and registers, the explanations given being usually supported by medieval instances. But it cannot be used uncritically, for the author does not appear to have been either a linguist or a philologist, and, although he usually refrains from etymological conjecture, he occasionally ventures with disastrous results. Thus, to take a few instances, he identifies *Prust* with *Priest,* but the medieval *le prust* is quite obviously the Norman form of Old Fr. *le proust,* the provost. He attempts to connect *Pullen* with the archaic Eng. *pullen,* poultry; but his early examples, *le pulein, polayn,* etc., are of course Fr. *Poulain,* i.e. *Colt.* Under *Fallows,* explained as "fallow lands," he quotes three examples of *de la faleyse,* i.e. Fr. *Falaise,* corresponding to our *Cliff, Cleeve,* etc.; *Pochin,* explained as the diminutive of some personal name, is the Norman form of the famous name *Poussin,* i.e. *Chick.* Or, coming to native instances, *le wenchel,* a medieval prototype of *Winkle,* is explained as for "periwinkle," whereas it is a common Middle-English word, originally a diminutive of *wench,* and means *Child.* The obsolete *Swordslipper,* now only *Slipper,* which he interprets as a maker of "sword-slips," orsheaths, was really a sword-sharpener, from Mid. Eng. *slipen,* cognate with Old Du. *slijpen,* to polish, sharpen, and Ger. *schleifen.* Sometimes a very simple problem is left unexplained, *e.g.* in the case of the name *Tyas,* where the medieval instances of *le tyeis* are to a student of Old French clearly *le tieis* or *tiois,* i.e. the German, cognate with Ger. *deutsch* and Ital. *tedesco.*

These examples are quoted, not in depreciation of a conscientious student to whose work my own compilation is greatly indebted, but merely to show that the etymological study of surnames has scarcely been touched at present, except by writers to whom philology is an unknown science. I have inserted, as a specimen problem (ch. xvi.), a little disquisition on the name *Rutter,* a cursory perusal of which will convince most readers that it is not much use making shots in this subject.

My aim has been to steer a clear course between a too learned and a too superficial treatment, and rather to show how surnames are formed than to adduce innumerable examples which the reader should be able to solve for himself. I have made no attempt to collect curious names, but have taken those which occur in the *London Directory* (1908) or have caught my eye in the newspaper or the streets. To go into proofs would have swelled the book beyond all reasonable proportions, but the reader may assume that, in the case of any derivation not expressly stated as a conjecture, the connecting links exist. In the various classes of names, I have intentionally omitted all that is obvious, except in the rather frequent case of the obvious being wrong. The index, which I have tried to make complete, is intended to replace to some extent those cross-references which are useful to students but irritating to the general reader. Hundreds of names are susceptible of two, three, or more explanations, and I do not profess to be exhaustive.

The subject-matter is divided into a number of rather short chapters, dealing with the various classes and subdivisions into which surnames fall; but the natural association which exists between names has often prevailed over rigid classification. The quotations by which obsolete words are illustrated are taken as far as possible from Chaucer, whose writings date from the very period when our surnames were gradually becoming hereditary. I have also quoted extensively from the *Promptorium Parvulorum*, our earliest English-Latin Dictionary (1440).

In ch. vii, on Anglo-Saxon names, I have obtained some help from a paper by the late Professor Skeat (*Transactions of the Philological Society*, 1907–10, pp. 57–85) and from the materials contained in Searle's valuable *Onomasticon Anglo-Saxonicum* (Cambridge, 1897). Among several works which I have consulted on French and German family names, the most useful have been Heintze's *Deutsche Familiennamen*, 3rd ed. (Halle a. S., 1908) and Kremers' *Beiträge zur Erforschung der französischen Familiennamen* (Bonn, 1910). The comparative method which I have adopted, especially in explaining nicknames (ch. xxi), will be found, I think, to clear up a good many dark points. Of books on names published in this country, only Bardsley's Dictionary has been of any considerable assistance, though I have gleaned some scraps of information here and there from other compilations. My real sources have been the lists of medieval names found in Domesday Book, the Pipe Rolls, the Hundred Rolls, and in the numerous historical records published by the Government and by various antiquarian societies.

ERNEST WEEKLEY.

NOTTINGHAM,
September 1913.

CONTENTS

CHAPTER XXI

CHAPTER XXII

CHAPTER XXIII

THE following dictionaries are quoted without further reference:

Promptorium Parvulorum (1440), ed. Mayhew (E.E.T.S., 1908).

PALSGRAVE, *L'Esclarcissement de la langue francoyse* (1530), ed. Génin (Paris, 1852).

COOPER, *Thesaurus Linguæ Romanæ et Britannicæ* (London, 1573).

COTGRAVE, *A Dictionarie of the French and English Tongues* (London, 1611).

The Middle English quotations, except where otherwise stated, are from Chaucer, the references being to the Globe edition.

THE ROMANCE OF NAMES

CHAPTER I

OF SURNAMES IN GENERAL

"The French and we termed them *Surnames*, not because they are the names of the *Sire*, or the father, but because they are *super-added* to Christian names."

(CAMDEN, *Remains concerning Britain.*)

THE study of the origin of family names is at the same time quite simple and very difficult. Its simplicity consists in the fact that surnames can only come into existence in certain well-understood ways. Its difficulty is due to the extraordinary perversions which names undergo in common speech, to the orthographic uncertainty of our ancestors, to the frequent coalescence of two or more names of quite different origin, and to the multitudinous forms which one single name can assume, such forms being due to local pronunciation, accidents of spelling, date of assumption, and many minor causes. It must always be remembered that the majority of our surnames come from the various dialects of Middle English, *i.e.* of a language very different from our own in spelling and sound, full of words that are now obsolete, and of others which have completely changed their form and meaning.

If we take any medieval roll of names, we see almost at a glance that four such individuals as—

John *filius Simon*
William *de la Moor*
Richard *le Spicer*
Robert *le Long*

exhaust the possibilities of English name-making—*i.e.* that every surname must be (i) personal, from a sire or ancestor, (ii) local, from place of residence,[1] (iii) occupative, from trade or office, (iv) a nickname, from bodily attributes, character, etc.

This can easily be illustrated from any list of names taken at random. The Rugby team chosen to represent the East Midlands against Kent (January 22, 1913) consisted of the following fifteen names: *Hancock; Mobbs, Poulton, Hudson, Cook; Watson, Earl; Bull, Muddiman, Collins, Tebbitt, Lacey, Hall, Osborne, Manton.* Some of these are simple, but others require a little knowledge for their explanation. There are seven personal names, and the first of these, *Hancock*, is rather a problem. This is usually explained as from Flemish *Hanke*, Johnny, while the origin of the suffix *-cock* has never been very clearly accounted for (see p. 65). With *Hancock* we may compare *Hankin.*

[1] This is by far the largest class, counting by names, not individuals, and many names for which I give another explanation have also a local origin. Thus, when I say that *Ely* is Old Fr. Élie, *i.e.* Elias, I assume that the reader will know without being told that it must have an alternative explanation from Ely in ambridgeshire.

But, while the Flemish derivation is possible for these two names, it will not explain *Hanson*,[1] which sometimes becomes *Hansom* (p. 36). According to Camden, there is evidence that *Han* was also used as a rimed form of *Ran*, short for Ranolf and Randolf (cf. Hob from Robert, Hick from Richard), very popular names in the north during the surname period. In *Hankin* and *Hancock* this *Han* would naturally coalesce with the Flemish *Hanke*. This would also explain the names *Hand* for *Rand*, and *Hands*, *Hance* for *Rands*, *Rance*. *Mobbs* is the same as *Mabbs* (cf. Moggy for Maggy), and *Mabbs* is the genitive of Mab, *i.e.* Mabel, for Amabel. We have the diminutive in *Mappin* and the patronymic in *Mapleson*. *Hudson* is the son of Hud, a very common medieval name, which seems to represent Anglo-Saxon Hudda (p. 75), though there is some evidence that it was also used for Richard. *Watson* is the son of *Wat*, i.e. Walter, from the Old N.E. Fr. Wautier (Gautier), regularly pronounced Water at one time—

> "My name is *Walter* Whitmore.
> How now! Why start'st thou? What! doth death affright?
> *Suffolk*. Thy name affrights me, in whose sound is death.
> A cunning man did calculate my birth,
> And told me that by *water* I should die."
>
> (2 *Henry VI*, iv. 1.)

Hence the name *Waters*, which has not usually any connection with water; while *Waterman*, though sometimes occupative, is also formed from Walter, like *Hickman* from Hick (see p. 64). *Collins* is from Colin, a French diminutive of Col, *i.e.* Nicol or Nicolas.

[1] The existence of such place-names as *Hanbury*, *Hanley*, *Hanwell*, *Hanworth*, *Handsworth*, etc., precludes a purely Flemish origin for *Han*.

Tebbitt is a diminutive of Theobald, a favourite medieval name which had the shortened forms *Teb, Tib, Tub,* whence a number of derivatives. But names in *Teb-* and *Tib-* may also come from Isabel (p. 94). *Osborne* is the Anglo-Saxon name Osbeorn.

Of course, each of these personal names has a meaning, *e.g.* Amabel, ultimately Latin, means lovable, and Walter, a Germanic name, means "rule army" (Modern Ger. *walten* and *Heer*), but the discussion of such meanings lies outside our subject. It is, in fact, sometimes difficult to distinguish between the personal name and the nickname. Thus *Pagan,* whence *Payn,* with its diminutives *Pannell, Pennell,* etc., *Gold, Good, German,* whence *Jermyn, Jarman,* and many other apparent nicknames, occur as personal names in the earliest records. Their etymological origin is in any case the same as if they were nicknames.

To return to our football team, *Poulton, Lacey, Hall,* and *Manton* are local. There are several villages in Cheshire and Lancashire named *Poulton,* i.e. the town or homestead (p. 123) by the pool. *Lacey* occurs in *Domesday Book* as *de Laci,* from some small spot in Normandy, probably the hamlet of Lassy (Calvados). *Hall* is due to residence near the great house of the neighbourhood. If Hall's ancestor's name had chanced to be put down in Anglo-French as *de la sale,* he might now be known as *Sale,* or even as *Saul.* *Manton* is the name of places in Lincolnshire and Northamptonshire, so that this player, at any rate, has an ancestral qualification for the East Midlands.

The only true occupative name in the list is *Cook,* for *Earl* is a nickname. *Cook* was perhaps the last occupative title to hold its own against the inherited name. Justice Shallow, welcoming Sir John Falstaff, says—

"Some pigeons, Davy; a couple of short-legged hens, a joint of mutton, and any pretty little tiny kickshaws. Tell William *Cook*" (2 *Henry IV*, v. i.).

And students of the *Ingoldsby Legends* will remember that—

"Ellen Bean ruled his cuisine.—He called her Nelly *Cook*."
(*Nell Cook*, l. 32.)

There are probably a goodly number of housewives of the present day who would be at a loss if suddenly asked for "cook's" name in full. It may be noted that *Lequeux* means exactly the same, and is of identical origin, archaic Fr. *le queux*, Lat. *coquus*, while *Kew* is sometimes for Anglo-Fr. *le keu*, where *keu* is the accusative of *queux* (see p. 9, *n.*).

The nicknames are *Earl*, *Bull*, and *Muddiman*. Nicknames such as *Earl* may have been acquired in various ways (see p. 144). *Bull* and *Muddiman* are singularly appropriate for Rugby scrummagers, though the first may be from an inn or shop sign, rather than from physique or character. It is equivalent to *Thoreau*, Old Fr. *toreau* (*taureau*). *Muddiman* is for *Moodyman*, where moody has its older meaning of valiant; cf. its German cognate *mutig*. The weather on the day in question gave a certain fitness both to the original meaning and the later form.

The above names are, with the exception of *Hancock*, *Hudson*, and *Muddiman*, easy to solve; but it must not be concluded that every list is as simple, or that the obvious is always right. The first page of Bardsley's *Dictionary of Surnames* might well serve as a danger-signal to cocksure writers on this subject. The names *Abbey* and *Abbott* would naturally seem to go back to an ancestor who lived in or near an abbey, and to another who had been nicknamed the abbot. But *Abbey* is usually from the Anglo-French entry *le abbé*, the abbot, and *Abbott* is often a diminutive of Ab, standing for Abel, or Abraham, the first of which was a favourite medieval font-name. Francis *Holyoak* describes himself on the title-page of his Latin Dictionary (1612) as Franciscus *de Sacra Quercu*, but his name comes from the holly oak, or holm oak (see p. 118). On the other hand, *Holliman* generally occurs in early rolls as *hali* or *holi man*, *i.e.* holy man.

It may be stated here, once for all, that etymologies of names which are based on medieval latinizations, family mottoes, etc., are always to be regarded with suspicion, as they involve the reversing of chronology, or the explanation of a name by a pun which has been made from it. We find *Lilburne* latinized as *de insula fontis*, as though it were the impossible hybrid *de l'isle burn*, and *Beaufoy* sometimes as *de bella fide*, whereas *foy* is the Old French for beech, from Lat. *fagus*. *Napier* of Merchiston had the motto *n'a pier*, "has no equal," and described himself on title-pages as the Nonpareil, but his ancestor was a servant who looked after the napery. With Holyoak's rendering of his own name we may compare Parkinson's "latinization" of his name in his famous book on gardening (1629), which bears the title *Paradisi in Sole Paradisus Terrestris*, i.e. the Earthly Paradise of "Park in Sun."

Many noble names have an anecdotic "explanation." I learnt at school that *Percy* came from pierce-eye, in allusion to a treacherous exploit at Alnwick. The *Lesleys* claim descent from a hero who overthrew a Hungarian champion—

> "Between the *less lee* and the mair
> He slew the knight and left him there."
>
> (*Quentin Durward*, ch. xxxvii.)

Similarly, the great name of *Courtenay*, *Courtney*, of French local origin, is derived in an Old French epic from *court nez*, short nose, an epithet conferred on the famous Guillaume d'Orange, who, when the sword of a Saracen giant removed this important feature, exclaimed undauntedly—

> "Mais que mon nés ai un poi acorcié,
> Bien sai mes nons en sera alongié."[1]
> (*Li Coronemenz Looïs*, l. 1159.)

I read lately in some newspaper that the original *Lockhart* took the "heart" of the Bruce to the Holy Land in a "locked" casket. Practically every famous Scottish name has a yarn connected with it, the gem perhaps being that which accounts for *Guthrie*. A Scottish king, it is said, landed weary and hungry as the sole survivor of a shipwreck. He approached a woman who was gutting fish, and asked her to prepare one for him. The kindly fishwife at once replied, "I'll gut three." Whereupon the king, dropping into rime with a readiness worthy of Mr. Wegg, said—

> "Then *gut three*, Your name shall be,"

and conferred a suitable estate on his benefactress.

After all, truth is stranger than fiction. There is quite enough legitimate cause for wonderment in the fact that *Tyas* is letter for letter the same name as *Douch*, or that *Strangeways*, from a district in Manchester which, lying between the Irwell and the Irk, was formerly subject to floods, is etymologically *strong-wash*. The Joannes *Acutus* whose tomb stands in Florence is the great free-lance captain Sir John

[1] "Though I have my nose a little shortened, I know well that my name will be thereby lengthened."

Hawkwood, "omitting the *h* in Latin as frivolous, and the *k* and *w* as unusual" (Verstegan, *Restitution of Decayed Intelligence*, ch. ix), which makes him almost as unrecognizable as that Peter Gower, the supposed founder of freemasonry, who turned out to be Pythagoras.

Many names are susceptible of two, three, or more explanations. This is especially true of some of our commonest monosyllabic surnames. *Bell* may be from Anglo-Fr. *le bel* (*beau*), or from a shop sign, or from residence near the church or town bell. It may even have been applied to the man who pulled the bell. Finally, the ancestor may have been a lady called Isabel, a supposition which does not necessarily imply illegitimacy (see p. 92). *Ball* is sometimes the shortened form of the once favourite Baldwin. It is also from a shop sign, and perhaps most frequently of all is for *bald*. The latter word is properly *balled*, i.e., marked with a *ball*,[1] or white streak, a word of Celtic origin; cf. piebald, i.e., balled like a (mag)pie, and the bald-faced stag. From the same word we get the augmentative *Ballard*, used, according to Wyclif, by the little boys who unwisely called to an irritable prophet—

"Stey up *ballard*" (2 Kings ii. 23).

The name may also be personal, Anglo-Sax. Bealheard. *Rowe* may be local, from residence in a row (cf. Fr. *Delarue*), or it may be an accidental spelling

[1] Halliwell notes that the nickname *Ball* is the name of a horse in Chaucer and Tusser, of a sheep in the *Promptorium Parvulorum*, and of a dog in the Privy Purse Expenses of Henry VIII. In each case the name alludes to a white mark, or what horsy people call a star. A cow thus marked is called in Scotland a *boasand* cow, and from the same word comes the obsolete *bawson*, badger.

of the nickname *Roe*, which also survives in the Mid. English form *Ray* (p. 223). But *Row* was also the shortened form of Rowland, or Roland. *Cobb* is an Anglo-Saxon name, as in the local Cobham, but it is also from the first syllable of *Cobbold* (Cuthbeald) and the second of Jacob. It has the diminutives *Cobbin* and *Coppin*.

Or, to take some less common names, *House* not only represents the medieval *de la house*, but also stands for *Howes*, which, in its turn, may be the plural of *how*, a hill (p. 106), or the genitive of *How*, one of the numerous medieval forms of Hugh (p. 59). *Barnett* is sometimes local, but, in most cases, represents Bernard, many of our Barnetts being German Jews. But in William *del barnet*, who died in 1348, we have a variant of *Burnet*, burn head (see p. 115). *Rouse* is generally Fr. *roux*, i.e. the red, but it may also be the nominative[1] form of Rou, *i.e.* of Rolf, or Rollo, the sea-king who conquered Normandy. Was *Holman* the holy man, the man who lived near a *holm*, i.e. holly (p. 118), on a *holm*, or river island (p. 117), or in a *hole*, or hollow? All these origins have equal claims.

As a rule, when an apparent nickname is also susceptible of another solution, baptismal, local, or occupative, the alternative explanation is to be preferred, as the popular tendency has always been towards twisting names into significant words. Thus, to take an example of each class, *Diamond* is for an old personal name Dimond, *Portwine* is a corruption of Poitevin, the man from Poitou (p. 99), and *Tipler*,

[1] Old French had a declension in two cases. The nominative, which has now almost disappeared, was usually distinguished by *-s*. This survives in a few words, e.g. *fils*, and proper names such as *Charles*, *Jules*, etc.

which now suggests alcoholic excess, was, as late as the seventeenth century, the regular name for an ale-house keeper.

Thus in a very large number of cases there is a considerable choice for the modern bearer of a name. Any *Boon* or *Bone* who wishes to assert that—

> "Of Hereford's high blood he came,
> A race renown'd for knightly fame"
> (*Lord of the Isles*, vi. 15),

can claim descent from de Bohun. While, if he holds that kind hearts are more than coronets, he has an alternative descent from some medieval *le bon*. This adjective, used as a personal name, gave also *Bunn* and *Bunce*; for the spelling of the latter name cf. *Dance* for Dans, and *Pearce* for Piers, the nominative of Pierre (see p. 9, *n.*), which also survives in *Pears* and *Pearson*. *Swain* may go back to the father of Canute, or to some hoary-headed swain who, possibly, tended the swine. Not all the *Seymours* are *St. Maurs*. Some of them were once *Seamers*, i.e. tailors. *Gosling* is rather trivial, but it represents the romantic Jocelyn, in Normandy Gosselin, a diminutive of the personal name Josse, Lat. Jodocus. *Goss* is usually for goose, but any *Goss*, or *Gossett*, unwilling to trace his family back to John *Goose*, "my lord of Yorkes fole,"[1] may likewise choose the French Josse or Gosse. *Goss* may also be a dialect pronunciation of gorse, the older form of which has given the name *Gorst*. *Coward*, though humble, cow-herd, is no more timid than *Craven*, the name of a district in the West Riding of Yorkshire.

Mr. *Chucks*, when in good society, "seldom bowed,

[1] Privy Purse Expenses of Elizabeth of York (1502).

sir, to anything under *three* syllables" (*Peter Simple*, ch. xvii.). But the length of a name is not necessarily an index of a noble meaning. As will be seen (pp. 74, 5), a great number of our monosyllabic names belong to the oldest stratum of all. The boatswain's own name, from Norman-Fr. *chouque*, a tree-stump, is identical with the rather aristocratic *Zouch* or *Such*, from the usual French form *souche*. *Stubbs*, which has the same meaning, may be compared with *Curzon*, Fr. *courson*, a stump, a derivative of *court*, short. *Pomeroy* has a lordly ring, but is the Old French for *Applegarth* or *Appleyard* (p. 142), and *Camoys* means flat-nosed, Fr. *camus*—

> "This wenche thikke and wel y-growen was,
> With *kamuse* nose, and eyen greye as glas."
> (A, 3973.)

Kingsley, speaking of the name assumed by John Briggs, says—

> "*Vavasour* was a very pretty name, and one of those which is [*sic*] supposed by novelists and young ladies to be aristocratic; why so is a puzzle; as its plain meaning is a tenant farmer and nothing more or less" (*Two Years Ago*, ch. xi.).

The word is interesting, because it is one of the few instances of a Latin genitive plural having passed into French. It represents a Vulgar Lat. *vassus vassorum*, vassal of vassals.

On the other hand, many a homely name has a complimentary meaning. Mr. Wegg did not like the name *Boffin*, but its oldest form is *bon-fin*, good and fine. In 1273 Mr. *Bumble's* name was spelt *bon-bel*, good and beautiful. With these we may group *Bunker*, of which the oldest form is *bon-quer* (*bon cœur*), and *Boffey*, which corresponds to the common

French name *Bonnefoy,* good faith; while the much more assertive *Beaufoy* means simply fine beech (p. 6). With *Bunker* we may compare *Goodhart* and *Cordeaux,* the oldest form of the latter being the French name *Cœurdoux.* *Momerie* and *Mummery* are identical with *Mowbray,* from Monbrai in Normandy. *Molyneux* impresses more than *Mullins,* of which it is merely the dim., Fr. *moulins,* mills. The Yorkshire name *Tankard* is a perversion of Tancred. *Stiggins* goes back to the illustrious Anglo-Saxon name Stigand, as *Wiggins* does to *wigand,* a champion. *Cadman* represents Caedmon, the name of the poet-monk of Whitby. *Segar* and *Sugar* are imitative forms of the Anglo-Sax. Sægær, of which the normal modern representative is *Sayers.* *Giblett* is not a name one would covet, but it stands in the same relationship to Gilbert as *Hamlet* does to Hamo.

A small difference in spelling makes a great difference in the look of a name. The aristocratic *Coke* is an archaic spelling of *Cook,* the still more lordly *Herries* sometimes disguises *Harris,* while the modern *Brassey* is the same as de Bracy in *Ivanhoe.* The rather grisly *Nightgall* is a variant of *Nightingale.* The accidental retention of particles and articles is also effective, e.g. *Delmar, Delamere, Delapole,* impress more than *Mears* and *Pool,* and *Larpent* (Fr. l'arpent), *Lemaître,* and *Lestrange* more than *Acres, Masters,* and *Strange.* There are few names of less heroic sound than *Spark* and *Codlin,* yet the former is a contraction of the picturesque Sparrow-hawk, used as a personal name by the Anglo-Saxons, while the latter can be traced back *via* the earlier forms *Quodling* (still found), Querdling, Querdelyoun to Cœur de Lion.

CHAPTER II

A MEDIEVAL ROLL

"Quelque diversité d'herbes qu'il y ait, tout s'enveloppe sous le nom de salade ; de mesme, sous la considération des noms, je m'en voys faire icy une galimafree de divers articles."

(MONTAIGNE, *Essais*, i. 46.)

JUST as, in studying a new language, the linguist finds it most helpful to take a simple text and hammer out in detail every word and grammatical form it contains, so the student of name-lore cannot do better than tackle a medieval roll and try to connect every name in it with those of the present day. I give here two lists of names from the Hundred Rolls of 1273. The first contains the names of London and Middlesex jurymen, most of them, especially the Londoners, men of substance and position. The second is a list of cottagers resident in the village of Steeple Claydon in Bucks. Even a cursory perusal of these lists should suffice to dispel all recollection of the nightmare "philology" which has been so much employed to obscure what is perfectly simple and obvious ; while a very slight knowledge of Latin and French is all that is required to connect these names of men who were dead and buried before the Battle of Crecy with those to be found in any modern directory. The brief indications supplied under each name will be found in a fuller form in the various chapters of the book to which references are given.

For simplicity I have given the modern English form of each Christian name and expanded the abbreviations used by the official compilers. It will be noticed that English, Latin, and Anglo-French are used indifferently, that *le* is usually, though not always, put before the trade-name or nickname, that *de* is put before place-names and *at* before spots which have no proper name. The names in the right-hand column are only specimens of the, often very numerous, modern equivalents.

London Jurymen

Hundred Rolls	Modern Form
William **Dibel.**	**Dibble** (Theobald).

Initial *t*- and *d*- alternate (p. 32) according to locality. In *Tennyson*, for *Denison*, son of Denis, we have the opposite change. The forms assumed by Theobald are very numerous (p. 4). Besides *Dibble* we have the shorter *Dibb*. It is almost certain that to the same name we owe both *Double* and *Treble*, the latter with the intrusive -*r*- which is not unusual in names (p. 88, *n*. 1)

Baldwin **le Bocher.** **Butcher, Booker,** etc.

On the various forms of this name, see p. 149.

Robert **Hauteyn.** **Auty.**

A Yorkshire name. The omission or addition of an aspirate is very common (p. 38). Cf. *Harnett* for *Arnett*, dim. of Arnold.

Henry **le Wimpler.**

The name has apparently disappeared with the garment. But it is never safe to assert that a surname is quite extinct.

Hundred Rolls — Modern Form

Stephen **le Feron.** — **Fearon.**

From Old Fr. *féron*, smith, from *férir*, to smite. In a few cases French has *-on* as an agential suffix (p. 171).

William **de Paris.** — **Paris, Parris, Parish.**

The commoner modern form *Parish* is seldom to be derived from our word *parish*. This rarely occurs, while the entry *de Paris* is, on the other hand, very common.

Roger **le Wyn.** — **Wynne** (white).

A Celtic nickname, identical with *Gwynne*. For other common nicknames of Celtic origin, see p. 216.

Matthew **de Pomfrait.** — **Pomfret.**

The usual pronunciation of Pontefract, broken bridge, one of the few English place-names of purely Latin origin (p. 120). The Old French form would be *pont-frait*.

Richard **le Paumer.** — **Palmer.**

A man who had made pilgrimage to the Holy Land (p. 167). The modern spelling is restored, but the *-l-* remains mute. It is just possible that this name sometimes means tennis-player, as tennis, Fr. *le jeu de paume*, once played with the palm of the hand, is of great antiquity.

Walter **Poletar.** — **Poulter.**

A dealer in poults, *i.e.* fowls. For the lengthened form *poulterer*, cf. *fruiterer* for *fruiter*, and see p. 155.

Reginald **Aurifaber.** — **Goldsmith.**

The French form *orfèvre* has also given the name *Offer*.

Hundred Rolls	Modern Form
Henry **Deubeneye.**	**Daubeney, Dabney.**

Fr. *d'Aubigny*. One of the many cases in which the French preposition has been incorporated in the name. Cf. *Danvers*, for *d'Anvers*, Antwerp, and see p. 100.

Richard **Knotte.** **Knott.**

From Scandinavian Cnut, Canute. This name is also local, from *knot*, a hillock, and has of course become confused (p. 30) with the nickname *Nott*, with cropped hair (p. 210).

> "Thou *nott*-pated fool."
>
> (1 *Henry IV*, ii. 4.)

Walter **le Wyte.** **White.**

The large number of *Whites* is partly to be accounted for by their having absorbed the name *Wight* (p. 214) from Mid. Eng. *wiht*, valiant.

Adam **le Sutel.** **Suttle.**

Both Eng. *subtle* and Fr. *subtil* are restored spellings, which do not appear in nomenclature (see p. 29).

Fulk **de Sancto Edmundo.** **Tedman.**

The older form would be *Tednam*. Bury St. Edmund's is sometimes referred to as Tednambury. For the mutilation of the word *saint* in place-names, see p. 34.

William **le Boteler.** **Butler.**

More probably a bottle-maker than what we understand by a butler, the origin being of course the same.

Hundred Rolls	Modern Form
Gilbert **Lupus.**	**Wolf.**

Wolf, and the Scandinavian Ulf, are both common as personal names before the Conquest, but a good many modern bearers of the name are German Jews (see p. 55). Old Fr. *lou* (loup) is one source of *Low*.

Stephen **Juvenis.** **Young.**

Senex is rarely found. The natural tendency was to distinguish the younger man from his father. *Senior* is generally to be explained differently (see p. 145).

William **Braciator.** **Brewer.**

The French form *brasseur* also survives as *Bracher* and *Brasher*, the latter being also confused with *Brazier*, the worker in brass.

John **de Cruce.** **Cross, Crouch.**

A man who lived near some outdoor cross. The form *crouch* survives in Crutched Friars. Hence also the name *Croucher*.

Matthew **le Candeler.** **Candler, Chandler.**

Initial *c-* for *ch-* shows Norman or Picard origin (see p. 32).

Henry **Bernard.** **Barnard, Barnett.**

The change from *-er-* to *-ar-* is regular; cf. *Clark*, and see p. 32. The endings *-ard*, *-ald*, are generally changed to *-ett*; cf. *Everett* for Everard, *Barrett* for Berald, *Garrett* for Gerard, Garrard, whence the imitative *Garrison* for Garretson.

Hundred Rolls | Modern Form

William **de Bosco.** **Bush, Busk, Buss.**

> "For there is neither *busk* nor hay (p. 124)
> In May that it nyl shrouded bene."
> (*Romaunt of the Rose*, 54.)

The name might also be translated as *Wood.* The corresponding name of French origin is *Boyce* or *Boyes,* Fr. *bois* (see p. 140).

Henry **de Sancta Ositha.** **Toosey.**

Cf. Fulk de Sancto Edmundo (*supra*), and cf. Tooley St. for St. Olave St. (see p. 34).

Walter **ate Stede.** **Stead.**

In this case the preposition has not coalesced, as in *Adeane,* at the dean, i.e. hollow, *Agate,* at gate, etc. (see p. 104).

William **le Fevere.** **Wright, Smith.**

The French name survives as *Feaver* and *Fevyer.* Cf. also the Lat. *Faber,* which is not always a modern German importation (see p. 105, *n.*).

Thomas **de Cumbe.** **Combe, Coombes.**

A West-country name for a hollow in a hillside (see p. 106).

John **Stace.** **Stace, Stacey.**

Generally for Eustace, but sometimes perhaps for Anastasia, as we find Stacey used as a female name (see p. 33).

Richard **le Teynturier.** **Dyer, Dyter, Dexter.**

Dexter represents Mid. Eng. *dighester,* with the feminine agential suffix (see p. 149).

Hundred Rolls — Modern Form

Henry **le Waleys.** — **Wallis, Walsh, Welch.**

Literally the foreigner, but especially applied by the English to the Western Celts. *Quelch* represents the Welsh pronunciation. With *Wallis* cf. *Cornwallis,* Mid. Eng. *le cornwaleis* (see p. 96).

John **le Bret.** — **Brett, Britton.**

An inhabitant of Brittany, perhaps resident in that Breton colony in London called Little Britain. Bret is the Old French nominative of Breton (see p. 80, *n.* 1).

Thomas **le Clerc.** — **Clark.**

One of our commonest names. We now spell the common noun *clerk* by etymological reaction, but educated people pronounce the word as it was generally written up to the eighteenth century (see p. 32).

Stephen **le Hatter.**

The disappearance of this name is a curious problem (see p. 151). The name *Capper* exists, though it is not very common.

Thomas **le Batur.** — **Thresher.**

But, being a Londoner, he was more probably a gold-beater, or perhaps a beater of cloth. The name *Beater* also survives.

Alexander **de Leycestre.** — **Leicester, Lester.**

For the simpler spelling, once usual and still adopted by those who chalk the names on the mail-vans at St. Pancras, cf. such names as *Worster, Wooster, Gloster,* etc. (see p. 99).

Hundred Rolls	Modern Form
Robert **le Noreys.**	**Norris, Nurse.**

Old Fr. *noreis*, the Northerner (see p. 97), or *norice* (nourrice), the nurse, foster-mother (see p. 185).

Reginald **le Blond.** **Blount, Blunt.**

Fr. *blond*, fair. We have also the dim. *Blundell*. The corresponding English name is *Fairfax*, from Mid. Eng. *fax*, hair (see p. 214).

Randolf **ate Mor.** **Moor.**

With the preposition retained (see p. 104) it has given the Latin-looking *Amor*.

Matthew **le Pevrier.** **Pepper.**

For the reduction of pepperer to *Pepper* cf. *Armour* for armourer, and see p. 155.

Godfrey **le Furmager.** **Cheeseman, Firminger.**

From Old Fr. *formage* (fromage). The intrusion of the *n* in *Firminger* is regular ; cf. *Massinger*, messenger, from Fr. *messager*, and see p. 35.

Robert **Campeneys.** **Champness, Champneys.**

Old Fr. *champeneis* (champenois), of Champagne (see p. 99).

John **del Pek.** **Peck, Peake, Pike, Pick.**

A name taken from a hill-top, but often applied specifically to the Derbyshire Peak (see p. 107).

Richard **Dygun.** **Dickens.**

A diminutive of Dig, for Dick (see p. 63).

Hundred Rolls	Modern Form
Peter **le Hoder.**	**Hodder.**

A maker of hods or a maker of hoods? The latter is more likely.

Alan **Allutarius.** **Whittier.**

Lat. *alutarius*, a white tawer. Similarly, Mid. Eng. *stan-heawere*, stone-hewer, is contracted to *Stanier*, now swallowed up by *Stainer*. The simple tawer is also one origin of the name *Tower*.

Peter **le Rus.** **Russ, Rush, Rouse.**

Fr. *roux*, of red complexion. Cf. the dim. *Russell*, Fr. *Rousseau* (see p. 214).

MIDDLESEX JURYMEN

Roger **de la Hale.** **Hall, Hale, Hales.**

One of our commonest local surnames. But it has two interpretations, from *hall* and *heal* (p. 116).

Walter **de la Hegge.** **Hedge, Hedges.**

Other forms of the same word are *Hay*, *Hayes*, *Haig*, *Haigh*, *Hawes* (see p. 124).

John **Rex.** **King.**

One of our commonest nicknames, the survival of which is easily understood (see p. 144).

Stephen **de la Novele Meyson.** **Newhouse.**

Cf. also *Newbigging*, from Mid. Eng. *biggen*, to build (see p. 133).

Randolf **Pokoc.** **Pocock, Peacock.**

The simple *Poe*, Lat. *pavo*, has the same meaning (see p. 218).

Hundred Rolls	Modern Form
William **de Fonte.**	**Spring, Wells, Weller, Attewell.**

This is the more usual origin of the name *Spring* (see p. 90).

Robert **del Perer.** **Perrier.**

Old Fr. *périer* (poirier), pear-tree. Another origin of *Perrier* is, through French, from Lat. *petrarius*, a stone-hewer.

Adam **de la Denne.** **Denne, Dean, Dene.**

A Mid. English name for valley (see p. 112).

Robertus **filius Gillelmi.** **Wilson.**

For other possible names to be derived from a father named William, see p. 63.

William **filius Radolfi.** **Rawson.**

A very common medieval name, Anglo-Sax. Rædwulf, the origin of our *Ralph, Relf, Rolfe, Roff*, and of Fr. *Raoul.* Some of its derivatives, e.g. *Rolls,* have got mixed with those of Roland. To be distinguished from Randolf or *Randall,* of which the shorter form is *Ran* or *Rand,* whence *Rankin, Rands, Rance,* etc.

Steeple Claydon Cottagers

Andrew **Colle.** **Collins, Colley.**

For Nicolas (see p. 57).

William **Neuman.** **Newman, Newcomb.**

A man recently settled in the village (see p. 106).

Adam **ate Dene.** **Dean, Denne, Adeane.**

The separate *at* survives in *a'Court* and *a'Beckett,* at the beck head; cf. Allan *a'Dale* (see p. 104).

Hundred Rolls	Modern Form
Ralph **Mydevynter.**	**Midwinter.**

An old name for Christmas (see p. 89).

William **ate Hull.** **Athill, Hill, Hull.**

The form *hul* for *hil* occurs in Mid. English (see p. 106).

Gilbert **Sutor.** **Sutor, Souter.**

On the poor representation of the shoemaker see p. 151.

Walter **Maraud.**

It is easy to understand the disappearance of this name—

"A rogue, begger, vagabond; a varlet, rascall, scoundrell, base knave" (Cotgrave);

but it may be represented by *Marratt, Marrott,* unless these are from Mary (p. 93).

Nicholas **le P.ker.**

This may be expanded into *Parker,* a park-keeper, *Packer,* a wool-packer, or the common medieval *Porker,* a swine-herd, now disguised as *Parker.*

John **Stegand.** **Stiggins.**

Anglo-Saxon names survived chiefly among the peasantry (see p. 12).

Roger **Mercator.** **Marchant, Chapman.**

The restored modern spelling *merchant* has affected the pronunciation of the common noun (see p. 32). The more usual term *Chapman* is cognate with *cheap, chaffer, Chipping, Copenhagen,* Ger. *kaufen,* to buy, etc.

Hundred Rolls | Modern Form

Adam **Hoppe.** **Hobbs, Hobson, Hopkins.**

An example of the interchange of *b* and *p* (see p. 35). Hob is usually regarded as one of the rimed forms from Robert (see p. 62).

Roger **Crom.** **Crum, Crump.**

Lit. crooked, cognate with Ger. *krumm*. The final -*p* of *Crump* is excrescent (see p. 35).

Stephen **Cornevaleis.** **Cornwallis, Cornish.**

A name which would begin in Devonshire (see p. 96).

Walter **de Ibernia.** **Ireland.**

A much more common name than *Scotland*, which has been squeezed out by *Scott* (see p. 96).

Matilda **filia Matildæ.** **Mawson** (for Maud-son), **Till, Tilley, Tillett, Tillotson,** etc.

One of the favourite girl-names during the surname period (see p. 93).

Ralph **Vouler.** **Fowler.**

A West-country pronunciation ; cf. *Vowle* for *Fowell*, *Vokes* for *Foakes* (p. 61), *Venn* for *Fenn*, etc.

John **filius Thomæ.** **Thompson, Tompkins, Tomlin,** etc.

One of the largest surname families. It includes *Toulmin*, a metathesis of *Tomlin*. In *Townson* and *Tonson* it coalesces with Tony, Anthony.

Henry **Bolle.** **Bull.**

In this case evidently a nickname (see p. 5).

Hundred Rolls	Modern Form
Roger **Gyle.**	**Gill.**

For names in *Gil-* see p. 59. The form in the roll may, however, represent an uncomplimentary nickname, " guile."

Walter **Molendarius.** **Miller, Mellor, Milner.**

In *Milne, Milner,* we have the oldest form, representing Vulgar Lat. *molina,* mill; cf. *Kilner,* from kiln, Lat. *culina,* kitchen. *Millard* (p. 180) is no doubt sometimes the same name with excrescent *-d.*

Thomas **Berker.** **Barker.**

A man who stripped bark, also a tanner. But as a surname reinforced by the Norman form of Fr. *berger,* a shepherd (see p. 150).

Matthew **Hedde.** **Head.**

Sometimes local, at the head, but here a nickname; cf. *Tate, Tait,* sometimes from Fr. *tête* (see p. 126).

Richard **Joyet.** **Jowett, Jewett.**

A diminutive either of Joy or of Julian, Juliana. But it is possible that Joy itself is not the abstract noun, but a shortened form of Julian.

Adam **Kyg.** **Ketch, Keach.**

An obsolete adjective meaning lively (see p. 212).

Simon **filius Johannis Nigelli.** **Johnson, Jones, Jennings,** etc.

The derivatives of John are innumerable and not to be distinguished from those of Joan, Jane (see p. 95).

In the above lists occur examples of all the ways in which surnames could be formed. At the time of compilation they were not hereditary. Thus the last man on the list is Simon *Johnson*, but his father was John *Neilson*, or *Nelson* (see p. 95), and his son would be —— *Simpson*, *Sims*, etc. This would go on until, at a period varying with the locality, the wealth and importance of the individual, etc., one name in the line would become accidentally petrified and persist to the present day. The chain could, of course, be broken at any time by the assumption of a name from one of the other three classes.

CHAPTER III

SPELLING AND SOUND

"Do you spell it with a V or a W?" inquired the judge.
"That depends upon the taste and fancy of the speller, my lord," replied Sam. "I never had occasion to spell it more than once or twice in my life, but I spells it with a V."

(*Pickwick*, ch. xxxiv.)

MANY people are particular about the spelling of their names. I am myself, although, as a student of philology, I ought to know better. The greatest of Englishmen was so careless in the matter as to sign himself *Shagsper*, a fact usually emphasized by Baconians when speaking of the illiterate clown of Stratford-on-Avon. Equally illiterate must have been the learned Dr. Crown, who, in the various books he published in the latter half of the seventeenth century, spelt his name indifferently Cron, Croon, Croun, Crone, Croone, Croune. The modern spelling of any particular name is a pure accident. Before the Elementary Education Act of 1870 a considerable proportion of English people did not spell their names at all. They trusted to the parson and the clerk, who did their best with unfamiliar names. Even now old people in rural districts may find half a dozen orthographic variants of their own names among the sparse documentary records of their lives. Dugdale the antiquary is said to have found more than 130 variants of *Mainwaring* among the parchments of that family. Bardsley quotes, under the name *Blenkinsop*—

"On April 23, 1470, Elizabeth *Blynkkynesoppye*, of *Blynkkynsoppe*, widow of Thomas *Blynkyensope*, of *Blynkkensope*, received a general pardon"—

four variants in one sentence. In the List of Foreign Protestants and Aliens in England (1618) we have Andrian *Medlor* and Ellin *Medler* his wife, Johan *Cosen* and Abraham *Cozen*, brethren. The death of Sarah *Inward*, daughter of Richard *Inwood*, was registered in 1685.

Medieval spelling was roughly phonetic, *i.e.* it attempted to reproduce the sound of the period and region, and even men of learning, as late as the eighteenth century, were very uncertain in matters of orthography. The spelling of the language is now practically normalized, although in conformity with no sort of principle; but the family name, as a private possession, has kept its freedom. Thus, if we wish to speak poetically of a meadow, I suppose we should call it a *lea*, but the same word is represented by the family names *Lea*, *Lee*, *Ley*, *Leigh*, *Legh*, *Legge*, *Lay*, *Lye*, perhaps the largest group of local surnames we possess.

In matters of spelling we observe various tendencies. One is the retention of an archaic form, which does not necessarily affect pronunciation. Late Mid. English was fond of *y* for *i*, of double consonants, and of final *-e*. All these appear in the names *Thynne* (thin) and *Wyllie* (wily). Therefore we should not deride the man who writes himself *Smythe*. But in some cases the pronunciation suffers, *e.g.* the name *Fry* represents Mid. Eng. *fri*, one of the forms of the adjective that is now written *free*. *Burt* represents Anglo-Sax. *beorht*, the normal result of which is *Bright*. We now write *subtle* and *perfect*, artificial words, in the second of which the pronunciation has been changed in accordance with the restored spelling; but the older forms survive in the names *Suttle* and *Parfitt*—

> "He was a verray *parfit*, gentil knyght."
> (A, 72.)

The usual English pronunciation of names like *Mackenzie, Menzies, Dalziel,* is due to the substitution by the printer of a *z* for an obsolete letter [1] that represented a soft palatal sound more like *y.*

We have an archaic plural ending in *Knollys* (*Knowles*), the plural of knoll, and in *Sandys,* and an archaic spelling in *Sclater* for *Slater* or *Slatter,* for both slat and slate come from Old Fr. *esclat* (éclat), a splinter. With Knollys and Sandys we may put *Pepys,* for the existence of the dims. *Pipkin, Peppitt,* and *Peppiatt* points to the medieval name Pipun, corresponding to the royal Pépin. *Streatfeild* preserves variant spellings of street and field. In *Gardiner* we have the Old Northern French word which now, as a common noun, gardener, is assimilated to garden, the normal French form of which appears in *Jardine.*

Such orthographic variants as *i* and *y, Simons, Symons, ph* and *f, Jephcott, Jeffcott, s* and *c, Pearse, Pearce, Rees, Reece, Sellars* (cellars), *ks* and *x, Dickson, Dixon,* are a matter of taste or accident. Initial letters which became mute often disappeared in spelling, e.g.

[1] This substitution has led one writer on surnames, who apparently confuses bells with beans, to derive the obsolete name Billiter, whence Billiter's Lane in the City, from "*Belzetter*, i.e., the *bell-setter*." The Mid. Eng. "*bellezeter*, campanarius" (*Prompt. Parv.*), was a bell-founder, from a verb related to *gey*sir, in*got*, and Ger. *giessen*, to pour. Robert le *bellegeter* was a freeman of York in 1279.

Wray, a corner (p. 127), has become hopelessly confused with *Ray*, a roe, *Knott*, from Cnut, *i.e.* Canute, or from dialect knot, a hillock, with *Nott*, crop-haired. *Knowlson* is the son of *Nowell* (see p. 89) or of Noll, *i.e.* Oliver. Therefore, when Mr. X. asserts that his name has always been spelt in such and such a way, he is talking nonsense. If his great-grandfather's will is accessible, and a document of any length, he will probably find two or three variants in that alone. The great Duke of Wellington, as a younger man, signed himself Arthur Wesley—

> "He was colonel of Dad's regiment, the Thirty-third foot, after Dad left the army, and then he changed his name from *Wesley* to *Wellesley*, or else the other way about"
>
> (KIPLING, *Marklake Witches*);

and I know two families the members of which disagree as to the orthography of their names. We have a curious affectation in such spellings as *ffrench*, *ffoulkes*, etc., where the *ff* is merely the method of indicating the capital letter in early documents.

The telescoping of long names is a familiar phenomenon. Well-known examples are Cholmondeley, *Chumley*, Marjoribanks, *Marchbanks*, Mainwaring, *Mannering*. Less familiar are Auchinleck, *Affleck*, Boutevilain, *Butlin*, Postlethwaite, *Posnett*, Sudeley, *Sully*, Wolstenholme, *Woosnam*. *Ensor* is from the local Edensor, Cavendish was regularly *Candish* for the Elizabethans, while Cavenham in Suffolk has given the surname *Canham*. Daventry has become *Daintree*, *Dentry*, and probably the imitative *Dainty*, while *Stenson* is for Stevenson. It is this tendency which makes the connection between surnames and village names so difficult to establish in many cases, for the artificial name as it occurs in the gazetteer often gives little clue to the local pronunciation. It is easy to recognize Bickenhall or Bickenhill in *Bicknell* and Puttenham in *Putnam,* but the identity of *Wyndham* with Wymondham is only clear when we know the local pronunciation of the latter name. *Milton* and *Melton* are often telescoped forms of *Middleton.*

Dialectic variants must also be taken into account. *Briggs* and *Rigg* represent the Northern forms of *Bridges* and *Ridge,* and *Philbrick* is a disguised fell-bridge. In *Egg* we have rather the survival of the Mid. English spelling of *Edge. Braid, Lang, Strang,* are Northern variants of *Broad, Long, Strong. Auld* is for Old, while *Tamson* is for Thompson and *Dabbs* for Dobbs (Robert). We have the same change of vowel in *Raper,* for *Roper. Venner* generally means hunter, Fr. *veneur,* but sometimes represents the West-country form of *Fenner,* the fen-dweller; cf. *Vidler* for fiddler, and *Vanner* for *Fanner,* the winnower.

We all know the difficulty we have in catching a new and unfamiliar name, and the subterfuges we employ to find out what it really is. In such cases we do not get the help from association and analogy which serves us in dealing with language in general, but find ourselves in the position of a foreigner or child hearing an unfamiliar word for the first time. We realize how many imperceptible shades there are between a short *i* and a short *e,* or between a fully voiced *g* and a voiceless *k,* examples suggested to me by my having lately understood a Mr. Riggs to be a Mr. Rex.

We find occurring in surnames examples of those consonantal changes which do not violate the great phonetic law that such changes can only occur regularly within the same group, *i.e.* that a labial cannot alternate with a palatal, or a dental with either. It is thus that we find *b* alternating with *p*, *Hobbs* and *Hopps* (Robert), *Bullinger* and *Pullinger*, Fr. *boulanger*; *g* with *k*, *Cutlack* and *Goodlake* (Anglo-Sax. Guthlac), *Diggs* and *Dix* (Richard), *Gipps* and *Kipps* (Gilbert), *Catlin* and *Gatling* (Catherine); *j* with *ch*, *Jubb* or *Jupp* and *Chubb* (Job); *d* with *t*, *Proud* and *Prout* (see p. 213), *Dyson* and *Tyson* (Dionisia), and also with *th*, *Carrodus* and *Carruthers* (a hamlet in Dumfries). The alternation of *c* and *ch* or *g* and *j* in names of French origin is dialectic, the *c* and *g* representing the Norman-Picard pronunciation, e.g. *Campion* for *Champion*, *Gosling* for *Joslin*. In some cases we have shown a definite preference for one form, e.g. *Chancellor* and *Chappell*, but *Carpenter* and *Camp*. In English names *c* is northern, *ch* southern, e.g. *Carlton*, *Charlton*, *Kirk*, *Church*.

There are also a few very common vowel changes. The sound *er* usually became *ar*, as in *Barclay* (Berkeley), *Clark*, *Darby*, *Garrard* (Gerard), *Jarrold* (Gerald), *Harbord* (Herbert), *Jarvis* (Gervase), *Marchant*, *Sargent*, etc., while *Larned*, our great-grandfathers' pronunciation of "learned," corresponds to Fr. *Littré*. Thus *Parkins* is the same name as *Perkins* (Peter), and these also give *Parks* and *Perks*, the former of which is usually not connected with *Park*. To Peter, or rather to Fr. Pierre, belong also *Parr*, *Parry* and *Perry*, though *Parry* is generally Welsh (see p. 66). The dims. *Parrott*, *Perrott*, etc., were sometimes nicknames, the etymology being the same, for our word *parrot* is from Fr. *pierrot*. To the freedom with which this sound is spelt, e.g. in *Herd*, *Heard*, *Hird*, *Hurd*, we also owe *Purkiss*; cf. *appurtenance* for older *appartenance*. The letter *l* seems also to exercise a demoralizing influence on the adjacent vowel. Juliana became

Gillian, and from this, or from the masculine form Julian, we get *Jalland*, *Jolland*, and the shortened *Gell*, *Gill* (see p. 59), and *Jull*. *Gallon*, which Bardsley groups with these, is more often a French name, from the Old German Walo, or a corruption of the still commoner French name *Galland*, likewise of Germanic origin.

We find also such irregular vowel changes as *Flinders* for Flanders, and conversely *Packard* for Picard. *Pottinger* (see p. 35) sometimes becomes *Pettinger* as Portugal gives *Pettingall*. The general tendency is towards that thinning of the vowel that we get in *mister* for *master* and Miss Miggs's *mim* for *ma'am*. *Biddulph* for Botolf is an example of this. But in *Royle* for the local *Ryle* we find the same broadening which has given *boil*, a swelling, for earlier *bile*.

Among phonetic changes which occur with more or less regularity are those called aphesis, epenthesis, epithesis, assimilation, dissimilation, and metathesis, convenient terms which are less learned than they appear. Aphesis is the loss of the unaccented first syllable, as in *'baccy* and *'tater*. It occurs almost regularly in words of French origin, e.g. *squire* and *esquire*, *prentice* and *apprentice*. When such double forms exist, the surname invariably assumes the popular form, e.g. *Prentice*, *Squire*. Other examples are *Bonner*, i.e. debonair, *Jenner*, *Jenoure*, for Mid. Eng. *engenour*, engineer, *Cator*, *Chaytor*, Old Fr. *acatour* (*acheteur*), a buyer—

> "A gentil maunciple was ther of a temple,
> Of which *achatours* mighte take exemple" (A. 567),

Spencer, dispenser, a spender, *Stacey* for Eustace, *Vick* and *Veck* for *Levick*, i.e. *l'évêque*, the bishop, *Merrick* for Almeric, *Pottinger* for the obsolete *potigar*, an apothecary, etc. The institution now known as the "orspittle" was called by our unlettered forefathers the "spital," hence the names *Spittle* and *Spittlehouse*. A well-known amateur goal-keeper has the appropriate name *Fender*, for defender.

Many names beginning with *n* are due to aphesis, e.g. *Nash* for *atten ash*, *Nalder*, *Nelms*, *Nock*, *atten oak*, *Nokes*, *Nye*, *atten ey*, at the island, *Nangle*, *atten angle*, *Nind* or *Nend*, *atten ind* or *end*. With these we may compare *Twells*, *at wells*, and the numerous cases in which the first part of a personal name is dropped, e.g. *Tolley*, Bartholomew, *Munn*, Edmund, *Pott*, Philpot, dim. of Philip (see p. 87) and the less common *Facey*, from Boniface, and *Loney*, from Appolonia, the latter of which has also given *Applin*.

When a name compounded with Saint begins with a vowel, we get such forms as *Tedman*, St. Edmund, *Tobin*, St. Aubyn, *Toosey*, St. Osith, *Toomer*, St. Omer, *Tooley*, St. Olave; cf. *Tooley St.* for St. Olave St. and *tawdry* from St. Audrey. When the saint's name begins with a consonant, we get, instead of aphesis, a telescoped pronunciation, e.g. *Selinger*, St. Leger, *Seymour*, St. Maur, *Sinclair*, St. Clair, *Semark*, St. Mark, *Semple*, St. Paul, *Simper*, St. Pierre, *Sidney*, probably for St. Denis, with which we may compare the educated pronunciation of *St. John*. These names are all of local origin, from chapelries in Normandy or England.

Epenthesis is the insertion of a sound which facilitates pronunciation, such as that of *b* in Fr. *chambre*, from Lat. *camera*. The intrusive sound may be a vowel or a consonant as in the names *Henery*, *Hendry*, perversions of *Henry*.[1] To *Hendry* we owe the northern

[1] On the usual fate of this name in English, see p. 38.

Henderson, which has often coalesced with *Anderson,* from Andrew. These are contracted into *Henson* and *Anson,* the latter also from Ann and Agnes (see p. 88). Intrusion of a vowel is seen in *Greenaway, Hathaway,* heath way, *Treadaway,* trade (i.e. trodden) way, etc., also in *Horniman, Alabone,* Alban, *Minister,* minster, etc. But epenthesis of a consonant is more common, especially *b* or *p* after *m,* and *d* after *n.* Examples are *Gamble* for the Anglo-Saxon name Gamel, *Hamblin* for *Hamlin,* a double diminutive of Hamo, *Simpson, Thompson,* etc., and *Grindrod,* green royd (see p. 111). There is also the special case of *n* before *g* in such names as *Firminger* (see p. 148), *Massinger* (p. 185), *Pottinger* (p. 176), etc.

Epithesis, or the addition of a final consonant, is common in uneducated speech, e.g. *scholard, gownd, garding,* etc. I say " uneducated," but many such forms have been adapted by the language, e.g. *sound,* Fr. *son,* and we have the name *Kitching* for kitchen. The usual additions are *-d, -t,* or *-g* after *n,* e.g. *Simmonds,* Simon, *Hammond, Hammant,* Fr. Hamon, *Hind,* a farm labourer, of which the older form is *Hine* (p. 164), *Collings* for Collins, *Jennings,* Fr. Jeannin, dim. of Jean, *Aveling* from the female name Avelina or Evelyn. *Neild* is for *Neil,* Nigel. We have epithetic *-b* in *Plumb,* the man who lived by the plum-tree and epithetic *-p* in *Crump* (p. 24).

Assimilation is the tendency of a sound to imitate its neighbour. Thus the *d* of *Hud* (p. 3) sometimes becomes *t* in contact with the sharp *s,* hence *Hutson*; *Tomkins* tends to become *Tonkins,* whence *Tonks,* if the *m* and *k* are not separated by the epenthetic *p,* *Tompkins.* In *Hopps* and *Hopkins* we have the *b* of Hob assimilated to the sharp *s* and *k,* while in *Hobbs* we pronounce a final *-z*. It is perhaps under the influence of the initial labial that *Milson*, son of Miles, sometimes becomes *Milsom*, and *Branson*, son of Brand, appears as *Bransom*.

The same group of names is affected by dissimilation, *i.e.* the instinct to avoid the recurrence of the same sound. Thus *Ranson*, son of Ranolf or Randolf, becomes *Ransom* [1] by dissimilation of one *n*, and *Hanson*, son of Han (see p. 3), becomes *Hansom*. In *Sansom* we have Samson assimilated to *Sanson* and then dissimilated. Dissimilation especially affects the sounds *l, n, r*. *Bullivant* is found earlier as *bon enfaunt* (*Goodchild*), just as a braggart Burgundian was called by Tudor dramatists a *burgullian*.[2] *Glazebrook* (see p. 115) is sometimes a dissimilation of *Grazebrook* (grass). Those people called *Salisbury* who do not hail from Salesbury in Lancashire must have had an ancestor *de Sares-bury*, for such was the earlier name of Salisbury (Sarum). A number of occupative names have lost the last syllable by dissimilation, e.g. *Pepper* for pepperer, *Armour* for armourer. For further examples see p. 155.

It may be noted here that, apart from dissimilation, the sounds *l, n, r,* have a general tendency to become confused, e.g. *Phillimore* is for Finamour (*Dearlove*), which also appears as *Finnemore* and *Fenimore*, the latter also to be explained from fen and moor. *Catlin* is from Catherine. *Balestier*, a cross-bow man, gives *Bannister*, and *Hamnet* and

[1] So also Fr. *rançon* gives Eng. *ransom*. The French surname *Rançon* is probably aphetic for *Laurançon*.

[2] "When was Bobadil here, your captain? that rogue, that foist, that fencing *burgullian*" (Jonson, *Every Man in his Humour*, iv. 2).

Hamlet both occur as the name of one of Shakespeare's sons. Janico or Jenico, Fr. Janicot, little Johnny, is now *Jellicoe*. We also get the change of *r* to *l* in Hal, for Harry, whence *Hallett, Hawkins* (Halkins), and the Cornish *Hockin*, Mal or Mol for Mary, whence *Malleson, Mollison*, etc., and *Pell* for Peregrine. This confusion is common in infantile speech, *e.g.* I have heard a small child express great satisfaction at the presence on the table of "blackbelly dam."

Metathesis, or the transposition of sound, chiefly affects *l* and *r*, especially the latter. Our word cress is from Mid. Eng. *kers*, which appears in *Karslake*, *Toulmin* is for *Tomlin*, a double dim., *-el-in*, of Tom, *Grundy* is for *Gundry*, from Anglo-Sax. Gundred, and Joe *Gargery* descended from a *Gregory*. *Burnell* is for *Brunel*, dim. of Fr. *brun*, brown, and *Thrupp* is for *Thorp*, a village (p. 122). *Strickland* was formerly Stirkland, *Cripps* is the same as *Crisp*, from Mid. Eng. *crisp*, curly. Prentis Jankin had—

> "*Crispe* here, shynynge as gold so fyn"
>
> (D. 304);

and of Fame we are told that—

> "Her heer was oundie (wavy) and *crips*."
>
> (*House of Fame*, iii. 296.)

Both names may also be short for Crispin, the etymology being the same in any case. *Apps* is sometimes for *asp*, the tree now called by the adjectival name aspen (cf. linden). We find Thomas *atte apse* in the reign of Edward III.

The letters *l, n, r* also tend to disappear from no other cause than rapid or careless pronunciation.

Hence we get *Home* for *Holme* (p. 117), *Ferris* for *Ferrers*, a French local name, *Batt* for Bartholomew, *Gatty* for Gertrude, *Dallison* for *d'Alençon*. The loss of *-r-* after a vowel is also exemplified by *Foster* for *Forster*, *Pannell* and *Pennell* for *Parnell* (sometimes), *Gath* for *Garth* (p. 124), and *Mash* for *Marsh*. To the loss of *n* before *s* we owe such names as *Pattison, Paterson*, etc., son of *Paton*, the dim. of Patrick, and *Robison* for Robinson, and also a whole group of names like *Jenks* and *Jinks* for *Jenkins* (John), *Wilkes* for *Wilkins, Gilkes, Danks, Perks, Hawkes, Jukes* for *Judkins* (p. 58), etc. Here I should also include *Biggs*, which cannot be connected with *Bigg*, for we do not find adjectival nicknames with *-s*. It seems to represent *Biggins*, from obsolete *biggin*, a building (p. 133).

The French nasal *n* often disappeared before *r*. Thus *denrée*, lit. a pennyworth, appears in Anglo-French as *darree*. Similarly *Henry* became *Harry*, except in Scotland, and the English Kings of that name were always called Harry by their subjects. It is to this pronunciation that we owe the popularity of *Harris* and *Harrison*, and the frequency of Welsh *Parry* as compared with *Penry*. A compromise between Henry and Harry is seen in *Hanrott*, from the French dim. Henriot.

The initial *h-*, which we regard with such veneration, is treated quite arbitrarily in surnames. We find a well-known medieval poet called indifferently *Occleve* and *Hoccleve*. *Harnett* is the same as *Arnett*, for Arnold, *Ewens* and *Hewens* are both from *Ewan*, cognate with Evan, of which *Heaven* is an imitative form. In *Hoskins*, from the medieval Osekin, a dim. of some Anglo-Saxon name such as Oswald (p. 69), the aspirate has definitely prevailed. The Devonshire name *Hexter* is for Exeter, *Arbuckle* is a corruption of Harbottle, in Northumberland. The Old French name Ancel appears as both *Ansell* and *Hansell*, and *Earnshaw* exists side by side with *Hearnshaw* (p. 110).

The loss of *h* is especially common when it is the initial letter of a suffix, e.g. *Barnum* for Barnham, *Haslam* (hazel), *Blenkinsop* for Blenkin's hope (see *hope*, p. 108), *Newall* for Newhall, *Windle* for Wind Hill, *Tickell* for Tick Hill, in Yorkshire, etc. *Pickles* might be of similar origin, but its oldest form, Pighkeleys, seems to mean rather hill-meadows. A man who minded sheep was once called a *Shepard*, or *Sheppard*, as he still is, though we spell it *shepherd*. The letter *w* disappears in the same way; thus *Greenish* is for Greenwich, *Horridge* for Horwich, *Aspinall* for Aspinwall, *Millard* for *Millward*, the mill-keeper, *Boxall* for Boxwell, *Caudle* for *Cauldwell* (cold); and the Anglo-Saxon names in *-win* are often confused with those in *-ing*, e.g. *Gooding*, *Goodwin*; *Golding*, *Goldwin*; *Gunning*, *Gunwin*, etc. In this way *Harding* has prevailed over the once equally common *Hardwin*.

Finally, we have to consider what may be called baby phonetics, the sound-changes which seem rather to transgress general phonetic laws. Young children habitually confuse dentals and palatals, thus a child may be heard to say that he has "dot a told." This tendency is, however, not confined to children. My own name, which is a very uncommon one, is a stumbling-block to most people, and when I give it in a shop the scribe has generally got as far as *Wheat-* before he can be stopped. We find both *Astill* and *Askell* for the medieval Asketil and *Thurtle* alternating with *Thurkle*, originally Thurketil (p. 74, *n*). *Berten-*

shaw is found for *Birkenshaw*, birch wood, *Bartley*, usually from Bartholomew, is sometimes for Berkeley, and both Lord Bacon and Horace Walpole wrote Twitnam for Twickenham. *Jeffcock*, dim. of Geoffrey, becomes *Jeffcott*, while *Glascock* is for the local *Glascott*. Here the palatal takes the place of the dental, as in *Brangwin* for Anglo-Sax. Brandwine. *Middlemas* is almost certainly for Michaelmas (see p. 89). We have the same change in *tiddlebat* for *stickleback*, a word which exemplifies another point in baby phonetics, viz. the loss of initial *s-*, as in the classic instance *tummy*. To this loss of *s-* we owe *Pillsbury* for the local *Spilsbury*, *Pink* for *Spink*, an obsolete word for the chaffinch, and, I think, *Tout* for *Stout*. The name *Stacey* is found as *Tacey* in old Notts registers. On the other hand, an inorganic *s-* is sometimes prefixed, as in *Sturgess* for the older Turgis. For the loss of *s-* we may compare Shakespeare's *parmaceti* (1 *Henry IV*. i. 3), and for its addition the adjective *spruce*, from Pruce, *i.e.* Prussia.

We also find the infantile confusion between *th* and *f*, e.g. in *Selfe*, which represents a personal name Seleth, probably from Anglo-Sax. *sælð*, bliss. Both Selve and Selthe occur in the Hundred Rolls. Perhaps also in *Fripp* for *Thripp*, a variant of *Thrupp*, for *Thorp*. *Bickerstaffe* is the name of a place in Lancashire, of which the older form appears in *Bickersteth*, and the local name *Throgmorton* is spelt by Camden Frogmorton.

Such are some of the commoner phenomena to be noticed in connection with the spelling and sound of our names. The student must always bear in mind that our surnames date from a period when nearly the whole population was uneducated. Their modern forms depend on all sorts of circumstances, such as local dialect, time of adoption, successive fashions in pronunciation and the taste and fancy of the speller. They form part of our language, that is, of a living and ever-changing organism. Some of us are old enough to remember the confusion between initial *v* and *w* which prompted the judge's question to Mr. Weller. The vulgar *i* for *a*, as in "*tike* the *kike*," has been evolved within comparatively recent times, as well as the loss of final -*g*, "*shootin* and *huntin*," in sporting circles. In the word *warmint*—

> "What were you brought up to be?"
> "A *warmint*, dear boy"
> (*Great Expectations*, ch. xl.),

we have three phonetic phenomena, all of which have influenced the form and sound of modern surnames, e.g. in *Winter*, sometimes for *Vinter*, i.e. vintner, *Clark* for *Clerk*, and *Bryant* for *Bryan*; and similar changes have been in progress all through the history of our language.

In conclusion it may be remarked that the personal and accidental element, which has so much to do with the development of surnames, releases this branch of philology to some extent from the iron rule of the phonetician. Of this the preceding pages give examples. The name, not being subject as other words are to a normalizing influence, is easily effected by the traditional or accidental spelling. Otherwise *Fry* would be pronounced *Free*. The *o* is short in *Robin* and long in *Probyn*, and yet the names are the same (p. 62). *Sloper* and *Smoker* mean a maker of slops and smocks respectively, and *Smale* is an archaic spelling of *Small*, the modern vowel being in each case lengthened by the retention of an archaic spelling. The late Professor Skeat rejects Bardsley's identification of *Waring* with Old Fr. Garin or Warin, because the original vowel and the suffix are both different. But *Mainwaring*, which is undoubtedly from *mesnil Warin* (p. 142), shows Bardsley to be right.

CHAPTER IV

BROWN, JONES, AND ROBINSON

" *Talbots* and *Stanleys, St. Maurs* and such-like folk, have led armies and made laws time out of mind ; but those noble families would be somewhat astonished—if the accounts ever came to be fairly taken—to find how small their work for England has been by the side of that of the *Browns.*"

(*Tom Brown's Schooldays*, ch. i.)

Brown, Jones, and *Robinson* have usurped in popular speech positions properly belonging to *Smith, Jones* and *Williams.* But the high position of *Jones* and *Williams* is due to the Welsh, who, replacing a string of *Aps* by a simple genitive at a comparatively recent date, have given undue prominence to a few very common names ; cf. *Davies, Evans,* etc. If we consider only purely English names, the triumvirate would be *Smith, Taylor,* and *Brown.* Thus, of our three commonest names, the first two are occupative and the third is a nickname. French has no regular equivalent, though *Dupont* and *Durand* are sometimes used in this way—

" Si Chateaubriand avait eu nom *Durand* ou *Dupont,* qui sait si son *Génie du Christianisme* n'eût point passé pour une capucinade?'

(F. Brunetière)

The Germans speak of *Müller, Meyer* and *Schulze,* all rural names, and it is perhaps characteristic that two of them are official. *Meyer* is an early loan from Lat. *major,* and appears to have originally meant something like overseer. Later on it acquired the meaning of farmer, in its proper sense of one who farms, *i.e.* manages on a profit-sharing system, the property of another. It is etymologically the same as our *Mayor, Mair,* etc. *Schulze,* a village magistrate, is cognate with Ger. *Schuld,* debt, and our verb *shall.*

Taking the different classes of surnames separately, the six commonest occupative names are *Smith, Taylor, Clark, Wright, Walker, Turner.* If we exclude *Clark,* as being more often a nickname for the man who could read and write, the sixth will be *Cooper,* sometimes spelt *Cowper.* The commanding position of *Smith* is due to the fact that it was applied to all workers in, or *smiters* of, metal. The modern Smiths no doubt include descendants of medieval blacksmiths, white-smiths, brownsmiths, locksmiths, and many others, but the compounds are not common as surnames. We find, however, *Shoosmith, Shearsmith,* and *Nasmyth,* the last being more probably for earlier *Knysmith,* i.e. knife-smith, than for nail-smith, which was supplanted by *Naylor.* *Grossmith* I guess to be an accommodated form of the Ger. *Grobschmied,* blacksmith, lit. rough smith, and *Goldsmith* is very often a Jewish name for Ger. *Goldschmid.* *Wright,* obsolete perhaps as a trade name, has given many compounds, including *Arkwright,* a maker of bins, or *arks* as they were once called, *Tellwright,* a tile maker, and many others which need no interpretation. The high position of *Taylor* is curious, for there were other names for the trade, such as *Seamer, Shapster, Parmenter* (p. 170), and neither *Tailleur* nor *Letailleur* are particularly common in French. The explanation is that this name has absorbed the medieval *Teler* and *Teller,* weaver, ultimately belonging to Lat. *tela,* a web; cf. the very common Fr. *Tellier* and *Letellier*. In some cases also the Mid. Eng. *teygheler*, *Tyler*, has been swallowed up. *Walker*, i.e. trampler, meant a cloth fuller, but another origin has helped to swell the numbers of the clan—

> " *Walkers* are such as are otherwise called foresters. They are foresters assigned by the King, who are *walkers* within a certain space of ground assigned to their care " (Cowel's *Interpreter*).

Cooper, a derivative of Lat. *cupa* or *cuppa*, a vessel, is cognate with the famous French name *Cuvier*, which has given our *Cover*, though this may also be for coverer, *i.e.* tiler (see p. 155).

Of occupative names which have also an official meaning, the three commonest are *Ward*, *Bailey*, and *Marshall*. *Ward*, originally abstract, is the same word as Fr. *garde*. *Bailey*, Old Fr. *bailif* (*bailli*), ranges from a Scottish magistrate to a man in possession. It is related to *bail* and to *bailey*, a ward in a fortress, as in Old Bailey. *Bayliss* appears to be from the Old French nominative *bailis* (p. 9, *n.*). *Marshall* (p. 183) may stand for a great commander or a shoeing-smith, still called farrier-marshal in the army. The first syllable is cognate with *mare* and the second means servant. *Constable*, Lat. *comes stabuli*, stableman, has a similar history.

The commonest local names naturally include none taken from particular places. The three commonest are *Hall*, *Wood* and *Green*, from residence by the great house, the wood, and the village green. Cf. the French names *Lasalle*, *Dubois*, *Dupré*. *Hall* has sometimes given *Hale* and *Hales* (p. 21), and, in its Old French translation, *Sale*. Next to these come *Hill*, *Moore*, and *Shaw* (see p. 110); but *Lee* would probably come among the first if all its variants were taken into account (p. 28).

Of baptismal names used unaltered as surnames the six commonest are *Thomas, Lewis, Martin, James, Morris, Morgan.* Here again the Welsh element is strong, and four of these names, ending in *-s,* belong also to the next group, *i.e.* the class of surnames formed from the genitive of baptismal names. The frequent occurrence of *Lewis* is partly due to its being adopted as a kind of translation of the Welsh Llewellyn, but the name is often a disguised Jewish Levi, and has also absorbed the local *Lewes.* Next to the above come *Allen, Bennett, Mitchell,* all of French introduction. *Mitchell* may have been reinforced by *Mickle,* the northern for *Bigg.* It is curious that these particularly common names, *Martin, Allen, Bennett* (Benedict), *Mitchell* (Michael), have formed comparatively few derivatives and are generally found in their unaltered form. Three of them are from famous saints' names, while *Allen,* a Breton name which came in with the Conquest, has probably absorbed to some extent the Anglo-Saxon name *Alwin* (p. 72). *Martin* is in some cases an animal nickname, the *marten.* Among the genitives *Jones, Williams,* and *Davi(e)s* lead easily, followed by *Evans, Roberts,* and *Hughes,* all Welsh in the main. Among the twelve commonest names of this class those that are not preponderantly Welsh are *Roberts, Edwards, Harris, Phillips,* and *Rogers.* Another Welsh patronymic, *Price* (p. 66), is among the fifty commonest English names.

The classification of names in *-son* raises the difficult question as to whether *Jack* represents Fr. *Jacques,* or whether it comes from *Jankin, Jenkin,* dim. of John.[1]

[1] See E. B. Nicholson, *The Pedigree of Jack.*

Taking *Johnson* and *Jackson* as separate names, we get the order *Johnson, Robinson, Wilson, Thompson, Jackson, Harrison.* The variants of *Thompson* would put it a place or two higher. Names in *-kins* (see p. 48) are of comparatively late appearance and are not so common as those in the above classes. It would be hard to say which English font-name has given the largest number of family names. In Chapter V. will be found some idea of the bewildering and multitudinous forms they assume. It has been calculated, I need hardly say by a German professor, that the possible number of derivatives from one given name is 6,000, but fortunately most of the seeds are abortive.

Of nicknames *Brown, Clark,* and *White* are by far the commonest. Then comes *King,* followed by the two adjectival nicknames *Sharp* and *Young.*

The growth of towns and facility of communication are now bringing about such a general movement that most regions would accept *Brown, Jones* and *Robinson* as fairly typical names. But this was not always so. *Brown* is still much commoner in the north than in the south, and at one time the northern *Johnson* and *Robinson* contrasted with the southern *Jones* and *Roberts,* the latter being of comparatively modern origin in Wales (p. 43). Even now, if we take the farmer class, our nomenclature is largely regional,[1] and the directories even of our great manufacturing towns represent to a great extent the medieval population of the rural district around them. The names *Daft* and *Turney,* well known in Nottingham, appear in the county in the Hundred Rolls. *Cheetham,* the name of a place now absorbed in Manchester, is as a surname ten times

[1] See Guppy, *Homes of Family Names.*

more numerous there than in London, and the same is true of many characteristic north-country names, such as the *Barraclough*, *Murgatroyd*, and *Sugden* of Charlotte Brontë's *Shirley*. The transference of *Murgatroyd* (p. 111) to Cornwall, in Gilbert and Sullivan's *Ruddigore*, must have been part of the intentional topsy-turvydom in which those two bright spirits delighted. Diminutives in *-kin*, from the Old Dutch suffix *-ken*, are still found in greatest number on the east coast that faces Holland, or in Wales, where they were introduced by the Flemish weavers who settled in Pembrokeshire in the reign of Henry I. It is in the border counties, Cheshire, Shropshire, Hereford, and Monmouth, that we find the old Welsh names such as *Gough*, *Lloyd*, *Onion* (Enion), *Vaughan* (p. 216). The local *Gapp*, an opening in the cliffs, is pretty well confined to Norfolk, and *Puddifoot* belongs to Bucks and the adjacent counties as it did in 1273. The hall changes hands as one conquering race succeeds another—

"Where is Bohun? Where is de Vere? The lawyer, the farmer, the silk mercer, lies *perdu* under the coronet, and winks to the antiquary to say nothing" (Emerson, *English Traits*),

but the hut keeps its ancient inhabitants. The descendant of the Anglo-Saxon serf who cringed to Front de Bœuf now makes way respectfully for Isaac of York's motor, perhaps on the very spot where his own fierce ancestor first exchanged the sword for the ploughshare long before Alfred's day.

CHAPTER V

THE ABSORPTION OF FOREIGN NAMES

"I was born in the year 1632, in the city of York, of a good family, though not of that country, my father being a foreigner of Bremen, who settled first at Hull. He got a good estate by merchandize, and leaving off his trade, lived afterwards at York, from whence he married my mother, whose relations were named Robinson, a very good family in that country, and from whom I was called Robinson Kreutznaer; but by the usual corruption of words in English, we are now called—nay, we call ourselves and write our name—Crusoe" (*Robinson Crusoe*, ch. i.).

ANY student of our family nomenclature must be struck by the fact that the number of foreign names now recognizable in England is out of all proportion to the immense number which must have been introduced at various periods of our history. Even the expert, who is often able to detect the foreign name in its apparently English garb, cannot rectify this disproportion for us. The number of names of which the present form can be traced back to a foreign origin is inconsiderable when compared with the much larger number assimilated and absorbed by the Anglo-Saxon.

The great mass of those names of French or Flemish origin which do not date back to the Conquest or to medieval times are due to the immigration of Protestant refugees in the sixteenth and seventeenth centuries. It is true that many names for which Huguenot ancestry is claimed were known in England long before the Reformation. Thus, *Bulteel* is the name of a refugee family which came from Tournay about the year 1600, but the same name is found in the Hundred Rolls of 1273. The *Grubbe* family, according to Burke, came from Germany about 1450, after the Hussite persecution; but we find the name in England two centuries earlier, "without the assistance of a foreign persecution to make it respectable" (Bardsley, *Dictionary of English Surnames*). The *Minet* family is known to be of Huguenot origin, but the same name also figures in the Hundred Rolls. The fact is that there was all through the Middle Ages a steady immigration of foreigners, whether artisans, tradesmen, or adventurers, some of whose names naturally reappear among the Huguenots. On several occasions large bodies of Continental workmen, skilled in special trades, were brought into the country by the wise policy of the Government. Like the Huguenots later on, they were protected by the State and persecuted by the populace, who resented their habits of industry and sobriety.

During the whole period of the religious troubles in France and Flanders, starting from about the middle of the sixteenth century, refugees were reaching this country in a steady stream; but after the Revocation of the Edict of Nantes they arrived in thousands, and the task of providing for them and helping on their absorption into the population became a serious problem. Among the better class of these immigrants was to be found the flower of French intellect and enterprise, and one has only to look through an Army or Navy list, or to notice the names which are prominent in the Church, at the Bar, and in the higher walks of industry and commerce, to realize the madness of Louis XIV. and the wisdom of the English Government.

Here are a few taken at random from Smiles's *History of the Huguenots*—*Bosanquet, Casaubon, Chenevix Trench, Champion de Crespigny, Dalbiac, Delane, Dollond, Durand, Fonblanque, Gambier, Garrick, Layard, Lefanu, Lefroy, Ligonier, Luard, Martineau, Palairet, Perowne, Plimsoll, Riou, Romilly*—all respectable and many distinguished, even cricket being represented. These more educated foreigners usually kept their names, sometimes with slight modifications which do not make them unrecognizable. Thus, *Bouverie*, literally "ox-farm," is generally found in its unaltered form, though the *London Directory* has also examples of the perverted *Buffery*. But the majority of the immigrants were of the artisan class and illiterate. This explains the extraordinary disappearance, in the course of two centuries, of the thousands of French names which were introduced between 1550 and 1700.

We have many official lists of these foreigners, and in these lists we catch the foreign name in the very act of transforming itself into English. This happens sometimes by translation, e.g. *Poulain* became *Colt*, *Poisson* was reincarnated as *Fish*, and a refugee bearing the somewhat uncommon name *Petitœil* transformed himself into *Little-eye*, which became in a few generations *Lidley*. But comparatively few surnames were susceptible of such simple treatment, and in the great majority of cases the name underwent a more or less arbitrary perversion which gave it a more English physiognomy. Especially interesting from this point of view is the list of—"Straungers residing and dwellinge within the city of London and the liberties thereof," drawn up in 1618. The names were probably taken down by the officials of the different wards, who, differing themselves in intelligence and orthography, produced very curious results. As a rule the Christian name is translated, while the surname is either assimilated to some English form or perverted according to the taste and fancy of the individual constable. Thus, *John Garret*, a Dutchman, is probably *Jan Gerard*, and *James Flower*, a milliner, born in Rouen, is certainly *Jaques Fleur*, or *Lafleur*. *John de Cane* and *Peter le Cane* are *Jean Duquesne* and *Pierre Lequesne* (Norman *quêne*, oak), though the former may also have come from *Caen*. *John Buck*, from Rouen, is *Jean Bouc*, and *Abraham Bushell*, from Rochelle, was probably a *Boussel* or *Boissel*. *James King* and *John Hill*, both Dutchmen, are obvious translations of common Dutch names, while *Henry Powell*, a German, is *Heinrich Paul*. *Mary Peacock*, from Dunkirk, and *John Bonner*, a Frenchman, I take to be *Marie Picot* and *Jean Bonheur*, while *Nicholas Bellow* is surely *Nicolas Belleau*. *Michael Leman*, born in Brussels, may be French *Leman* or *Lemoine*, or perhaps German *Lehmann*.

To each alien's name is appended that of the monarch whose subject he calls himself, but a republic is outside the experience of one constable who leaves an interrogative blank after *Cristofer Switcher*, born at *Swerick* (Zurich) in *Switcherland*. The surname so ingeniously created appears to have left no pedagogic descendants. In some cases the harassed Bumble has lost patience, and substituted a plain English name for foreign absurdity. To the brain which christened Oliver Twist we owe *Henry Price*, a subject of the King of Poland, *Lewis Jackson*, a "Portingall," and *Alexander Faith*, a steward to the Venice Ambassador, born in the dukedom of Florence.

In the returns made outside the bounds of the city

proper the aliens have added their own signatures, or in some cases made their marks. *Jacob Alburtt* signs himself as *Jacob Elbers,* and *Croft Castell* as *Kraft Kassels. Harman James* is the official translation of *Hermann Jacobs, Mary Miller* of *Marija Moliner,* and *John Young* of *Jan le Jeune. Gyllyam Spease,* for *Wilbert Spirs,* seems to be due to a Welsh constable, and *Chrystyan Wyhelhames,* for *Cristian Welselm,* looks like a conscientious attempt at Williams. One registrar, with a phonetic system of his own, has transformed the Dutch *Moll* into the Norman-French *Maule,* and has enriched his list with *Jannacay Yacopes* for *Jantje Jacobs. Lowe Luddow,* who signs himself *Louij Ledou,* seems to be *Louis Ledoux.* An alien who writes himself *Jann Eisankraott* (Ger. *Eisenkraut* ?) cannot reasonably complain at being transformed into *John Isacrocke,* but the substitution of *John Johnson* for *Jansen Vandrusen* suggests that this individual's case was taken at the end of a long day's work.

These examples, taken at random, show how the French and Flemish names of the humbler refugees lost their foreign appearance. In many cases the transformation was etymologically justified. Thus, some of our *Druitts* and *Drewetts* may be descended from *Martin Druett,* the first name on the list. But this is probably the common French name *Drouet* or *Drouot,* assimilated to the English *Druitt,* which we find in 1273. And both are diminutives of Drogo, which occurs in *Domesday Book,* and is, through Old French, the origin of our *Drew.* But in many cases the name has been so deformed that one can only guess at the continental original. I should conjecture, for instance, that the curious name *Shoppee* is a corruption of *Chappuis,* the Old French for a carpenter, and that

Jacob Shophousey, registered as a German cutler, came from *Schaffhausen*. In this particular region of English nomenclature a little guessing is almost excusable. The law of probabilities makes it mathematically certain that the horde of immigrants included representatives of all the very common French family names, and it would be strange if *Chappuis* were absent.

This process of transformation is still going on in a small way, especially in our provincial manufacturing towns, in which most large commercial undertakings have slipped from the nerveless grasp of the Anglo-Saxon into the more capable and prehensile fingers of the foreigner—

> "Hilda then learnt that Mrs. Gailey had married a French modeller named *Canonges* . . . and that in course of time the modeller had informally changed the name to *Cannon*, because no one in the five towns could pronounce the true name rightly."
> (Arnold Bennett, *Hilda Lessways*, i. 5.)

This occurs most frequently in the case of Jewish names of German origin. Thus, *Löwe* becomes *Lowe* or *Lyons*, *Meyer* is transformed into *Myers*, *Goldschmid* into *Goldsmith*, *Kohn* into *Cowan*, *Levy* into *Lee* or *Lewis*, *Salamon* into *Salmon*, *Hirsch* or *Hertz* into *Hart*, and so on. Sometimes a bolder flight is attempted—

> "*Leopold Norfolk Gordon* had a house in Park Lane, and ever so many people's money to keep it up with. As may be guessed from his name, he was a Jew."
> (Morley Roberts, *Lady Penelope*, ch. ii.)

The Jewish names of German origin which are now so common in England mostly date from the beginning of the nineteenth century, when laws were passed in Austria, Prussia and Bavaria to compel all Jewish families to adopt a fixed surname. Many of them chose personal names, e.g. *Jakobs, Levy, Moses,* for this purpose, while others named themselves from their place of residence, e.g. *Cassel, Speyer* (Spires), *Hamburg,* often with the addition of the syllable *-er,* e.g. *Darmesteter, Homburger.* Some families preferred descriptive names such as *Selig* (see p 209), *Sonnenschein, Goldmann,* or invented poetic and gorgeous place-names such as *Rosenberg, Blumenthal, Goldberg, Lilienfeld.* The oriental fancy also showed itself in such names as *Edelstein,* jewel, *Glückstein,*[1] luck stone, *Rubinstein,* ruby, *Goldenkranz,* golden wreath, etc. It is owing to the existence of the last two groups that our fashionable intelligence is now often so suggestive of a wine-list. Among animal names adopted the favourites were *Adler,* eagle, *Hirsch,* hart, *Löwe,* lion, and *Wolf,* each of which is used with symbolic significance in the Old Testament.

[1] Our *Touchstone* would seem also to be a nickname. The obituary of a Mr. Touchstone appeared in the *Manchester Guardian,* December 12, 1912.

CHAPTER VI

TOM, DICK AND HARRY

"*Watte* vocat, cui *Thomme* venit, neque *Symme* retardat,
*Bette*que, *Gibbe* simul, *Hykke* venire jubent;
Colle furit, quem *Geffe* juvat nocumenta parantes,
Cum quibus ad dampnum *Wille* coire vovet.
Grigge rapit, dum *Dawe* strepit, comes est quibus *Hobbe*,
Lorkyn et in medio non minor esse putat:
Hudde ferit, quem *Judde* terit, dum *Tebbe* minatur,
Jakke domosque viros vellit et ense necat."

(GOWER, *On Wat Tyler's Rebellion*.)

GOWER'S lines on the peasant rebels give us some idea of the names which were most popular in the fourteenth century, and which have consequently impressed themselves most strongly on our modern surnames. It will be noticed that one member of the modern triumvirate,[1] Harry, or Hal, is absent. The great popularity of this name probably dates from a rather later period and is connected with the exploits of Henry V. Moreover, all the names, with the possible exception of Hud, are of French introduction and occur rarely before the Conquest. The Old Anglo-Saxon names did survive, especially in the remoter parts of the country, and have given us many surnames (see ch. vii.), but even in the Middle Ages people had a

[1] The three names were not definitely established till the nineteenth century. Before that period they had rivals. French says *Pierre* et *Paul*, and German *Heinz* und *Kunz*, *i.e.* Heinrich and Conrad.

preference for anything that came over with the Conqueror. French names are nearly all of German origin, the Celtic names and the Latin names which encroached on them having been swept away by the Frankish invasion, a parallel to the wholesale adoption of Norman names in England. Thus our name *Harvey*, no longer usual as a font-name, is Fr. Hervé, which represents the heroic German name Hartwig, to the second syllable of which belongs such an apparently insignificant name as *Wigg*. The disappearance of Latin names is not to be regretted, for the Latin nomenclature was of the most unimaginative description, while the Old German names are more like those of Greece. Thus Ger. Ludwig, which has passed into most of the European languages (Louis, Lewis, Ludovico, etc), is from Old High Ger. *hlut-wig*, renowned in fight, equivalent to the Greek Clytomachus, with one-half of which it is etymologically cognate.

Some of the names in Gower's list, e.g. *Watte* (p. 3), *Thomme, Symme, Geffe* (p. 61), *Wille, Jakke*, are easily recognized. *Bette* is for *Bat*, Bartholomew, a name which has given *Batty, Batten, Bates, Bartle* (cf. Bartlemas), *Bartlett, Badcock, Badman*, and many other names, but its popularity is not easy to account for. *Gibbe* is for Gilbert. *Hick* is rimed on Dick (p. 62). *Colle*[1] is for Nicolas. *Grig* is for Gregory, whence *Gregson* and Scottish *Grier*. *Dawe*, for David, alternated with *Day* and *Dow*, which appear as first element in many surnames, though *Day* has another origin (p. 177) and *Dowson* sometimes belongs to the female name *Douce*, sweet. *Hobbe* is a rimed

[1] It is doubtful whether Scottish *Colin* is a dim. of this. It may be the same Celtic name which has sometimes given the Irish *Cullen*.

form from Robert. *Lorkyn*, or *Larkin*, is for Lawrence, for which we also find *Law*, *Lay*, and *Low*, whence *Lawson*, *Lowson*, *Laycock*, *Locock*, etc. For *Hudde* see pp. 3, 75. *Judde*, from the very popular *Jordan*, has given *Judson*, *Judkins*, and the contracted *Jukes*. It is probable that *Jordan* (Fr. Jourdain, Ital. Giordano) is an Old German personal name mistakenly associated with the sacred river of Palestine. *Tebbe* is for Theobald (p. 4).

Many people, in addressing a small boy with whom they are unacquainted, are in the habit of using Tommy as a name to which any small boy should naturally answer. In some parts of Polynesia the natives speak of a white Mary or a black Mary, *i.e.* woman, just as the Walloons round Mons speak of Marie bon bec, a shrew, Marie grognon, a Mrs. Gummidge, Marie quatre langues, a chatterbox, and several other Maries still less politely described. We have the modern silly Johnny for the older silly Billy, while Jack Pudding is in German Hans Wurst, John Sausage. Only the very commonest names are used in this way, and, if we had no further evidence, the rustic Dicky bird, Robin redbreast, Hob goblin, Tom tit, Will o' the Wisp, Jack o' lantern, etc., would tell us which have been in the past the most popular English font-names. During the Middle Ages there was a kind of race among half a dozen favourite names, the prevailing order being John, William, Thomas, Richard, Robert, with perhaps Hugh as sixth.

Now, for each of these there is a reason. John, a favourite name in so many languages (Jean, Johann, Giovanni, Evan, Yves, Ivan, etc.), as the name of the Baptist and of the favoured disciple, defied even the unpopularity of our one King of that name. The special circumstances attending the birth and naming of the Baptist probably supplied the chief factor in its triumph. For some time after the Conquest William led easily. We usually adopted the *W-* form from the north-east of France, but Guillaume has also supplied a large number of surnames in *Gil-*, which have got inextricably mixed up with those derived from Gilbert, Gillian (Juliana), and Giles. *Gilman* represents the French dim. Guillemin, the local-looking *Gilham* is simply Guillaume, and *Wilmot* corresponds to Fr. Guillemot. The doubting disciple held a very insignificant place until the shrine of St. Thomas of Canterbury became one of the holy places of Christendom. To Thomas belong *Macey*, *Massie*, *Machin*, and *Masson*, dims. of French aphetic forms, but the first two are also local, from Macé or Macey, and the second two are sometimes alternative forms of *Mason*. Robert and Richard were both popular Norman names. The first was greatly helped by Robin Hood and the second by the Lion-Heart. The name Hugh was borne by several saints, the most famous of whom in England was the child-martyr, St. Hugh of Lincoln, said to have been murdered by the Jews *c.* 1250. It had a dim. *Huggin* and also the forms *Hew* and *How*, whence *Hewett*, *Hewlett*, *Howitt*, *Howlett*, etc., while from the French dim. Huchon we get *Hutchin* and its derivatives, and also *Houchin*. Hugh also appears in the rather small class of names represented by *Littlejohn*, *Meiklejohn*,[1] etc. We find

[1] This formation seems to be much commoner in French. In the "Bottin" I find Grandblaise, Grandcollot (Nicolas), Grandgeorge, Grandgérard, Grandguillaume, Grandguillot, Grandjacques, Grandjean, Grandperrin (Pierre), Grandpierre, Grandremy, Grandvincent, and Petitcolin, Petitdemange (Dominique), Petitdidier (Desiderius), Petit-Durand, Petit-étienne (Stephen), Petit-Gérard, Petit-Huguenin, Petitjean, Petitperrin, Petit-Richard.

Goodhew, *Goodhue*. Cf. *Gaukroger*, i.e. awkward Roger, and *Goodwillie*. *Goodrich* and *Goodrick* may in some cases belong to Richard. Only the very commonest names occur in such compounds.

Most of the other names in Gower's list have been prolific. We might add to them Roger, whence *Hodge* and *Dodge*, *Humfrey*, which did not lend itself to many variations, and Peter, from the French form of which we have many derivatives (see p. 32), including perhaps the Huguenot *Perowne*, Fr. Perron, but this can also be local, du Perron, the etymology, Lat. *petra*, rock, remaining the same.

The absence of the great names Alfred[1] and Edward is not surprising, as they belonged to the conquered race. Though Edward was revived as the name of a long line of Kings, its contribution to surnames has been small, most names in *Ed-*, *Ead-*, e.g. *Ede*, *Eden*, *Edison*, *Edkins*, *Eady*, etc., belonging rather to the once popular female name Eda or to Edith, though in some cases they are from Edward or other Anglo-Saxon names having the same initial syllable. James is a very rare name in medieval rolls, being represented by Jacob, and no doubt partly by Jack (see p. 46). It is—

> "Wrested from Jacob, the same as Jago[2] in Spanish, Jaques in French; which some Frenchified English, to their disgrace, have too much affected" (Camden).

It appears in *Gimson*, *Jemmett*, and the odd-looking *Gem*, while its French form is somewhat disguised in *Jeakes* and *Jex*.

[1] The name *Alured* is due to misreading of the older *Alvred*, *v* being written *u* in old MSS. *Allfrey* is from the Old French form of the name.

[2] *Jago* is found, with other Spanish names, in Cornwall; cf. *Bastian* or *Basten*, for Sebastian.

The force of royal example is seen in the popularity under the Angevin kings of Henry, or Harry, Geoffrey and Fulk, the three favourite names in that family. For Harry see p. 38. Geoffrey, from Ger. Gottfried, Godfrey, has given us a large number of names in *Geff-*, *Jeff-*, and *Giff-*, *Jiff-*, and probably also *Jebb*, *Gepp* and *Jepson*, while to *Fulk* we owe *Fewkes*, *Foakes*, *Fowkes*, *Vokes*, etc., and perhaps in some cases *Fox*. But it is impossible to catalogue all the popular medieval font-names. Many others will be found scattered through this book as occasion or association suggests them.

Three names whose poor representation is surprising are *Arthur*, *Charles* and *George*, the two great Kings of medieval romance and the patron saint of Merrie England. All three are fairly common in their unaltered form, and we find also *Arter*. But they have given hardly any derivatives, though *Atkins*, generally from *Ad-*, i.e. Adam, may sometimes be from Arthur (cf. Bat for Bart, Matty for Martha, etc.). Arthur is a rare medieval font-name, a fact no doubt due to the sad fate of King John's nephew. Its modern popularity dates from the Duke of Wellington, while Charles and George were raised from obscurity by the Stuarts and the Brunswicks. To these might be added the German name Frederick, the spread of which was due to the fame of Frederick the Great. It gave, however, in French the dissimilated *Ferry*, one source of our surnames *Ferry*,[1] *Ferris*, though the former is generally local.

[1] "For Frideric, the English have commonly used Frery and Fery, which hath been now a long time a Christian name in the ancient family of Tilney, and lucky to their house, as they report." (Camden.)

If, on the other hand, we take from Gower's list a name which is to-day comparatively rare, *e.g.* Gilbert, we find it represented by a whole string of surnames, e.g. *Gibbs, Gibson, Gibbon, Gibbins, Gilbey, Gilpin, Gipps,* to mention only the most familiar. From the French dim. Gibelot we get the rather rare *Giblett*; cf. *Hewlett* for Hew-el-et, *Hamlet* for Ham-el-et (Hamo), etc.

In forming patronymics from personal names, it is not always the first syllable that is selected. In *Toll, Tolley, Tollett,* from Bartholomew, the second has survived, while *Philpot,* dim. of Philip, has given *Potts.* From Alexander we get *Sanders* and *Saunders.* But, taking, for simplicity, two instances in which the first syllable survived, we shall find plenty of instruction in those two pretty men Robert and Richard. We have seen (p. 60) that Roger gave *Hodge* and *Dodge,* which, in the derivatives *Hodson* and *Dodson* have coalesced with names derived from Odo and the Anglo-Sax. Dodda (p. 76). Similarly Robert gave *Rob, Hob*[1] and *Dob,* and Richard gave *Rick, Hick* and *Dick.* Hob, whence *Hobbs,* was sharpened into Hop, whence *Hopps.* The diminutive *Hopkin,* passing into Wales, gave *Popkin,* just as ap-Robin became *Probyn,* ap-Hugh *Pugh,* ap-Owen *Bowen,* etc. In the north *Dobbs* became *Dabbs* (p. 31). Hob also developed another rimed form Nob (cf. to "hob-nob" with anyone), whence *Nobbs* and *Nabbs,* the latter, of course, being sometimes rimed on *Abbs,* from Abel or Abraham. Bob is the latest variant and has not formed many surnames. Richard has a larger family than Robert, for, besides *Rick, Hick* and

[1] I believe, however, that Hob is in some cases from Hubert, whence *Hubbard, Hibbert, Hobart,* etc.

Dick, we have *Rich* and *Hitch*, *Higg* and *Digg*. The reader will be able to continue this genealogical tree for himself.

The full or the shortened name can become a surname, either without change, or with the addition of the genitive *-s* or the word *-son*,[1] the former more usual in the south, the latter in the north. To take a simple case, we find as surnames *William*, *Will*, *Williams*, *Wills*, *Williamson*, *Wilson*. From the short form we get diminutives by means of the English suffixes *-ie* or *-y* (these especially in the north), *-kin*, and the French suffixes *-et*, *-ot* (often becoming *-at* in English), *-in*, *-on* (often becoming *-en* in English). Thus *Willy*, *Wilkin*, *Willett*. I give a few examples of surnames formed from each class—

Ritchie (Richard), *Oddy* (Odo, whence also *Oates*), *Lambie*[2] (Lambert), *Jelley* (Julian);

Dawkins, *Dawkes* (David), *Hawkins*, *Hawkes* (Hal), *Gifkins* (Geoffrey), *Perkins*, *Perks* (Peter), *Rankin* (Randolf);

Gillett (Gil, see p. 59), *Collett* (Nicholas), *Bartlett* (Bartholomew), *Ricketts* (Richard), *Marriott*, *Marryat* (Mary), *Elliott* (Elias, see p. 85), *Wyatt* (Guy), *Perrott* (Peter);

Collins (Nicholas), *Jennings* (John, see p. 95), *Copping* (Jacob, see p. 9), *Rawlin* (Raoul, the French form of Radolf, whence *Rolf*, *Ralph*, *Relf*), *Paton* (Patrick), *Sisson* (Siss, *i.e.* Cecilia), *Gibbons* (Gilbert), *Beaton* (Beatrice).

[1] This suffix has squeezed out all the others, though Alice John*son* is theoretically absurd. In Mid. English we find daughter, father, mother, brother and other terms of relationship used in this way, *e.g.*, in 1379, Agnes *Dyconwyfdowson*, the wife of Dow's son Dick. *Dawbarn*, child of David, is still found. See also p. 193.

[2] *Lamb* is also, of course, a nickname; cf. *Agnew*, Fr. *agneau*.

In addition to the suffixes and diminutives already mentioned, we have the two rather puzzling endings *-man* and *-cock*. *Man* occurs as an ending in several Germanic names which are older than the Conquest, e.g. *Ashman, Harman, Coleman,* and the simple *Mann* is also an Anglo-Saxon personal name. It is sometimes to be taken literally, e.g. in *Goodman,* i.e. master of the house (Matt. xx. 11), *Longman, Youngman,* etc. In *Hickman, Homan* (How, Hugh), etc., it may mean servant of, as in *Ladyman, Priestman,* or may be merely an augmentative suffix. In *Coltman, Runciman,* it is occupative, the man in charge of the colts, rouncies or nags. Chaucer's shipman—

"Rood upon a *rouncy* as he kouthe" (A. 390).

In *Bridgeman, Pullman,* it means the man who lived near, or had some office in connection with, the bridge or pool. But it is often due to the imitative instinct. *Dedman* is for the local Debenham, and *Lakeman* for Lakenham, while *Wyman* represents the old name Wymond, and *Bowman* and *Beeman* are sometimes for the local Beaumont (cf. the pronunciation of Belvoir). But the existence in German of the name *Bienemann* shows that *Beeman* may have meant bee-keeper. *Sloman* is either imitative for Solomon or means the man in the slough (p. 113), and *Godliman* is an old familiar spelling of Godalming. We of course get doubtful cases, e.g. *Sandeman* may be, as explained by Bardsley, the servant of Alexander (p. 62), but it may equally well represent Mid. Eng. *sandeman,* a messenger, and *Lawman, Layman,* are rather to be regarded as derivatives of *Lawrence* (p. 58) than what they appear to be.

Many explanations have been given of the suffix

-cock, but I cannot say that any of them have convinced me. Both *Cock* and the patronymic *Cocking* are found as early personal names. The suffix was added to the shortened form of font-names, e.g. *Alcock* (Allen), *Hitchcock* (Richard), was apparently felt as a mere diminutive, and took an *-s* like the diminutives in *-kin,* e.g. *Willcocks, Simcox.* In *Hedgecock, Woodcock,* etc., it is of course a nickname. The modern *Cox* is one of our very common names, and the spelling *Cock, Cocks, Cox,* can be found representing three generations in the churchyard of Invergowrie, near Dundee.

The two names *Bawcock* and *Meacock* had once a special significance. Pistol, urged to the breach by Fluellen, replies—

> "Good *bawcock,* bate thy rage! use lenity, sweet chuck"
> (*Henry V.,* iii. 2);

and Petruchio, pretending that his first interview with Katherine has been most satisfactory, says—

> "'Tis a world to see
> How tame, when men and women are alone,
> A *meacock* wretch can make the curstest shrew."
> (*Taming of the Shrew,* ii. 1.)

These have been explained as Fr. *beau coq,* which is possible, and *meek cock,* which is absurd. As both words are found as surnames before Shakespeare's time, it is probable that they are diminutives which were felt as suited to receive a special connotation, just as a man who treats his thirst generously is vulgarly called a *Lushington. Bawcock, Bocock,* can easily be connected with Baldwin, while *Meacock, Maycock,* belong to the personal name *May* or *Mee,* shortened from the Old Fr. *Mahieu* (p. 86).

Although we are not dealing with Celtic names, a few words as to the Scottish, Irish, and Welsh surnames which we find in our directories may be useful. Those of Celtic origin are almost invariably patronymics. The Scottish and Irish *Mac*, used like the Anglo-Fr. *Fitz-*, means relative, and is ultimately related to the *-mough* of *Watmough* (see p. 193) and to the word *maid*. In *MacNab*, son of the abbot, and *MacPherson*, son of the parson, we have curious hybrids. In Manx names, such as *Quilliam* (Mac William), *Killip* (Mac Philip), *Clucas* (Mac Lucas), we have aphetic forms of *Mac*. The Irish *O'* has the same meaning as *Mac*, and is related to the first part of Ger. *Oheim*, uncle, of Anglo-Sax. *eam* (see *Eames*, p. 193), and of Lat. *avus*, grandfather. *Oe* or *oye* is still used for grandchild in Scottish—

"There was my daughter's wean, little Eppie Daidle, my *oe*, ye ken" (*Heart of Midlothian*, ch. iv.).

The names of the Lowlands of Scotland are pretty much the same as those of northern England, with the addition of a very large French element, due to the close historical connection between the two countries. Examples of French names, often much corrupted, are *Bethune* (Pas de Calais), often corrupted into *Beaton*, the name of one of the Queen's Maries, *Boswell* (Bosville, Seine Inf.), *Bruce* (Brieux, Orne), *Comyn*, *Cumming* (Comines, Nord), *Grant* (*le grand*), *Rennie* (René), etc.

Welsh *Ap* or *Ab*, reduced from an older *Map*, ultimately cognate with *Mac*, gives us such names as *Probyn*, *Powell* (Howell, Hoel), *Price* (Rhys), *Pritchard*, *Prosser* (Rosser), *Prothero* (Roderick), *Bedward*, *Beddoes* (Eddowe), *Blood* (Lud, Lloyd), *Bethell* (Ithel), *Benyon*

(Enion), whence also *Bunyan* and the local-looking *Baynham*. *Onion* and *Onions* are imitative forms of Enion. *Applejohn* and *Upjohn* are corruptions of Ap-john. The name *Floyd*, sometimes *Flood*, is due to the English inability to grapple with the Welsh *Ll*—

> "I am a gentylman and come of Brutes [Brutus'] blood,
> My name is ap Ryce, ap Davy, ap *Flood*."
> (Andrew Boorde, *Book of the Introduction of Knowledge*, ii. 7.)

While Welsh names are almost entirely patronymic, Cornish names are very largely local. They are distinguished by the following prefixes and others of less common occurrence: *Caer-*, fort, *Lan-*, church, *Pen-*, hill, *Pol-*, pool, *Ros-*, heath, *Tre-*, settlement, e.g. *Carthew, Lanyon, Penruddock, Polwarth, Rosevear, Trethewy*. Sometimes these elements are found combined, e.g. in *Penrose*.

A certain number of Celtic nicknames and occupative names which are frequently found in England will be mentioned elsewhere (pp. 173, 216). In *Gilchrist*, Christ's servant, *Gildea*, servant of God, *Gillies*, servant of Jesus, *Gillespie*, bishop's servant, *Gilmour*, big servant, *Gilroy*, red servant, we have the Highland "gillie." Such names were originally preceded by *Mac-*, e.g. *Gilroy* is the same as *MacIlroy*; cf. *MacLean*, for *Macgil-ian*, son of the servant of John. To the same class of formation belong Scottish names in *Mal*, e.g. *Malcolm*, and Irish names in *Mul*, e.g. *Mulholland*, in which the first element means tonsured servant, shaveling, and the second is the name of a saint.

CHAPTER VII

GODERIC AND GODIVA

"England had now once more (A.D. 1100) a King born on her own soil, a Queen of the blood of the hero Eadmund, a King and Queen whose children would trace to Ælfred by two descents. Norman insolence mocked at the English King and his English Lady under the English names of *Godric* and *Godgifu*." [1]

(FREEMAN, *Norman Conquest*, v. 170.)

IN dealing with surnames we begin after the Conquest, for the simple reason that there were no surnames before. Occasionally an important person has come down in history with a nickname, *e.g.* Edmund Ironside, Harold Harefoot, Edward the Confessor; but this is exceptional, and the Anglo-Saxon, as a rule, was satisfied with one name. It is probable that the majority of names in use before the Conquest, whether of English or Scandinavian origin, were chosen because of their etymological meaning, e.g. that the name Beornheard (*Bernard*, *Barnard*, *Barnett*) was given to a boy in the hope that he would grow up a warrior strong, just as his sister might be called Æthelgivu, noble gift. The formation of these old names is both interesting and, like all Germanic nomenclature, poetic.

As a rule the name consists of two elements, and the number of those elements which appear with great frequency is rather limited. Some themes occur only

[1] "Godricum eum, et comparem Godgivam appellantes" (William of Malmesbury, *Gesta Regum Anglorum*).

in the first half of the name, e.g. *Æthel-*, whence Æthelstan, later *Alston*; *Ælf-*, whence Ælfgar, now *Elgar* and *Agar* (*Æthel-* and *Ælf-* soon got confused, so that *Allvey* and *Elvey* may represent either Æthelgifu or Ælfgifu, or, Latinized, Ethelgiva and Elgiva); *Cuth-*, whence Cuthbeald, now *Cobbold*[1]; *Cyne-*, whence Cynebeald, now *Kimball* and *Kemble*, both of which are also local; *Folc-*, whence Folcheard and Folchere, now *Folkard* and *Fulcher*; *Gun-*, whence Gundred, now *Gundry* and *Grundy* (p. 37); *Os-*, whence *Osbert, Osborn, Osgood*. Other themes only occur as the second half of the name. Such are *-gifu*, in Godgifu, *i.e.* Godiva, whence *Goodeve*; *-lac* in Guthlac, now *Goodlake* and *Goodluck* (p. 197); *-laf* in Deorlaf, now *Dearlove*; *-wacer* in Euerwacer, now *Earwaker*.

Other themes, and perhaps the greater number, may occur indifferently first and second, e.g. *beald, god, here, sige, weald, win, wulf* or *ulf*. Thus we have complete reversals in Bealdwine, whence *Baldwin*, and Winebeald, whence *Winbolt*, Hereweald, whence *Herald, Harold, Harrod*, and Wealdhere, whence *Walter* (p. 3). With these we may compare Goldman and Mangold, the latter of which has given *Mangles*. So also we have Sigeheard, whence *Siggers*, and Wulfsige, now *Wolsey*, Wulfnoth, now the imitative *Wallnutt*, and Beorhtwulf, later Bardolph and *Bardell*. The famous name *Havelock* was borne by the hero of a medieval epic, "Havelock the Dane," but *Dunstan* is usually for the local Dunston. On the other hand, *Winston* is a personal name, Winestan, whence *Winstanley*.

These examples show that the pre-Norman names are by no means unrepresented in the twentieth

[1] This is also the origin of *Cupples*, and probably of *Keble* and *Kibbles*. It shares *Cobbett* and *Cubitt* with Cuthbeorht.

century, but, in this matter, one must proceed with caution. To take as examples the two names that head this chapter, there is no doubt that Goderic and Godiva are now represented by *Goodrich* and *Goodeve*, but these may also belong to the small group mentioned on p. 59, and stand for good Richard and good Eve. Also *Goodrich* comes in some cases from Goodrich, formerly Gotheridge, in Hereford, which has also given *Gutteridge*. Moreover, it must not be forgotten that our medieval nomenclature is preponderantly French, as the early rolls show beyond dispute, so that, even where a modern name appears susceptible of an Anglo-Saxon explanation, it is often safer to refer it to the Old French cognate, for the Germanic names introduced into France by the Frankish conquerors, and the Scandinavian names which passed into Normandy, contained very much the same elements as our own native names, but underwent a different phonetic development. Thus I would rather explain *Bawden*, *Bowden*, *Boulden*, *Boden*, and the dims. *Body* and *Bodkin*, as Old French variants from the Old Ger. Baldawin than as coming directly from Anglo-Saxon. *Boyden* undoubtedly goes back to Old Fr. Baudouin. Practically all the names given in Gower's lines (p. 56), and many others to which I have ascribed a continental origin, are found occasionally in England before the Conquest, but the weight of evidence shows that they were either adopted in England as French names or were corrupted in form by the Norman scribes and officials. To take other examples, our *Tibbald*, *Tibbles*, *Tibbs* suggest the Fr. Thibaut rather than the natural development of Anglo-Sax. Thiudbeald, i.e. Theobald; and *Ralph*, *Relf*, *Roff*, etc., show the regular Old French development of Rædwulf,

Radolf. Tibaut Wauter, *i.e.* Theobald Walter, who lived in Lancashire in 1242, had both his names in Old French.

As a matter of fact, the various ways of forming nicknames, or descriptive names, are all used in the pre-Conquest personal names. We find *Orme,* i.e. serpent or dragon (cf. Great Orme's Head), Wulf, i.e. *Wolf*, Hwita, i.e. *White,* and its derivative Hwiting, now *Whiting*, Sæmann, i.e. *Seaman*, Bonda, i.e. *Bond*, Leofcild, dear child, now *Leifchild*, etc. But, except in the case of *Orme,* so common as the first element of place-names, I doubt the survival of these personal names into the surname period and regard *White*, *Seaman*, *Bond*, *Leifchild* as rather new epithets of Mid. English formation. *Whiting* is of course Anglo-Saxon, *-ing* being the regular patronymic suffix. Cf. *Browning*, *Benning*, *Dering*, *Dunning*, *Gunning* *Hemming*, *Kipping*, *Manning*, *Spalding*, and many others which occur in place-names. But not all names in *-ing* are Anglo-Saxon, e.g. *Baring* is German; cf. Behring, of the Straits, while *Jobling* is Fr. Jobelin, a double dim. of Job.

I will now give a few examples of undoubted survival of these Anglo-Saxon compounds, showing how the suffixes have been corrupted and simplified. Among the commonest of these suffixes are *-beald*, *-beorht*, *-cytel* (p. 74, *n.*), *-god*, *-heard*, *-here*, *-man*, *-mund*, *-ræd*, *-ric*, *-weald*, *-weard*, *-wine*,[1] which survive in *Rumball* and *Rumbold* (Rumbeald), *Allbright*[2] and *Allbutt* (Ealdbeorht, *i.e.* Albert), *Arkle* (Earncytel), *Allgood* and *Elgood* (Ælfgod), *Everett* (Eoforheard, *i.e.*

[1] Bold, bright, kettle, good, strong, army, man, protection, counsel, powerful, ruling, guard, friend.

[2] Albert is of modern German introduction.

Everard), *Gunter* (Gundhere), *Harman* (Hereman), *Redmond*[1] (Rædmund), *Aldred* (Æthelræd or Ealdræd), *Aldridge*, and the perversion *Allwright* (Æthelric or Ealdric), *Thorold* (Thurweald), and, through Fr. Turold, *Turrell, Terrell*, and *Tyrrell, Harward* and *Harvard* (Hereweard), *Lewin* (Leofwine). In popular use some of these endings got confused, e.g. *Rumbold* probably sometimes represents Rumweald, while *Kennard* no doubt stands for Cœnweard as well as for Cœnheard. *Man* and *mund* were often interchanged (p. 64), so that from Eastmund come both *Esmond* and *Eastman*. *Gorman* represents Gormund, and *Almond* (p. 97) is so common in the Middle Ages that it must sometimes be from Æthelmund.

Sometimes the modern forms are imitative. Thus *Allchin* is for Alcuin, and *Goodyear*,[2] *Goodier* and *Goodair* represent Godhere, while *Goodbeer, Godbehere, Gotobed* are classed by Bardsley under Godbeorht, which has also given *Godber*. But in these three names the face value of the words can also be accepted (pp. 153, 203, 206). Wisgar or Wisgeard has given the imitative *Whisker* and *Vizard*, and, through French, the Scottish *Wishart*, which is thus the same as the famous Norman Guiscard. *Garment* and *Rayment* are for Garmund and Regenmund, *i.e.* Raymond.

Other names which can be traced directly to the group of Anglo-Saxon names dealt with above are *Elphick* (Ælfheah), which in Norman French gave Alphege, *Elmer* (Ælfmær), *Allnutt* (Ælfnoth), *Alwin, Elwin, Elvin* (Ælfwine), *Aylmer* (Æthelmær), *Aylward*

[1] Pure Anglo-Saxon, like the names of so many opponents of English tyranny. *Parnell* is of course not Irish (p. 94).

[2] This may, however, be taken literally. There is a German name *Gutjahr* and a Norfolk name *Feaveryear*.

(Æthelweard), *Kenrick* (Cœnric), *Collard* (Ceolheard), *Colvin* (Ceolwine), *Darwin* (Deorwine), *Edridge* (Eadric), *Aldwin*, *Auden*, and the patronymic *Alderson* (Ealdwine), *Falstaff* (Fastwulf), *Filmer* (Filumær), *Frewin* (Freowine), *Garrard*, *Garrett*, *Jarrold* (Gærheard, Gærweald), but probably these are through French, *Garbett* (Garbeald, which, in Italian, became Garibaldi), *Gatliffe* (Geatleof), *Goddard* (Godheard), *Goodliffe* (Godleof), *Gunnell* (Gunhild), *Gunner*[1] (Gunhere), *Haines* (Hagene), *Haldane* (Hælfdene), *Hastings* (Hæsten, the Danish chief who gave his name to Hastings, formerly Hæstinga-ceaster), *Herbert* (Herebeorht), *Herrick* (Hereric), *Hildyard* (Hildegeard), *Hubert*, *Hubbard*, *Hobart*, *Hibbert* (Hygebeorht), *Ingram* (Ingelram), *Lambert* (Landbeorht), *Lugard* (Leofgar), *Lemon* (Leofman), *Leveridge* (Leofric), *Loveridge* (Luferic), *Maynard* (Mægenheard), *Maidment* (Mægenmund), *Rayner* (Regenhere), *Raymond* (Regenmund), *Reynolds* (Regenweald), *Seabright* (Sigebeorht and Sæbeorht), *Sayers*[2] (Sægær), *Sewell* (Sæweald or Sigeweald), *Seward* (Sigeweard), *Turbot* (Thurbeorht), *Thoroughgood* (Thurgod), *Walthew* (Waltheof), *Warman* (Wærmund), *Wyberd* (Wigbeorht), *Wyman* (Wigmund), *Willard* (Wilheard), *Winfrey* (Winefrith), *Ulyett* and *Woollett* (Wulfgeat), *Wolmer* (Wulfmær), *Woolridge* (Wulfric).

[1] It is unlikely that this name is connected with *gun*, a word of too late appearance. It may be seen over a shop in Brentford, perhaps kept by a descendant of the thane of the adjacent Gunnersbury.

[2] The simple *Sayer* is also for "assayer," either of metals or of meat and drink—"*essayeur*, an essayer; one that tasts, or takes an essay; and particularly, an officer in the mint, who touches every kind of new coyne before it be delivered out" (Cotgrave). Robert *le sayer*, goldsmith, was a London citizen *c.* 1300.

In several of these, e.g. *Fulcher, Hibbert, Lambert, Reynolds,* the probability is that the name came through French. Where an alternative explanation is possible, the direct Anglo-Saxon origin is generally the less probable. Thus, although Colling occurs as an Anglo-Saxon name, *Collings* is generally a variant of *Collins* (cf. *Jennings* for Jennins), and though *Hammond* is etymologically Haganmund, it is better to connect it with the very popular French form Hamon. *Simmonds* might come from Sigemund, but is more likely from Simon with excrescent *-d* (see p. 35).

In many cases the Anglo-Saxon name was a simplex instead of a compound. The simple Cytel[1] survives as *Chettle, Kettle, Chell, Kell,* whence *Kelsey* (see *ey,* p. 116). *Brand* also appears as *Braund,* Grim is common in place-names, and from Grima we have *Grimes.* Cola gives *Cole,* the name of a monarch of ancient legend, to be distinguished from the derivatives of Nicolas (p. 57), Gunna is now *Gunn,* Serl has given the very common *Searle,* and Wicga is *Wigg.* From Haco we have *Hack* and the dim. *Hackett.*

To these might be added many examples of pure adjectives, such as Freo, *Free,* Froda (prudent), *Froude,* Goda, *Good,* Leof (dear), *Leif, Leaf,* Read (red), *Read, Reid, Reed,* Rica, *Rich,* Rudda (ruddy), *Rudd* and *Rodd,* Snel (swift, valiant), *Snell,* Swet, *Sweet,* etc., or epithets such as Boda (messenger), *Bode,* Cempa (warrior), *Kemp,* Cyta, *Kite,* Dreng (warrior), *Dring,* Eorl, *Earl,* Godcild, *Goodchild,* Nunna, *Nunn,* Oter, *Otter,* Puttoc

[1] Connected with the kettle or cauldron of Norse mythology. The renowned Captain Kettle, described by his creator as a Welshman, must have descended from some hardy Norse pirate. Many names in this chapter are Scandinavian.

(kite), *Puttock*, Sæfugel, *Seafowl*, Spearhavoc, *Sparhawk*, *Spark* (p. 12), Tryggr (true), *Triggs*, Unwine (unfriend), *Unwin*, etc. But most of these had died out as personal names and, in medieval use, were nicknames pure and simple.

Finally, there is a very large group of Anglo-Saxon dissyllabic names, usually ending in *-a*, which appear to be pet forms of the longer names, though it is not always possible to establish the connection. Many of them have double forms with a long and short vowel respectively. It is to this class that we must refer the large numbers of our monosyllabic surnames, which would otherwise defy interpretation. Anglo-Sax. Dodda gave *Dodd*, while Dodson's partner *Fogg* had an ancestor Focga. Other examples are Bacga, *Bagg*, Benna, *Benn*, Bota, *Boot* and dim. *Booty*, Botta, *Bott*, whence *Botting*, Bubba, *Bubb*, Budda, *Budd*, Bynna, *Binns*, Cobba, *Cobb*, Coda, *Coad*, Codda, *Codd*, Cuffa, *Cuff*, Deda, *Deedes*, Duda, *Dowd*, Duna, *Down*, Dunna, *Dunn*, Dutta, *Dutt*, whence *Dutton*, Eada, *Eade*, *Edes*, etc., Ebba, *Ebbs*, Eppa, *Epps*, Hudda, *Hud*, whence *Hudson*, Inga, *Inge*, Sibba, *Sibbs*, Sicga, *Siggs*, Tata, *Tate* and *Tait*, Tidda, *Tidd*, Tigga, *Tigg*, Toca, *Tooke*, Tucca, *Tuck*, Wada, *Wade*, Wadda, *Waddy*, etc. Similarly French took from German a number of surnames formed from shortened names in *-o*, with an accusative in *-on*, e.g. Old Ger. Bodo has given Fr. Bout and Bouton, whence our *Butt* and *Button*.

But the names exemplified above are very thinly represented in early records, and, though their existence in surnames derived from place-names (*Dodsley*, *Bagshaw*, *Bensted*, *Budworth*, *Cobham*, *Ebbsworth*, etc.) would vouch for them even if they were not recorded, their comparative insignificance is attested by the fact that they form very few derivatives. Compare, for instance, the multitudinous surnames which go back to monosyllables of the later type of name, such as John and Hugh, with the complete sterility of the names above. Therefore, when an alternative derivation for a surname is possible, it is usually ten to one that this alternative is right. *Dodson* is a simplified *Dodgson*, from Roger (p. 62); *Benson* belongs to Benedict, sometimes to Benjamin; *Cobbett* is a disguised *Cuthbert* or *Cobbold* (cf. *Garrett*, p. 17); *Down* is usually local, at the down or dune; *Dunn* is medieval *le dun*, a colour nickname; names in *Ead-*, *Ed-*, are usually from the medieval female name Eda (p. 60); *Sibbs* generally belongs to Sybilla or Sebastian; *Tait* must sometimes be for Fr. *Tête*, probably from an inn sign; *Tidd* is an old pet form of Theodore; and *Wade* is more frequently *at wade*, i.e. ford. Even *Ebbs* and *Epps* are much more likely to be shortened forms of Isabella, usually reduced to Ib or Ibbot (p. 94).

To sum up, we may say that the Anglo-Saxon element in our surnames is much larger than one would imagine from Bardsley's Dictionary, and that it accounts, not only for names which have a distinctly Anglo-Saxon suffix or a disguised form of one, but also for a very large number of monosyllabic names which survive in isolation and without kindred. In this chapter I have only given sets of characteristic examples, to which many more might be added. It would be comparatively easy, with some imagination and a conscientious neglect of evidence, to connect the greater number of our surnames with the Anglo-Saxons. Thus *Honeyball* might very well represent the Anglo-Sax. Hunbeald, but, in the absence of links, it is better to regard it as a popular perversion of Hannibal (p. 82). In dealing with this subject, the *via media* is the safe one, and one cannot pass in one stride from Hengist and Horsa to the Reformation period.

Matthew Arnold, in his essay on the *Function of Criticism at the Present Time,* is moved by the case of poor *Wragg,* who was "in custody," to the following wail—

> "What a touch of grossness in our race, what an original shortcoming in the more delicate spiritual perceptions, is shown by the natural growth amongst us of such hideous names—*Higginbottom, Stiggins, Bugg!*"

But this is the poet's point of view. Though there may have been "no *Wragg* by the Ilissus," it is not a bad name, for, in its original form *Ragg,* it is the first element of the heroic Ragnar, and probably unrelated to *Raggett,* which is the medieval *le ragged. Bugg,* which one family exchanged for Norfolk Howard, is the Anglo-Saxon Bucga, a name no doubt borne by many a valiant warrior. *Stiggins,* as we have seen (p. 12), goes back to a name great in history, and *Higginbottom* (p. 114) is purely geographical.

CHAPTER VIII

PALADINS AND HEROES

> "Morz est Rollanz, Deus en ad l'anme es ciels.
> Li Emperere en Rencesvals parvient. . . .
> Carles escriet: 'U estes vus, bels niés?
> U l'Arcevesques e li quens Oliviers?
> U est Gerins e sis cumpainz Geriers?
> Otes u est e li quens Berengiers?
> Ives e Ivories que j'aveie tant chiers?
> Qu'est devenuz li Guascuinz Engeliers,
> Sansun li dux e Anseïs li fiers?
> U est Gerarz de Russillun li vielz,
> Li duze per que j'aveie laissiet?' "[1]
>
> (*Chanson de Roland*, l. 2397.)

It is natural that many favourite names should be taken from those of heroes of romançe whose exploits were sung all over Europe by wandering minstrels. Such names, including those taken from the Round Table legends, usually came to us through French, though a few names of the British heroes are Welsh, e.g. *Cradock* from Caradoc (Caractacus) and *Maddox* from Madoc. But the Round Table stories were

[1] "Dead is Roland, God has his soul in heaven. The Emperor arrives at Roncevaux. . . . Charles cries: 'Where are you, fair nephew? Where the archbishop (Turpin) and Count Oliver? Where is Gerin and his comrade Gerier? Where is Odo and count Berenger? Ivo and Ivory whom I held so dear? What has become of the Gascon Engelier? Samson the duke and Anseis the proud? Where is Gerard of Roussillon the old, the twelve peers whom I had left?' "

versified much later than the true Old French *Chansons de Geste*, which had a basis in the national history, and not many of Arthur's knights are immortalized as surnames. We have *Tristram*, *Lancelot*, whence *Lance*, *Percival*, Gawain in *Gavin*, and *Kay*. But the last named is, like *Key*, more usually from the word we now spell "quay," though *Key* and *Keys* can also be shop-signs, as of course *Crosskeys* is. *Linnell* and *Lyell* are for Lionel, as *Neil*,[1] *Neal* for Nigel. The ladies have fared better. *Vivian*, which is sometimes from the masculine Vivien, is found in Dorset as *Vye*. and Isolt and Guinevere, which long survived as font-names in Cornwall, have given several names. From Isolt come *Isard*, *Isitt*, *Izzard*, *Izod*, and many other forms, while Guinever appears as *Genever*, *Jennifer*, *Gaynor*, *Gilliver*, *Gulliver*,[2] and the imitative *Juniper*. It is probably also the source of *Genn* and *Ginn*, though these may come also from Eugenia or from Jane. The later prose versions of the Arthurian stories, such as those of Malory, are full of musical and picturesque names like those used by Mr. Maurice Hewlett, but this artificial nomenclature has left no traces in our surnames.

Of the paladins the most popular was Roland or Rowland, who survives as *Rowe*, *Rowlinson*, *Rolls*, *Rollit*, etc., sometimes coalescing with the derivations of Raoul, another epic hero. Gerin or Geri gave *Geary*, and *Oates* is the nominative (see p. 80, *n.* 1) of Odo, an important Norman name. Berenger appears as *Barringer* and *Bellinger* (p. 36). The simple *Oliver* is

[1] But the Scottish Neil is a Gaelic name often exchanged for the unrelated Nigel.

[2] There is also an Old Fr. Gulafre which will account for some of the Gullivers.

fairly common, but it also became *Ollier* and *Olver*. But perhaps the largest surname family connected with the paladins is derived from the Breton Ives or Ivon,[1] whose name appears in that of two English towns. It is the same as Welsh Evan, and the Yvain of the Arthurian legends, and has given us *Ives*, *Ivison*, *Ivatts*, etc. The modern surname *Ivory* is usually an imitative form of *Every*, or *Avery* (p. 82). Gerard has a variety of forms in *Ger-* and *Gar-*, *Jer-* and *Jar-* (see p. 32). The others do not seem to have survived, except the redoubtable Archbishop *Turpin*, whose fame is probably less than that of his namesake Dick.

Besides the paladins, there are many heroes of Old French epic whose names were popular during the two centuries that followed the Conquest. Ogier le Danois, who also fought at Roncevaux, has given us *Odgers*; Fierabras occasionally crops up as *Firebrace*; Aimeri de Narbonne, from Almaric,[2] whence Ital. Amerigo, is in English *Amery*, *Emery*, *Imray*, etc.; Renaud de Montauban is represented by *Reynolds* (p. 74) and *Reynell*. The famous *Doon* de Mayence may have been an ancestor of Lorna, and the equally famous Garin, or Warin, de Monglane has given us *Waring*, sometimes *Warren*, and the diminutives *Garnett* and *Warnett*. He shares *Gerring* with the paladin Gerin. Milo becomes *Miles*, with dim. *Millett*, and some of its derivatives have got mixed with the local *Mill* and the font-name Millicent. Amis and Amiles were the Orestes and Pylades of Old French epic and

[1] A number of Old French names had an accusative in *-on* or *-ain*. Thus we find *Otes*, *Oton*, *Ives*, *Ivain*, and feminines such as *Ide*, *Idain*, all of which survive as English surnames.

[2] A metathesis of Amalric, which is found in Anglo-Saxon.

the former survives as *Ames, Amies,* and *Amos.* We have also *Berner* from Bernier, *Bartram* from Bertran, *Farrant,* with many variants, from Ferrand, *i.e.,* Ferdinand, *Terry* and *Terriss* from Thierry, the French form of Ger. Dietrich (Theodoric), which, through Dutch, has given also *Derrick.* Garnier, from Ger. Werner, is our *Garner* and *Warner,* though these have other origins (pp. 154, 185). Dru, from Drogo, has given *Drew,* with dim. *Druitt* (p. 53), and *Druce,* though the latter may also come from the town of Dreux. *Walrond* and *Waldron* are for Waleran, usually Galeran, and King Pippin had a retainer named *Morant.* Saint Leger appears as *Ledger, Lediard,* etc., and sometimes in the shortened *Legg.* Among the heroines we have *Orbell* from Orable, while Blancheflour may have suggested *Lillywhite*; but the part played by women in the *Chansons de Geste* was insignificant.

As this element in our nomenclature has hitherto received no attention, it may be well to add a few more examples of names which occur very frequently in the *Chansons de Geste* and which have undoubted representatives in modern English. *Allard* was one of the Four Sons of Aymon. The name is etymologically identical with *Aylward* (p. 73), but in the above form has reached us through French. Acard or Achard is represented by *Haggard, Haggett,* and *Hatchard, Hatchett,* though *Haggard* probably has another origin (p. 221). *Harness* is imitative for Harnais, Herneis. *Clarabutt* is for Clarembaut ; cf. *Archbutt* for Archembaut, the Old French form of Archibald, *Archbold.* *Durrant* is Durand, still a very common French surname. *Ely* is Old Fr. Élie, *i.e.* Elias (p. 85), which had the dim. Elyot.[1] We also find Old Fr. Helye,

[1] For other names belonging to this group see p. 85

whence our *Healey*. Enguerrand is telescoped to *Ingram*, though this may also come from the English form Ingelram. *Fawkes* is the Old Fr. Fauques, nominative (see p. 80, *n*. 1) of Faucon, *i.e.* falcon. *Galpin* is contracted from *Galopin*, a famous epic thief, but it may also come from the common noun *galopin*—

> "*Galloppins*, under cookes, or scullions in monasteries."
> (Cotgrave.)

In either case it means a "runner." *Henfrey* is from Heinfrei or Hainfroi, identical with Anglo-Sax Haganfrith, and *Manser* from Manesier. *Neame* (p. 193) may sometimes represent Naime, the Nestor of Old French epic and the sage counsellor of Charlemagne. *Richer*, from Old Fr. Richier, has generally been absorbed by the cognate Richard. *Aubrey* and *Avery* are from Alberic. An unheroic name like *Siggins* may be connected with several heroes called Seguin.

Nor are the heroes of antiquity altogether absent. Along with Old French national and Arthurian epics there were a number of romances based on the legends of Alexander, Cæsar, and the tale of Troy. Alexander, or *Saunder*, was the favourite among this class of names, especially in Scotland. *Cayzer* was generally a nickname, its later form *Cæsar* being due to Italian influence,[1] and the same applies to *Hannibal*,[2] when it is not an imitative form of the female name Annabel, also corrupted into *Honeyball*. Both Dionisius and Dionisia were once common, and have survived as *Dennis*, *Dennett*, *Denny*, and from the shortened *Dy*.

[1] Julius Cesar, physician to Queen Elizabeth, was a Venetian (Bardsley).

[2] But the frequent occurrence of this name and its corruptions in Cornwall suggest that it may really have been introduced by Carthaginian sailors.

we get *Dyson*. But this Dionisius was the patron saint of France. Apparent names of heathen gods and goddesses are almost always due to folk-etymology, e.g. *Bacchus* is for *bake-house*, and the ancestors of Mr. Wegg's friend *Venus* came from Venice. *Virgil* is of Italian origin and *Homer* is Old Fr. *heaumier*, helmet maker.

CHAPTER IX

THE BIBLE AND THE CALENDAR

"'Now you see, brother Toby,' he would say, looking up, 'that Christian names are not such indifferent things;—had Luther here been called by any other name but Martin, he would have been damn'd to all eternity'" (*Tristram Shandy*, ch. xxxv).

THE use of biblical names as font-names does not date from the Puritans, nor are surnames derived from Abraham, Isaac and Jacob necessarily Jewish. The Old Testament names which were most popular among the medieval peasants from whom we nearly all spring were naturally those connected with the most picturesque episodes of sacred history. Taking as an example the father of all men, we find derived from the name *Adam* the following: *Adams, Adamson, Adcock, Addis, Addison, Adds, Addy, Ade, Ades, Adey, Adie, Ady, Addey, Aday, Adee, Addyman, Adkin, Adkins, Adkinson, Adnett,*[1] *Adnitt, Adnet, Adnot, Atkin, Atkins, Atkinson,* and the northern *Aitken,* etc This list, compiled from Bardsley's *Dictionary of Surnames,* is certainly not exhaustive. Probably *Taddy* is rimed on Addy as *Taggy* is on Aggy (Agnes). To put together all the derivatives of John or Thomas would be a task almost beyond the wit of man. Names in *Abb-, App-,* may come from either Abraham or Abel, and from *Abbs* we also have *Nabbs.* Cain was of

[1] Adenet (little Adam) le Roi was an Old French epic hero.

course unpopular. The modern *Cain, Cane, Kain* represents the town of Caen or Norman *quesne, quêne,* an oak. Moses appears in the French form *Moyes* (Moïse) as early as 1273, and still earlier as *Moss.* Of the patriarchs the favourites were perhaps Jacob and Joseph, the name *Jessop* from the latter having been influenced by Ital. Giuseppe. Benjamin has sometimes given *Benson* and *Bennett,* but these are generally for Benedict (p. 46). The Judges are poorly represented, except *Samson,* a name which has obviously coalesced with the derivatives of Samuel. David had, of course, an immense vogue, especially in Wales (for some of its derivatives see p. 57), and Solomon was also popular, the modern *Salmon* not always being a Jewish name. But almost the favourite Old Testament name was Elijah, Elias, which, usually through its Old French form Élie, whence *Ely,* is the parent of *Ellis, Elliot,* and many other names in *El-,* some of which, however, have to be shared with Ellen and Alice (p. 95). Job was also popular, and is easily recognized in *Jobson, Jobling,* etc., but less easily in *Chubb* (p. 32) and *Jupp.* The intermediate form was the obsolete Joppe. Among the prophetic writers Daniel was an easy winner, *Dann, Dance* (p. 10), *Dannatt, Dancock,* etc. *Balaam* is an imitative spelling of the local Baylham.

In considering these Old Testament names it must be remembered that the people did not possess the Bible in the vernacular. The teaching of the parish priests made them familiar with selected episodes, from which they naturally took the names which appeared to contain the greatest element of holiness or of warlike renown. It is probable that the mystery plays were not without influence; for the personal name was not always a fixed quantity, and just as John Carter, moving from Bingham to Nottingham, might become John Bingham, so Humfrey, after playing the part of Abel, might find his name changed accordingly.

This would apply with still more force to names taken from the legends of saints and martyrs on which the miracle plays were based. We even find the names *Saint*, *Martyr*[1] and *Postill*, the regular aphetic form of apostle (p. 33), just as we find *King* and *Pope*. Camden, speaking of the freedom with which English names are formed, quotes a Dutchman, who—

"When he heard of English men called God and Devil, said, that the English borrowed names from all things whatsoever, good or bad."

The medieval name Godde may of course be for *Good*, Anglo-Sax. Goda, which is the first element in *Goddard*, *Godfrey*, etc., but *Ledieu* is common enough in France. The name seems to be obsolete, unless it is disguised as *Goad*. The occurrence in medieval rolls of *Diabolus* and *le Diable* shows that *Deville* need not always be for de Eyville. There was probably much competition for this important part, and the name would not be always felt as uncomplimentary. The surname *Teufel* is found in German.

Coming to the New Testament, we find the four Evangelists strongly represented, especially the first and last. Matthew appears not only in an easily recognizable form, e.g. in *Matheson*, but also as *Mayhew* and *Mayo*, Old Fr. Mahieu. From the latter form we have the shortened *May* and *Mee*, whence *Mayes*, *Makins*, *Meakin*, *Meeson*, and sometimes *Mason*. Mark is one of the sources of *March*

[1] This may also be from Fr. *le martre*, the marten.

(p. 90), as Luke is of *Luck,* whence *Lucock, Luckett,* etc., though we more often find the learned form *Lucas.* Of John there is no need to speak. Of the apostles the great favourites, Simon, or Peter, John, and Bartholomew have already been mentioned. Almost equally popular was Philip, whence *Philp, Phipps, Phelps,* and the dim. *Philpot.* Here also belongs *Filkins.* Andrew flourished naturally in Scotland, its commonest derivative being *Anderson,* while *Dendy* is for the rimed form Dandy. Paul has of course had a great influence and is responsible for *Pawson* or *Porson, Pawling, Polson, Pollett,* and most names in *Pol-.*[1] It is also, in the form *Powell,* assimilated to the Welsh Ap Howel. Paul is regularly spelt Poule by Chaucer, and St. Paul's Cathedral is often called *Powles* in Tudor documents. Paul's companions are poorly represented, for *Barnby* is local, while names in *Sil-* and *Sel-* come from shortened form of Cecil, Cecilia, and Silvester. Another great name from the Acts of the Apostles is that of the protomartyr Stephen, among the numerous derivatives of which we must include *Stennett* and *Stimpson.*

Many non-biblical saints whose names occur very frequently have already been mentioned, *e.g.* Antony, Bernard, Gregory, Martin, Lawrence, Nicholas, etc. To these may be added Augustine, or *Austin,* Christopher, or Kit, with the dim. *Christie* and the imitative *Chrystal,* Clement, whence a large family of names in *Clem-,* Gervase or *Jarvis,* Jerome, sometimes represented by *Jerram,* and Theodore, or *Tidd* (cf. *Tibb* from Theobald), who becomes in Welsh *Tudor.* Vincent has given *Vince, Vincey* and *Vincett,* and *Baseley, Blazey*

[1] This does not of course apply to Cornish names in *Pol* (p. 67).

are from Basil and Blaise. The Anglo-Saxon saints are poorly represented, though probably most of them survive in a disguised form, e.g. *Price* is sometimes for *Brice*, Cuthbert has sometimes given *Cubitt* and *Cobbett*, and also *Cutts*. With an intrusive *r*[1] it has given *Crewdson* and *Cruden*. *Bottle* sometimes represents Botolf, *Neate* is for Neot, and Chad survives as *Cade* and in many local names, e.g. *Chadwick*. The Cornish *Tangye* is from the Breton St. Tanneguy. The Archangel Michael has given one of our commonest names, *Mitchell* (p. 46). This is through French, but we have also the contracted *Miall*[2]—

> "At Michael's term had many a *trial*,
> Worse than the dragon and St. *Michael*."
> (*Hudibras*, III. ii. 51.)

From Gabriel we have *Gabb*, *Gabbett*, etc. The common rustic pronunciation *Gable* has given *Cable* (p. 32).

Among female saints we find Agnes, pronounced *Annis*, the derivatives of which have become confused with those of Anne, or Nan, Catherine, whence *Catt*, *Catlin*, etc., Cecilia, Cicely, whence *Sisley*, and of course Mary and Margaret. For these see p. 93. St. Bride, or Bridget, survives in *Kirkbride*.

A very interesting group of surnames are derived from font-names taken from the great feasts of the Church, date of birth or baptism,[3] etc. These are more often French or Greco-Latin than English, a fact to be explained by priestly influence. Thus *Christmas*

[1] The letter *r*, so slightly sounded in English, is very irresponsible. It disappears in Fanny (Frances) and Biddy (Bridget), but intrudes itself in the scruff, formerly scuft, of the neck, and probably in *Scroggins* (p. 111).

[2] Cf. *Vialls* from Vitalis, a saint's name.

[3] Names of this class were no doubt also sometimes given to foundlings.

is much less common than *Noel* or *Nowell*, but we also find *Midwinter* (p. 23) and *Yule*. *Easter* has a local origin (from a place in Essex) and also represents Mid. Eng. *estre*, a word of very vague meaning for part of a building, originally the exterior, from Lat. *extra*. It survives in Fr. *les êtres d'une maison*. *Hester*, to which Bardsley gives the same origin, I should rather connect with Old Fr. *hestre* (*hêtre*), a beech. However that may be, the Easter festival is represented in our surnames by *Pascall*, Cornish *Pascoe*, and *Pask*, *Pash*, *Pace*, *Pack*. *Patch*, formerly a nickname for a jester (p. 187), from his motley clothes, is also sometimes a variant of *Pash*. And the dim. *Patchett* has become confused with *Padgett*, from Padge, a rimed form of Madge. *Pentecost* has been corrupted into *Pancoast* and the local-looking *Pankhurst*. Michaelmas is now *Middlemas* (see p. 40), and *Tiffany* is an old name for Epiphany. It comes from Greco-Latin *theophania* (while Epiphany represents *epiphania*), which gave the French female name Tiphaine, whence our *Tiffin*. *Lammas* (loaf mass) is also found as a personal name, but there is a place called Lammas in Norfolk. We have compounds of *day* in *Halliday* or *Holiday*, *Hayday*, for high day, *Loveday*, a day appointed for reconciliations, and *Hockaday*, for a child born during Hocktide, which begins on the 15th day after Easter. It was also called Hobday, though it is hard to say why, hence the name *Hobday*, unless this is to be taken as the *day*, or servant (see p. 177), in the service of Hob; cf. *Hobman*.

The days of the week are puzzling, the only one at all common being *Munday*, though most of the others are found in earlier nomenclature. We should rather expect special attention to be given to Sunday and

Friday, and, in fact, Sonntag and Freytag are by far the most usual in German, while Dimanche and its perversions are common in France, and Vendredi also occurs. This makes me suspect some other origin, probably local, for *Munday*, the more so as Fr. Dimanche, Demange, etc., is often for the personal name Dominicus, the etymology remaining the same as that of the day-name, the Lord's day. Parts of the day seem to survive in *Noon*, *Eve*, and *Morrow*, but *Noon* is local, Fr. Noyon (cf. *Moon*, earlier *Mohun*, from Moyon), *Eve* is the mother of mankind, and *Morrow* is for *moor-row*, i.e. the row of cottages on the moor.

We find the same difficulty with the names of the months. Several of these are represented in French, but our *March* has four other origins, from March in Cambridgeshire, from march, a boundary, from marsh, or from Mark; while *May* means in Mid. English a maiden (p. 195), and is also a dim. of Matthew (p. 86). The names of the seasons also present difficulty. *Spring* must often correspond to Fr. La Fontaine, but we find also *Lent*,[1] the old name for the season, and French has *Printemps*. *Summer* and *Winter*[2] are found very early as personal names, as are also *Frost* and *Snow*[3]; but why always *Summers* or *Somers* with *s* and *Winter* without? The latter has no doubt in many cases absorbed *Vinter*, vintner (see p. 41), but this will not account for the complete absence of genitive forms. And what has become of the other season? We should

[1] The cognate Ger. *Lenz* is fairly common, hence the frequency of *Lent* in America.

[2] Winter was one of Hereward's most faithful comrades.

[3] Two other common personal names were *Flint* and *Steel*.

not expect to find the learned word autumn, but neither *Fall* nor *Harvest*, the true English equivalents, are at all common as surnames.

I regard this group, days, months, seasons, as one of the least clearly accounted for in our nomenclature, and cannot help thinking that the more copious examples which we find in French and German are largely distorted forms due to the imitative instinct, or are susceptible of other explanations. This is certainly true in some cases, *e.g.* Fr. Mars is the regular French development of Medardus,[1] a saint to whom a well-known Parisian church is dedicated; and the relationship of Janvier to Janus may be *via* the Late Lat. *januarius*, for *janitor*, a doorkeeper.

[1] This was the saint who, according to Ingoldsby, lived largely on oysters obtained by the Red Sea shore. At his church in Paris were performed the 'miracles' of the Quietists in the seventeenth century. When the scenes that took place became a scandal, the government intervened, with the result that a wag adorned the church door with the following:

"De par le Roi, défense à Dieu
De faire miracle en ce lieu."

CHAPTER X

METRONYMICS

"During the whole evening Mr. Jellyby sat in a corner with his head against the wall, as if he were subject to low spirits."
(*Bleak House*, ch. iv.)

BARDSLEY first drew attention to the very large number of surnames derived from an ancestress. His views have been subjected to much ignorant criticism by writers who, taking upon themselves the task of defending medieval virtue, have been unwilling to accept this terrible picture of the moral condition of England, etc. This anxiety is misplaced. There are many reasons, besides illegitimacy, for the adoption of the mother's name. In medieval times the children of a widow, especially posthumous children, would often assume the mother's name. *Widdowson* itself is sufficiently common, and is usually to be taken literally, though, like *Widdows*, it is sometimes from Wido, *i.e.* Guy. Orphans would be adopted by female relatives, and a medieval Mrs. Joe Gargery would probably have impressed her own name rather than that of her husband on a medieval Pip. In a village which counted two Johns or Williams, and few villages did not, the children of one would assume, or rather would be given by the public voice, the mother's name. Finally, metronymics can be collected in hundreds by anyone who cares to work through a few early registers.

Thus, in the Lancashire Inquests 1205–1307 occur plenty of people described as the son of Alice, Beatrice, Christiana, Eda, Eva, Mariot, Matilda, Quenilda,[1] Sibilla, Ysolt. Even if illegitimacy were the only reason, that would not concern the philologist.

Female names undergo the same course of treatment as male names. Mary gave the diminutives Marion and Mariot, whence *Marriott.* It was popularly shortened into Mal (cf. Hal for Harry), which had the diminutive Mally. From these we have *Mawson* and *Malleson,* the former also belonging to Maud. Mal and Mally became Mol and Molly, hence *Mollison.* The rimed forms Pol, Polly are later, and names in *Pol-* usually belong to Paul (p. 87). The names *Morris* and *Morrison* occur too frequently to be altogether accounted for as from the font-name Maurice and the nickname Moorish, and are sometimes to be referred to Mary. Similarly Margaret, popularly Marget, became Mag, Meg, Mog, whence *Meggitt, Moxon,* etc. The rarity of *Maggot* is easily understood, but Poll Maggot was one of Jack Sheppard's accomplices and Shakespeare used *maggot-pie* for magpie (*Macbeth,* iii, 4). Meg was rimed into Peg, whence *Peggs,* Mog into Pog, whence *Pogson,* and Madge into Padge, whence *Padgett,* when this is not for *Patchett* (p. 89), or for the Fr. *Paget,* usually explained as *Littlepage.* The royal name Matilda appears in the contracted *Maud, Mould, Moule, Mott, Mahood* (Old Fr. Maheut). Its middle syllable *Till* gave *Tilly, Tillson* and the dim. *Tillet, Tillot,* whence *Tillotson.* From Beatrice we have *Bee, Beaton* and *Betts,* and the northern *Beattie,* which are not connected with the great name Elizabeth. This is in medieval rolls

[1] An Anglo-Saxon name, Cynehild, whence *Quennell.*

represented by its cognate Isabel, of which the shortened form was *Bell* (p. 8), or Ib, the latter giving *Ibbot, Ibbotson,* and the rimed forms *Tib-, Nib-, Bib-, Lib-.* Here also belong *Ebbs* and *Epps* rather than to the Anglo-Sax. Ebba.

Many names which would now sound somewhat ambitious were common among the medieval peasantry and are still found in the outlying parts of England, especially Devon and Cornwall. Among the characters in Mr. Eden Phillpotts's *Widecombe Fair* are two sisters named *Sibley* and *Petronell.* From Sibilla, now Sybil, come most names in *Sib-*, though this was used also as a dim. of Sebastian (see also p. 75), while Petronilla has given *Parnell, Purnell.* As a female name it suffered the eclipse to which certain names are accidentally subject, and became equivalent to wench. Reference to a "prattling Parnel" are common in old writers, and the same fate overtook it in French—

"Taisez-vous, *péronnelle*" (*Tartufe,* i. 1).

Mention has already been made of the survival of Guinevere (p. 79). From Cassandra we have *Cash, Cass, Case,* and *Casson,* from Idonia, *Ide, Iddins, Iddison*; these no doubt confused with the derivatives of Ida and also of Eda and Edith, for the slayer of Jack Cade is indifferently called *Iden* and *Edens. Pim,* as a female font-name, may be from Euphemia, and *Siddons* appears to belong to Sidonia, while the pretty name Avis or Avice has given *Haweis.* From Lettice, Lat. *lætitia,* joy, we have *Letts, Lettson,* while the corresponding *Joyce,* Lat. *jocosa,* merry, has become confused with Fr. Josse (see p. 10). *Anstey, Anstis,* is from Anastasia, *Dobell* from Dulcibella, *Precious* from Preciosa, and *Royce* from Rohesia.

It is often difficult to separate patronymics from metronymics. We have already seen (p. 60) that names in *Ed-* may be from Eda or from Edward, while names in *Gil-* must be shared between Julian, Juliana, Guillaume, Gilbert, and Giles. There are many other cases like Julian and Juliana, e.g. *Custance* is for Constance, but *Cust* may also represent the masculine Constant, while among the derivatives of Philip we must not forget the warlike Philippa. Or, to take pairs which are unrelated, *Kitson* may be from Christopher or from Catherine and *Mattison* from Matthew or from Martha, which became Matty and Patty, the derivatives of the latter coalescing with those of Patrick (p. 63). It is obvious that the derivatives of Alice would be confused with those of Allen, while names in *El-* may represent Elias or Eleanor. Also names in *Al-* and *El-* are sometimes themselves confused, *e.g.* the Anglo-Saxon Ælfgod appears both as *Allgood* and *Elgood*. More *Nelsons* are derived from Neil, *i.e.* Nigel, than from Nell, the rimed dim. of Ellen. *Emmett* is a dim. of Emma, but *Empson* may be a shortened *Emerson* from Emery (p. 80). The rather commonplace *Tibbles* stands for both Theobald and Isabella, and the same is true of all names in *Tib-* and some in *Teb-*. Lastly, the coalescence of John, the commonest English font-name, with Joan, the earlier form of Jane, was inevitable, while the French forms Jean and Jeanne would be undistinguishable in their derivatives. These names between them have given an immense number of surnames, the masculine or feminine interpretation of which must be left to the reader's imagination.

CHAPTER XI

LOCAL SURNAMES

"Now as men have always first given names unto places, so hath it afterwards grown usuall that men have taken their names from places" (VERSTEGAN, *Restitution of Decayed Intelligence*).

THERE is an idea cherished by some people that the possession of a surname which is that of a village or other locality points to ancestral ownership of that region. This is a delusion. In the case of quite small features of the landscape, e.g. *Bridge*, *Hill*, the name was given from place of residence. But in the case of counties, towns and villages, the name was usually acquired when the locality was left. Thus John Tiler leaving Acton, perhaps for Acton's good, would be known in his new surroundings as John Acton. A moment's reflection will show that this must be so. *Scott* is an English name, the aristocratic Scotts beyond the border representing a Norman family Escot, originally of Scottish origin. *English*, early spelt *Inglis*, is a Scottish name. The names *Cornish* and *Cornwallis* first became common in Devonshire, as *Devenish* did outside that county. *French* and *Francis*, Old Fr. *le franceis*, are English names, just as *Langlois* (l'Anglais) is common in France. For the same reason *Cutler* is a rare name in Sheffield, where all are cutlers. By exception the name *Curnow*, which is Cornish for a Cornishman, is fairly common in its native county, but it was perhaps applied especially to those inhabitants who could only speak the old Cornish language.

The local name may range in origin from a country to a plant (*France, Darbishire, Lankester, Ashby, Street, House, Pound, Plumptre, Daisy*), and, mathematically stated, the size of the locality will vary in direct proportion to the distance from which the immigrant has come. Terentius Afer was named from a continent. I cannot find a parallel in England, but names such as the nouns *France, Ireland, Pettingell* (Portugal), or the adjectives *Dench*, Mid. Eng. *densc*, Danish, *Norman, Welsh*, (*Walsh, Wallis*, etc.), *Allman* (Allemand), often perverted to *Almond*, were considered a sufficient mark of identification for men who came from foreign parts. But the untravelled inhabitant, if distinguished by a local name, would often receive it from some very minute feature of the landscape, *e.g.* Solomon *Daisy* may have been descended from a Robert *Dayeseye*, who lived in Hunts in 1273. It is not very easy to see how such very trifling surnames as this last came into existence, but its exiguity is surpassed in the case of a prominent French airman who bears the appropriately buoyant name of *Brindejonc*, perhaps from some ancestor who habitually chewed a straw.

An immense number of our countrymen are simply named from the points of the compass, slightly disguised in *Norris*, Anglo-Fr. *le noreis*,[1] *Sotheran*, the southron, and *Sterling*, for Easterling, a name given to the Hanse merchants. *Westray* was formerly *le westreis*. A German was to our ancestors, as he still is to sailors, a Dutchman, whence our name *Douch*,

[1] The corresponding *le surreis* is now probably obsolete.

Ger. *deutsch,* Old High Ger. *tiutisc,* which, through Old French *tieis,* has given *Tyas.*[1]

But not every local name is to be taken at its face value. *Holland* is usually from Holland in Lancashire and *England* is for Mid. Eng. *ing-land,* the land of Ing (cf. Ingulf, Ingold, etc.), a personal name which is the first element in many place-names, or from *ing,* a meadow by a stream. *Holyland* is not Palestine, but the holly-land. *Hampshire* is often for Hallamshire, a district in Yorkshire. *Dane* is a variant of Mid. Eng. *dene,* a valley, the inhabitant of Denmark having given us *Dench* (p. 97) and *Dennis* (*le daneis*). Visitors to Margate will remember the valley called the Dane, which stretches from the harbour to St. Peter's. *Saxon* is not racial, but a perversion of sexton (p. 167). Mr. Birdofredum Sawin, commenting on the methods employed in carrying out the great mission of the Anglo-Saxon race, remarks that—

> " *Saxons* would be handy
> To du the buryin' down here upon the Rio Grandy "
> (Lowell, *Biglow Papers*).

The name *Cockayne* was perhaps first given derisively to a sybarite—

> " Paris est pour le riche un pays de *Cocagne* " (Boileau, Let. 6),

but it may be an imitative form of Coken in Durham.

Names such as *Morris,* i.e. Moorish, but also from the personal name Maurice, or *Sarson,* i.e. Saracen, but also for Sara-son, are rather nicknames, due to complexion or to an ancestor who was mine host of the Saracen's Head. *Moor* is sometimes of similar origin.

[1] *Tyars,* or *Tyers,* which Bardsley puts with this, is Fr. *Thiers.* Lat. *tertius.*

Russ, like *Rush*, is one of the many forms of Fr. *roux*, red-complexioned (p. 21). *Pole* is for *Pool*, the native of Poland being called *Pollock*—

> "He smote the sledded *Polack* on the ice" (*Hamlet*, I. i).

As a rule it will be found that while most of our counties have given family names, sometimes corrupted, e.g. *Lankshear*, *Willsher*, *Cant*, *Chant*, for Kent, with which we may compare *Anguish* for Angus, the larger towns are rather poorly represented, the movement having always been from country to town, and the smaller spot serving for more exact description. An exception is *Bristow* (Bristol), Mid. Eng. *brig-stow*, the place on the bridge, the great commercial city of the west from which so many medieval seamen hailed; but the name is sometimes from Burstow (Surrey), and there were possibly smaller places called by so natural a name, just as the name *Bradford*, i.e. broad ford, may come from a great many other places than the Yorkshire wool town. *Rossiter* is generally for Rochester, but also for Wroxeter (Salop); Coggeshall is well disguised as *Coxall*, Barnstaple as *Bastable*, Maidstone as *Mayston*, Stockport as *Stopford*. On the other hand, there is not a village of any antiquity but has, or once had, a representative among surnames.

The provinces and towns of France and Flanders have given us many common surnames. From names of provinces we have *Burgoyne* and *Burgin*, *Champain* and *Champneys* (p. 20), *Gascoyne* and *Gaskin*, *Mayne*, *Mansell*, Old Fr. *Mancel* (*manceau*), an inhabitant of Maine or of its capital Le Mans, *Brett* and *Britton*, Fr. le Bret and le Breton, *Pickard* and *Power*, sometimes from Old Fr. *Pohier*, a Picard, *Peto*, formerly Peitow, from Poitou, *Poidevin* and *Puddifin*, for

Poitevin, *Loring*, Old Fr. *le Lohereng*, the man from Lorraine, assimilated to *Fleming*, *Hanway*, an old name for Hainault, *Brabazon*, le Brabançon, and *Brebner*, formerly le Brabaner, *Angwin*, for Angevin, *Flinders*, a perversion of Flanders, *Barry*, which is often for Berri, and others which can be identified by everybody.

Among towns we have *Allenson* and *Dallison*, Alençon, *Amyas*, Amiens (cf. Father Damien), *Ainger*, Angers, *Aris*, Arras, *Bevis*, Beauvais, *Bullen*, Boulogne, *Bloss*, Blois, *Callis* and *Challis*, Calais, *Challen*, Chalon, *Chaworth*, Cahors, *Druce*, Dreux, *Gaunt*, Gand (Ghent), *Luck*, Luick (Liège), *Loving*, Louvain, *Luckner*, Du. *Luykenaar*, man from Liège, *Malins*, Malines (Mechlin), *Raynes*, Rennes and Rheims, *Roan*, Rouen, *Sessions*, Soissons, *Stamp*, Old Fr. Estampes (Étampes), *Turney*, Tournay, etc. The name de Verdun is common enough in old records for us to connect with it both the fascinating Dolly and the illustrious Harry. To the above may be added, among German towns, *Cullen*, Cologne, and *Lubbock*, Lübeck, and, from Italy, *Janes*, Gênes (Genoa), *Janaway* or *Janways*, i.e. Genoese, and *Lambard* or *Lombard*. Familiar names of foreign towns were often anglicized. Thus we find Hamburg called *Hamborough*, Bruges *Bridges*, and Tours *Towers*.

To the town of Angers we owe, besides *Ainger*, the forbidding names *Anger* and *Danger*. In many local names of foreign origin the preposition *de* has been incorporated, e.g. *Dalmain*, d'Allemagne, sometimes corrupted into *Dallman* and *Dollman*, though these are also for *Doleman*, from the East Anglian *dole*, a boundary, *Danvers*, d'Anvers, Antwerp, *Devereux*, d'Évreux, *Daubeney*, *Dabney*, d'Aubigny, *Disney*, d'Isigny, etc. *Doyle* is a later form of *Doyley*, or *Dolley*, from d'Ouilli, and *Darcy* and *Durfey* were once d'Arcy and d'Urfé. *Dew* is sometimes for de Eu. Sir John de Grey, justice of Chester, had in 1246 two *Alice in Wonderland* clerks named Henry de Eu and William de Ho. This retention of the *de* is also common in names derived from spots which have not become recognized place-names; see p. 140. A familiar example, which has been much disputed, is the Cambridgeshire name *Death*, which some of its possessors prefer to write D'Aeth or De Ath. Bardsley rejects this, without, I think, sufficient reason. It is true that it occurs as *de Dethe* in the Hundred Rolls, but this is not a serious argument, for we find also *de Daubeney* (see p. 100), the original *de* having already been absorbed at the time the Rolls were compiled.

But to derive a name of obviously native origin from a place in France is a snobbish, if harmless, delusion. There are quite enough *moor leys* in England without explaining *Morley* by Morlaix. To connect the Mid. English nickname *Longfellow* with Longueville or the patronymic *Hansom* (p. 36) with Anceaumville betrays the same belief in phonetic epilepsy that inspires the derivation of *Barber* from the chapelry of Sainte-Barbe. The fact that there are at least three places in England called *Carrington* has not prevented one writer from seeking the origin of that name in the appropriate locality of Charenton.

CHAPTER XII

SPOT NAMES

"In *ford*, in *ham*, in *ley* and *tun*
The most of English surnames run"
(VERSTEGAN).

VERSTEGAN'S couplet, even if it be not strictly true, makes a very good text for a discourse on our local names. The *ham*, or home, and the *ton*, or town, originally an enclosure (cf. Ger. *Zaun*, hedge), were, at any rate in a great part of England, the regular nucleus of the village, which in some cases has become the great town and in others has decayed away and disappeared from the map. In an age when wool was our great export, flock keeping was naturally a most important calling, and the *ley*, or meadow land, would be quickly taken up and associated with human activity. When bridges were scarce, *fords* were important, and it is easy to see how the inn, the smithy, the cartwright's booth, etc., would naturally plant themselves at such a spot and form the commencement of a hamlet

Each of these four words exists by itself as a specific place-name and also as a surname. In fact *Lee* and *Ford* are among our commonest local surnames. In the same way the local origin of such names as *Clay* and *Chalk* may be specific as well as general. But I do not propose to deal here with the vast subject of our English village names, but only with the essential elements of which they are composed, elements which were often used for surnominal purposes long before the spot itself had developed into a village.[1] Thus the name *Oakley* must generally have been borne by a man who lived on meadow land which was surrounded or dotted with oak-trees. But I should be shy of explaining a given village called Oakley in the same way, because the student of place-names might be able to show from early records that the place was originally an *ey*, or island, and that the first syllable is the disguised name of a medieval churl. These four simple etymons themselves may also become perverted. Thus *-ham* is sometimes confused with *holm* (p. 117), *-ley*, as I have just suggested, may in some cases contain *-ey*, *-ton* occasionally interchanges with *-don* and *-stone*, and *-ford* with the French *-fort* (see p. 139).

In this chapter will be found a summary of the various words applied by our ancestors to the natural features of the land they lived on. To avoid too lengthy a catalogue, I have classified them under the three headings (1) Hill and Dale, (2) Plain and Wood-

[1] A good general account of our village names will be found in the Appendix to Isaac Taylor's *Names and their Histories*. It is reprinted as chapter xi of the same author's *Words and Places* (Everyman Library), in which new setting it shines, philologically, like a good deed in a naughty world. There are a few excellent monographs on the village names of various counties, *e.g.* Bedfordshire, Berkshire, Cambridgeshire, Hertfordshire, Huntingdonshire (Skeat), Oxfordshire (Alexander), Lancashire (Wyld and Hirst), West Riding of Yorkshire (Moorman), Staffordshire, Warwickshire, Worcestershire (Duignan), to which, by the time these lines are printed, may be added Nottinghamshire by my colleague Dr. H. Mutschmann. But the greater part of what has been done on this subject by earlier writers is, says Dr. Bradley, worthless.

land, (3) Water and Waterside, reserving for the next chapter the names due to man's interference with the scenery, *e.g.* roads, buildings, enclosures, etc. They are mostly Anglo-Saxon or Scandinavian, the Celtic name remaining as the appellation of the individual hill, stream, etc. (Helvellyn, Avon, etc.). The simple word has in almost all cases given a fairly common surname, but compounds are of course numerous, the first element being descriptive of the second, *e.g.* *Bradley*, broad lea, *Radley* and *Ridley*, red lea, *Brockley*, brook lea or badger lea (p. 225), *Beverley*, beaver lea, *Cleverley*, clover lea, *Hawley*, hedge lea, *Rawnsley*, raven's lea, and so *ad infinitum*. In the oldest records spot names are generally preceded by the preposition *at*, whence such names as *Attewell*, *Atwood*, but other prepositions occur, as in *Bythesea*, *Underwood* and the hybrid *Surtees*, on Tees. Cf. such French names as *Doutrepont*, from beyond the bridge.

One curious phenomenon, of which I can offer no explanation, is that while many spot names occur indifferently with or without *-s*, e.g. *Bridge*, *Bridges*; *Brook*, *Brooks*; *Platt*, *Platts*, in others we find a regular preference either for the singular or plural [1] form. Compare the following couples:

Field	*Meadows*
Lake	*Rivers*
Pool	*Mears* (meres)
Spring	*Wells*
Street	*Rhodes* [2] (roads)
Marsh	*Myers* [2] (mires)

[1] In some cases no doubt a plural, in others a kind of genitive due to the influence of personal names, such as *Wills*, *Perkins*, etc.

[2] These are often also Jewish names, from the island of Rhodes and from Ger. Meyer.

to which many more might be added. So we find regularly *Nokes* but *Nash* (p. 34), *Beech* but *Willows*. The general tendency is certainly towards the *-s* forms in the case of monosyllables, e.g. *Banks, Foulds, Hayes, Stubbs, Thwaites*, etc., but we naturally find the singular in compounds, e.g. *Windebank* (winding), *Nettlefold, Roundhay*, etc.

There is also a further problem offered by names in *-er*. We know that a *Waller* was a mason or wall-builder, but was a *Bridger* really a *Pontifex*,[1] did he merely live near the bridge, or was he the same as a *Bridgman*, and what was the latter? Did Sam *Weller's* ancestor sink wells, possess a well, or live near some-one else's well? Probably all explanations may be correct, for the suffix may have differed in meaning according to locality, but I fancy that in most cases proximity alone is implied. The same applies to many cases of names in *-man*, such as *Hillman, Dickman* (dyke), *Parkman*.

Many of the words in the following paragraphs are obsolete or survive only in local usage. Some of them also vary considerably in meaning, according to the region in which they are found. I have included many which, in their simple form, seem too obvious to need explanation, because the compounds are not always equally clear.

HILL AND DALE

We have a fair number of Celtic words connected with natural scenery, but they do not as a rule form

[1] An example of a Latinized name. Cf. *Sutor, Faber*, and the barbarous *Sartorius*, for *sartor*, a tailor. *Pontifex* may also be the latinized form of *Pope* or *Bishop*. It is not known why this title, bridge-builder, was given to high-priests.

compounds, and as surnames are usually found in their simple form. Such are *Cairn*, a stony hill, *Crag*, *Craig*, and the related *Carrick* and *Creagh*, *Glen* or *Glynn*, and *Lynn*, a cascade. Two words, however, of Celtic origin, *don*, or *down*, a hill, and *combe*, a hollow in the hills, were adopted by the Anglo-Saxons and enter into many compounds. Thus we find *Kingdon*, whence the imitative *Kingdom*, *Brandon*, from the name Brand (p. 74), *Ashdown*, etc. The simple *Donne* or *Dunne* is sometimes the Anglo-Saxon name Dunna, whence *Dunning*, or a colour nickname, while *Down* and *Downing* may represent the Anglo-Sax. Duna and Duning (see p. 76). From *combe*, used especially in the west of England, we have *Compton*, and such compounds as *Acomb*, at combe, *Addiscombe* (Adam), *Battiscombe* (Bartholomew), etc. But *Newcomb* is for *Newcome* (p. 22). See also *Slocomb* (p. 207).

The simple *Hill* and *Dale* are among our common surnames. *Hill* also appears as *Hull* and is easily disguised in compounds, e.g. *Brummel* for broom-hill, *Tootell* and *Tuttle* for Toothill, a name found in many localities and meaning a hill on which a watch was kept. It is connected with the verb to *tout*, originally to look out. We have *Dale* and its cognate *Dell* in *Swindell* (swine), *Tindall* (Tyne), *Twaddell*, *Tweddell* (Tweed), etc.—

"Mr. H. T. *Twaddle* announced the change of his name to *Tweeddale* in the *Times*, January 4, 1890" (Bardsley).

Other names for a hill are *Fell* (Scand.), found in the lake country, whence *Grenfell*; and *Hough* or *How* (Scand.), as in *Greenhow*, *Birchenough*, and *Goodenough*[1] (Godwin). This is often reduced to *-o*, as in

[1] Probably not a nickname. Its apparent opposite, *Badenough*, is for Badenoch in Scotland.

Clitheroe, *Shafto*, and is easily confused with *scough*, a wood (Scand.), as in *Briscoe* (birch), *Ayscough* (ash). In the north we also find *Law* and *Low*, with such compounds as *Bradlaugh*, *Whitelaw*, and *Harlow*. To these must be added *Barrow*, often confused with the related *borough* (p. 121). Both belong to the Anglo-Sax. *beorgan*, to protect, cover. The name *Leatherbarrow* means the hill, perhaps the burial mound, of *Leather*, Anglo-Sax. Hlothere, cognate with Lothair and Luther.

A hill-top was *Cope* or *Copp*. Chaucer uses it of the tip of the Miller's nose—

> "Upon the *cope* right of his nose he hade
> A werte, and thereon stood a toft of herys."
> (A. 554.)

Another name for a hill-top appears in *Peak*, *Pike*, *Peck*, or *Pick*, but the many compounds in *Pick-*, e.g. *Pickbourne*, *Pickford*, *Pickwick*, etc., suggest a personal name *Pick* of which we have the dim. in *Pickett* (cf. Fr. Picot) and the softened *Piggot*. We find *Peak* also as *Peach* and *Petch*, Anglo-French forms applied specifically to the Derbyshire Peak. A mere hillock or knoll has given the names *Knapp*, *Knollys* or *Knowles*, *Knock*, and *Knott*. But *Knapp* may also be for Mid. Eng. *cnape*, cognate with *knave* and with Low Ger. *Knappe*, squire—

> "Wer wagt es, Rittersmann oder *Knapp*',
> Zu tauchen in diesen Schlund ? "
> (Schiller, *Der Taucher*, l. 1.)

Redknap, the name of a Richmond boat-builder, is probably a nickname, like *Redhead*. A *Knapper* may have lived on a "knap," or may have been one of the Suffolk flint-knappers, who still prepare gun-flints for weapons to be retailed to the heathen. *Knock* and *Knocker* are both Kentish names, and there is a reef off Margate known as the Kentish Knock. We have the plural *Knox* (cf. *Bax*, p. 125). *Knott* is sometimes for Cnut, or Canute, which generally becomes *Nutt*. Both have got mixed with the nickname *Nott*.

A green knoll was also called *Toft* (Scand.), whence *Langtoft*, and the name was used later for a homestead. From *Cliff* we have *Clift*,[1] with excrescent *-t*, and the cognates *Cleeve* and *Clive*. Compounds of *Cliff* are *Radcliffe* (red), *Sutcliffe* (south), *Wyclif* (white). The *c-* sometimes disappears in compounds, e.g. *Cunliffe*, earlier *Cunde-clive*, and *Topliff*; but *Ayliffe* is for Ælfgifu or Æthelgifu and *Goodliffe* from Godleof (cf. Ger. Gottlieb). The older form of *Stone* appears in *Staines*, *Stanhope*, *Stanton*, etc. *Wheatstone* is either for white stone or for the local Whetstone (Middlesex). In *Balderstone*, *Johnston*, *Edmondstone*, *Livingstone*, the suffix is *-ton*, though the frequence of *Johnston* points to corruption from *Johnson*, just as in Nottingham we have the converse case of *Beeson* from the local *Beeston*. In *Hailstone* the first element is Mid. Eng. *hali*, holy. Another Mid. English name for a stone appears in *Hone*, now used only of a whetstone.

A hollow or valley in the hillside was called in the north *Clough*, also spelt *Clow*, *Cleugh* (Clim o' the Cleugh), and *Clew*. The compound *Fairclough* is found corrupted into *Faircloth*. Another northern name for a glen was *Hope*, whence *Allsop*, *Blenkinsop*, *Trollope*, the first element in each being probably the name of the first settler, and *Burnup*, *Hartopp* (hart), *Harrap* (hare), *Heslop* (hazel). *Gill* (Scand.), a ravine,

[1] This may also be from Mid. Eng. *clift*, a cleft.

has given *Fothergill, Pickersgill,* and *Gaskell,* from Gaisgill (Westmorland). These, like most of our names connected with mountain scenery, are naturally found almost exclusively in the north. Other surnames which belong more or less to the hill country are *Hole,* found also as *Holl, Hoole,* and *Hoyle,* but perhaps meaning merely a depression in the land, *Ridge,* and its northern form *Rigg,* with their compounds *Doddridge, Langridge, Brownrigg, Hazelrigg,* etc. But *Penkridge, Pankridge* are distortions of Pancras or Pancratius. From Mid. Eng. *raike,* a path, a sheep-track (Scand.), we get *Raikes* and *Greatorex,* found earlier as *Greatrakes,* the name of a famous faith-healer of the seventeenth century.

Woodland and Plain

The compounds of *Wood* itself are very numerous, e.g. *Braidwood, Harwood, Norwood, Sherrard* and *Sherratt* (Sherwood). But, in considering the frequency of the simple *Wood,* it must be remembered that we find people described as *le wode,* i.e. mad (cf. Ger. *Wut,* frenzy), and that *mad* and *madman* are found as medieval names—

> "Thou told'st me they were stolen unto this wood;
> And here am I, and *wode* within this wood,
> Because I cannot meet my Hermia."
> (*Midsummer Night's Dream,* ii. 1.)

As a suffix *-wood* is sometimes a corruption of *-ward,* e.g. *Haywood* is occasionally for *Hayward,* and *Allwood, Elwood* are for *Aylward,* Anglo-Sax. Æthelweard. Another name for a wood was *Holt,* cognate with Ger. *Holz*—

> "But right so as thise *holtes* and thise hayis,
> That han in winter dede ben and dreye,
> Revesten hem in grene whan that May is."
> (*Troilus and Criseyde*, iii. 351.)

Hurst or *Hirst* means a wooded hill (cf. Ger. *Horst*), and *Shaw* was once almost as common a word as wood itself—

> "Wher rydestow under this grene-wode *shawe*?"
> (D, 1386.)

Hurst belongs especially to the south and west, though *Hirst* is very common in Yorkshire; *Shaw* is found in the north and *Holt* in the east and south. We have compounds of *Shaw* in *Bradshaw*, *Crashaw* (crow), *Hearnshaw* or *Earnshaw* (heron), *Renshaw*[1] (raven), etc., of *Hurst* in *Buckhurst* (beech), *Brockhurst* (badger), and of *Holt* in *Oakshott*.

We have earlier forms of *Grove* in *Greaves*—

> "And with his stremes dryeth in the *greves*
> The silver dropes, hangynge on the leves" (A. 1495)—

and *Graves*, the latter being thus no more funereal than *Tombs*, from Thomas (cf. *Timbs* from Timothy). But *Greaves* and *Graves* may also be variants of the official *Grieves* (p. 181), or may come from Mid. Eng. *græfe*, a trench, quarry. Compounds are *Hargreave* (hare), *Redgrave*, *Stangrave*, the two latter probably referring to an excavation. From Mid. Eng. *strope*, a small wood, appear to come *Strode* and *Stroud*, compound *Bulstrode*, while *Struthers* is the cognate *strother*, marsh, still in dialect use. *Weald* and *wold*, the cognates of Ger. *Wald*, were applied rather to wild country in general than to land covered with trees. They are

[1] It is obvious that this may also be for raven's haw (p. 124). *Raven* was a common personal name and is the first element in *Ramsbottom* (p. 114), *Ramsden*.

probably connected with *wild*. Similarly the Late Lat. *foresta*, whence our *forest*, means only what is outside, Lat. *foris*, the town jurisdiction. From the Mid. Eng. *wæld* we have the names *Weld* and *Weale*, the latter with the not uncommon loss of final *-d*. *Scroggs* (Scand.) and *Scrubbs* suggest their meaning of brushwood. *Scroggins*, from its form, is a patronymic, and probably represents *Scoggins* with intrusive *-r-* (p. 88, *n*. 1). This is from Scogin, a name borne by a poet who was contemporary with Chaucer and by a court-fool of the fifteenth century—

> "The same Sir John, the very same. I saw him break *Skogan's* head at the court gate, when he was a crack, not thus high."
> (2 *Henry IV*., iii. 2.)

With *Scrubb* of cloudy ammonia fame we may compare Wormwood Scrubbs. *Shrubb* is the same word, and Shropshire is for Anglo-Sax. *scrob-scire*.

The two northern names for a clearing in the wood were *Royd* and *Thwaite* (Scand.). The former is cognate with the second part of Bai*reut* and Wernige*rode*, and with the *Rütli*, the small plateau on which the Swiss patriots took their famous oath. It was so called—

> "Weil dort die Waldung *ausgerodet* ward."
> (SCHILLER, *Wilhelm Tell*.)

Among its compounds are *Ackroyd* (oak), *Grindrod* (green), *Murgatroyd* (Margaret), *Learoyd* (lea), *Ormerod*, etc. We also find the name *Rodd*, which may belong here or to *Rudd* (p. 74), and both these names may also be for *Rood*, equivalent to *Cross* or *Crouch* (p. 17), as in Holyrood. *Ridding* is also related to *Royd*. *Hacking* may be a dim. of *Hack* (Haco), but we find also *de le hacking*, which suggests a forest clearing. *Thwaite*, from Anglo-Sax. *þwitan*, to cut, is found chiefly in Cumberland and the adjacent region in such compounds as *Braithwaite* (broad), *Hebbelthwaite*, *Postlethwaite*, *Satterthwaite*. The second of these is sometimes corrupted into *Ablewhite* as *Cowperthwaite* is into *Copperwheat*, for " this suffix has ever been too big a mouthful in the south " (Bardsley). A glade or valley in the wood was called a *Dean*, *Dene*, *Denne*, cognate with *den*. The compounds are numerous, e.g. *Borden* (boar), *Dibden* (deep), *Sowden*, *Sugden* (sow), *Hazeldean* or *Heseltine*, etc. From the fact that swine were pastured in these glades the names *Denman* and *Denyer* have been explained as equivalent to swineherd. As a suffix *-den* is often confused with *-don* (p. 106). At the foot of Horsenden Hill, near Harrow, two boards announce Horsen*don* Farm and Horsen*den* Golf-links. An opening in the wood was also called *Slade*—

> " And when he came to Barnesdale,
> Great heavinesse there hee hadd ;
> He found two of his fellowes
> Were slaine both in a *slade*."
>
> (*Robin Hood and Guy of Gisborne*.)

The maps still show Pond Slade in Richmond Park. The compound *Hertslet* may be for hart-slade.

Acre, a field, cognate with, but not derived from, Lat. *ager*, occurs in *Goodacre*, *Hardacre*, *Linacre*, *Whittaker*, etc., and *Field* itself gives numerous compounds, including *Butterfield* (bittern, p. 220), *Schofield* (school), *Streatfeild* (street), *Whitfield*. Pasture-land is represented above all by *Lea*, for which see p. 28. It is cognate with Hohen*lohe* and Water*loo*, while *Mead* and *Medd* are cognate with Zer*matt* (at the mead). *Brinsmead* thus means the same as *Brinsley*.

Marshy land has given the names *Carr* or *Kerr* (Scand.) and *Marsh*, originally an adjective, *merisc*, from *mer*, mere. *Marris* represents the cognate Fr. *marais*. The compounds *Tidmarsh* and *Titchmarsh* contain the Anglo-Saxon names Tidda and Ticca. *Moor* also originally had the meaning morass (*e.g.* in Sedgemoor), as Ger. *Moor* still has, so that *Fenimore* is pleonastic. The northern form is *Muir*, as in *Muirhead*. *Moss* was similarly used in the north; cf. moss-trooper and Solway Moss, but the surname *Moss* is generally for Moses (p. 85). From *slough* we get the names *Slow*, *Slowley*, and *Sloman* (also a perversion of *Solomon*), with which we may compare *Moorman* and *Mossman*. This seems to be also the most usual meaning of *Slack* or *Slagg*, also used of a gap in the hills—

> "The first horse that he rode upon,
> For he was raven black,
> He bore him far, and very far,
> But failed in a *slack*."
>
> (*Ballad of Lady Maisry*.)

Tye, or *Tighe*, means common land. *Platt* is a piece, or plot, of level country—

> "Oft on a *plat* of rising ground
> I hear the far-off curfew sound"
>
> (*Penseroso*, l. 73);

and shape is expressed by *Gore*, a triangular piece of land (cf. Kensington Gore), of which the older form *Gare*, *Geare*, also survives. In *Lowndes* we have *laund* or *lound*—

> "And to the *laund* he rideth hym ful right,
> For thider was the hart wont have his flight"
>
> (A. 1691)—

a piece of heath land, the origin of the modern word *lawn*. In *Lund* and *Lunn* it has become confused with the Old Norse *lundr*, a sacred grove. *Laund* itself is of French origin—

> "*Lande*, a land, or *laund;* a wild, untilled, shrubbie, or bushie plaine" (Cotgrave).

Its relation to *land* is uncertain, and it is not always possible to distinguish them in such compounds as *Acland*, *Buckland*, *Cleveland*, etc. The name *Lander* or *Launder* is unconnected with these (see p. 186). *Flack* is Mid. Eng. *flagge*, turf. *Snape* is a dialect word for winter pasture, and *Wong* means a meadow.

A rather uncouth-looking set of names, which occur chiefly on the border of Cheshire and Lancashire, are compounded from *bottom* or *botham*, a wide shallow valley suited for agriculture. Hotspur, dissatisfied with his fellow-conspirators' map-drawing, expresses his intention of damming the Trent so that—

> "It shall not wind with such a deep indent
> To rob me of so rich a *bottom* here."
>
> (1 *Henry IV*. iii. 1.)

The first element is sometimes the name of the settler, e.g. *Higginbottom* (Richard), *Rowbotham* (Roland). The first element of *Shufflebotham* is, in the Lancashire Assize Rolls (1176–1285), spelt *Schyppewalle-* and *Schyppewelle-*, where *schyppe* is for sheep, still so pronounced in dialect.

Water and Waterside

Very few surnames are taken, in any language, from the names of rivers. This is quite natural, for just as the man who lived on a hill became known as *Hill*, *Peake*, etc., and not as Skiddaw or Wrekin, so the man who lived by the waterside would be known as *Bywater, Rivers,* etc. No Londoner talks of going on the Thames. Another reason for the absence of such surnames is probably to be found in the fact that our river (and mountain) names are almost exclusively Celtic, and had no connotation for the English population. We have many apparent river names, but most of them are susceptible of another explanation. *Dee* may be for *Day* as *Deakin* is for *Daykin, Derwent* looks like *Darwin* (p. 73) or the local *Darwen* with excrescent *-t* (p. 41), *Humber* is *Humbert,* a French name corresponding to the Anglo-Sax. Hunbeorht, *Medway* is merely " mid-way," which is also the origin of the river name, and *Trent* is a place in Somerset. *Severn* I guess to be a perversion of Mid. Eng. *le severe,* which may mean what it appears to, though it is more probably the name of a sieve-maker, whence the name *Seaver.* This view as to river surnames is supported by the fact that we do not appear to have a single mountain surname, the apparent exception, *Snowdon,* being for *Snowden* (see *den,* p. 112).

Among names for streams we have *Beck,*[1] cognate with Ger. *Bach, Bourne,*[2] or *Burn,* cognate with Ger. *Brunnen, Brook,* related to *break, Crick,* a creek, *Fleet,* a creek, cognate with *Flood,* and *Syke,* a trench or rill. In *Beckett* and *Brockett* the suffix is *head* (p. 126). *Troutbeck, Birkbeck* explain themselves. In *Colbeck* we have cold, *Glazebrook* is for glassy brook, *Holbrook* contains hollow, and *Addenbrook* means " at the brook " (p. 104). We find *Brook* latinized as *Torrens. Aborn* is for *atte bourne,* and there are probably many

[1] The simple *Beck* is generally a German name of modern introduction (p. 149).

[2] Distinct from *bourne,* a boundary, Fr. *borne.*

places called *Blackburn* and *Otterburn*. *Firth*, an estuary, cognate with *fjord*, often becomes *Frith*, but this surname usually comes from *frith*, a park or game preserve (p. 124).

Another word for a creek, *wich* or *wick* (Scand.), cannot be distinguished from *wick*, a settlement. *Pond*, a doublet of *Pound* (p. 135), means a piece of water enclosed by a dam, while natural sheets of water are *Lake*, or *Lack*, not limited originally to a large expanse, *Mere*, whence *Mears* and the compound *Cranmer* (crane), and *Pool*, also *Pull* and *Pole*. We have compounds of the latter in *Poulton* (p. 4), *Pooley* (*ey*, p. 117), *Claypole*, and *Glasspool*. In Kent a small pond is called *Sole*, whence *Nethersole*. The bank of a river or lake was called *Over*, cognate with Ger. *Ufer*, whence *Overend*, *Overall* (hall), *Overbury*, *Overland*. The surname *Shore*, for *atte shore*, may refer to the sea-shore, but the word *sewer* was once regularly so pronounced and the name was applied to large drains in the fen country (cf. *Gott*, p. 129). *Beach* is a word of late appearance and doubtful origin, and as a surname is usually identical with *Beech*.

Spits of land by the waterside were called *Hook* (cf. Hook of Holland and Sandy Hook) and *Hoe* or *Hoo*, as in Plymouth Hoe, or the Hundred of Hoo, between the Thames and the Medway. From *Hook* comes *Hooker*, where it does not mean a maker of hooks, while *Homan* and *Hooman* sometimes belong to the second. Alluvial land by a stream was called *halgh*, *haugh*, whence sometimes *Hawes*. Its dative case gives *Hale* and *Heal*. These often become *-hall* in place-names. Compounds are *Greenhalgh*, *Greenall*, and *Featherstonehaugh*, perhaps our longest surname.

Ing, a low-lying meadow, Mid. Eng. *eng,* survives in *Greening* (also a patronymic, p. 71), and probably in *England* (p. 98). But *Inge* and *Ings,* the latter the name of one of the Cato Street conspirators, also represent an Anglo-Saxon personal name. Cf. *Ingall* and *Ingle,* from Ingold, or Ingwulf; cf. *Ingoldsby.*

Ey,[1] an island, survives as the last element of many names, and is not always to be distinguished from *hey* (*hay,* p. 124) and *ley.* Bill *Nye's* ancestor lived *atten ey* (p. 34). *Dowdney* or *Dudeney,* from the Anglo-Saxon name Duda, has probably swallowed up the very common French name Dieudonné, corresponding to Lat. Deodatus. In the north a river island was commonly called *Holm* (Scand.), also pronounced *Home, Hulme,* and *Hume,* in compounds easily confused with *-ham,* e.g. Durham was once Dun-holmr, hill island. Hence sometimes *Holman, Holmer,* and *Homer.* The very common *Holmes* is probably in most cases a tree-name (p. 118). In *Chisholm* the first element means pebble; cf. Chesil Beach. The names *Bent,* whence *Broadbent,* and *Crook* probably also belong sometimes to the river, but may have arisen from a turn in a road or valley. But *Bent* was also applied to a hill covered with bents, or rushes, and *Crook* is generally a nickname (p. 211). Lastly, the crossing of the unbridged stream has given us *Ford* or *Forth,* whence *Stratford* or *Strafford* (street), *Stanford* or *Stamford* (stone), etc. The alternative name was *Wade,* from which we have the compound *Grimwade.* The cognate *wath* (Scand.) has been swallowed up by *with* (Scand.), a wood, whence the name *Wythe. Askwith,* or *Asquith,* may thus be equivalent to *Ashford* or *Ashwood. Beckwith* probably means *Beckford.*

[1] Isle of Shepp*ey*, Mers*ea* Island, etc., are pleonasms.

Tree Names

In conclusion a few words must be said about tree names, so common in their simple form and in topographical compounds. Here, as in the case of most of the etymons already mentioned in this chapter, the origin of the surname may be specific as well as general, *i.e.* the name *Ash* may come from Ash in Kent rather than from any particular tree, the etymology remaining the same. Many of our surnames have preserved the older forms of tree names, *e.g.* the *lime* was once the *line*, hence *Lines, Lynes*, and earlier still the *Lind*, as in the compounds *Lyndhurst, Lindley*, etc. The older form of *Oak* appears in *Acland, Acton*, and variants in *Ogden* and *Braddock*, broad oak. We have ash in *Aston, Ascham*. The *holly* was once the *hollin*, whence *Hollins, Hollis, Hollings*; cf. *Hollingshead, Holinshed*. But *hollin* became colloquially *holm*, whence generally *Holmes*. *Homewood* is for holmwood. The holm oak, ilex, is so called from its holly-like leaves. For *Birch* we also find *Birk*, common in compounds. *Beech* often appears as *Buck*; cf. *buck*wheat, so called because the grains are of the shape of beech-mast. In *Poppleton, Popplewell* we have the dialect *popple*, a poplar. *Yeo* [1] sometimes represents *yew*, spelt *yowe* by Palsgrave.

In *Sallows* we have a provincial name for the willow, cognate with Fr. *saule* and Lat. *salix*. *Rowntree* is the *rowan*, or mountain ash, and *Bawtry* or *Bawtree* is a northern name for the elder. The older forms of *Alder* and *Elder*, in both of which the *-d-* is intrusive (p. 34),

[1] The *yeo* of *yeoman*, which is conjectured to have meant district, cognate with Ger. *Gau* in *Breisgau, Rheingau*, etc., is not found by itself.

appear in *Allerton* and *Ellershaw*. The *Hazel* is found also as the *Halse*, whence *Halsey*, the suffix being either *-ey* (p. 116) or *-hey*, *-hay* (p. 124). *Maple* is sometimes *Mapple* and *sycamore* is corrupted into *Sicklemore*.

Tree-names are common in all languages. *Beerbohm Tree* is pleonastic, from Ger. *Bierbaum*, for *Birnbaum*, pear-tree. A few years ago a prominent Belgian statesman bore the name *Vandepoerenboom*, rather terrifying till decomposed into "van den poerenboom." Its Mid. English equivalent appears in *Pirie*, originally a collection of pear-trees, but used by Chaucer for the single tree—

> "And thus I lete hym sitte upon the *pyrie*."
>
> (E. 2217.)

From trees we may descend gradually, via *Thorne*, *Bush*, *Furze*, *Gorst* (p. 10), *Ling*, etc., until we come finally to *Grace*, which in some cases represents grass, for we find William *atte grase* in 1327, while the name *Poorgrass*, in Mr. Hardy's *Far from the Madding Crowd*, seems to be certified by the famous French names *Malherbe* and *Malesherbes*. But *Savory* is the French personal name Savary.

The following list of trees is given by Chaucer in the Knight's tale—

> "The names that the trees highte,—
> As ook, firre, birch, aspe, alder, holm, popeler,
> Wylugh, elm, plane, assh, box, chasteyn, lynde, laurer,
> Mapul, thorn, bech, hasel, ew, whippeltre."
>
> (A. 2920.)

They are all represented in modern directories.

CHAPTER XIII

THE HAUNTS OF MAN

"One fels downe firs, another of the same
With crossed poles a little lodge doth frame:
Another mounds it with dry wall about,
And leaves a breach for passage in and out:
With turfe and furze some others yet more grose
Their homely sties in stead of walls inclose:
Some, like the swallow, mud and hay doe mixe
And that about their silly cotes they fixe:
Some heale (thatch) their roofes with fearn, or reeds, or rushes,
And some with hides, with oase, with boughs, and bushes."

(SYLVESTER, *The Devine Weekes.*)

IN almost every case where man has interfered with nature the resulting local name is naturally of Anglo-Saxon or, in some parts of England, of Scandinavian origin. The Roman and French elements in our topographical names are scanty in number, though the former are of frequent occurrence. The chief Latin contributions are *-chester*, *-cester*, *-caster*, Lat. *castrum*, a fort, or plural *castra*, a camp; *-street*, Lat. *via strata*, a levelled way; *-minster*, Lat. *monasterium*; and *-church* or *-kirk*, Greco-Lat. *kuriakon*, belonging to the Lord. *Eccles*, Greco-Lat. *ecclesia*, probably goes back to Celtic Christianity. *Street* was the high-road, hence *Greenstreet*. *Minster* is curiously corrupted in *Buckmaster* for Buckminster and *Kittermaster* for Kidderminster, while in its simple form it appears as *Minister* (p. 35). We have a few French place-names, e.g. *Beamish* (p. 139), *Beau-*

mont, *Richmond*, Richemont, and *Malpas* (Cheshire), the evil pass, with which we may compare *Maltravers*. We have the apparent opposite in *Bompas*, *Bumpus*, Fr. *bon pas*, but this was a nickname. Of late there has been a tendency to introduce the French *ville*, e.g. Bournville, near Birmingham. That part of Margate which ought to be called Northdown is known as Cliftonville, and the inhabitants of the opposite end of the town, dissatisfied with such good names as Westbrook and Rancorn, hanker after Westonville. But these philological atrocities are fortunately too late to be perpetuated as surnames.

I have divided the names in this chapter into those that are connected with (1) Settlements and Enclosures, (2) Highways and Byways, (3) Watercourses, (4) Buildings, (5) Shop Signs. And here, as before, names which neither in their simple nor compound form present any difficulty are omitted.

Settlements and Enclosures

The words which occur most commonly in the names of the modern towns which have sprung from early settlements are *borough* or *bury*,[1] *by*, *ham*, *stoke*, *stow*, *thorp*, *tun* or *ton*, *wick*, and *worth*. These names are all of native origin, except *by*, which indicates a Danish settlement, and *wick*, which is supposed to be a very early loan from Lat. *vicus*, cognate with Greek οἶκος, house. Nearly all of them are common, in their simple form, both as specific place-names and as surnames. *Borough*, cognate with Ger. *Burg*, castle, and related to *Barrow* (p. 107), has many variants, *Bury*, *Brough*, *Borrow*, *Berry*, whence *Berryman*, and *Burgh*, the last of which

[1] Originally the dative of *borough*.

has become *Burke* in Ireland, In *Atterbury* the preposition and article have both remained, while in *Thornber* the suffix is almost unrecognizable. *By*, related to *byre* and to the preposition *by*, is especially common in Yorkshire and Lincolnshire. It is sometimes spelt *bee*, e.g. *Ashbee* for *Ashby*. The simple *Bye* is not uncommon. *Ham* is cognate with *home*. In compounds it is sometimes reduced to *-um*, e.g. *Barnum*, *Holtum*, *Warnum*. *Allum* represents the usual Midland pronunciation of *Hallam*. *Cullum*, generally for Culham, may also represent the missionary Saint Colomb. In *Newnham* the adjective is dative, as in Ger. *Neuenheim*, at the new home. In *Bonham*, *Frankham*, and *Pridham* the suffix *-ham* has been substituted for the French *homme*, *bonhomme*, *franc homme*, *prudhomme*, while *Jerningham* is a perversion of the personal name Jernegan or Gernegan, as *Garnham* is of Gernon, Old French for *Beard* (see p. 199). *Stead* is cognate with Ger. *Stadt*, place, town, and with *staith*, as in *Bickersteth* (p. 40). *Armstead* means the dwelling of the hermit, *Bensted* the stead of Benna (p. 75) or Bennet.

Stoke is originally distinct from *Stock*, a stump, with which it has become fused in the compounds *Bostock*, *Brigstocke*. *Stow* appears in the compound *Bristol* (p. 99) and in *Plaistow*, play-ground (cf. *Playsted*). *Thorp*, cognate with Ger. *Dorf*, village, is especially common in the eastern counties—

> "By thirty hills I hurry down
> Or slip between the ridges,
> By twenty *thorps*, a little town,
> And half a hundred bridges."
>
> (Tennyson, *The Brook*, l. 5.)

It has also given *Thrupp* and probably *Thripp*, whence *Calthrop*, *Winthrop*, *Westrupp*, etc. *Ton*, later *Town*, gave also the northern *Toon*, still used in Scotland with something of its original sense (see p. 102). *Boston* is Botolf's town, *Gunston* Gunn's town. So also *Tarleton* (Thurweald), *Monkton* (monk), *Preston* (priest). *Barton* meant originally a barley-field, and is still used in the west of England for a paddock. *Wick* appears also as *Wych*, *Weech*. Its compounds cannot be separated from those of *wick*, a creek (p. 116). *Bromage* is for Bromwich, *Greenidge* for Greenwich, *Prestage* for Prestwich. *Killick* probably represents Kilnwick and *Physick* is imitative for *Fishwick*.

Worth was perhaps originally applied to land by a river or to a holm (p. 117); cf. Ger. *Donauwert*, *Nonnenwert*, etc. *Harmsworth* is for Harmondsworth; cf. *Ebbsworth* (Ebba), *Shuttleworth* (Sceotweald), *Wadsworth* (Wada). Sometimes we find a lengthened form, e.g. *Allworthy*, from *ald*, old (cf. *Aldworth*), *Langworthy*. *Brownsword* is folk-etymology for Brownsworth, and *Record* for Rickworth. *Littleworth* may belong to this class, but it may also be a disparaging nickname. This would make it equivalent to the imitative *Littleproud*, formerly Littleprow, from Old Fr. and Mid. Eng. *prou*, worth, value. To this group of words may be added two more, which signify a mart, viz. *Cheap* or *Chipp* (cf. Chepstow, Chipping Barnet, etc.) and *Staple*, whence *Huxtable*, *Stapleton*, etc. *Liberty*, that part of a city which, though outside the walls, shares in the city privileges, and *Parish* also occur as surnames, but the latter is usually for Paris.

Many other words connected with the delimitation of property occur commonly in surnames. *Croft* or *Craft*, a small field, is common in compounds such as *Beecroft* or *Bearcroft* (barley), *Haycraft* (see *hay*, p. 124),

Oscroft (ox), *Meadowcroft*,[1] *Rycroft*. *Fold* occurs usually as *Foulds*, but we have compounds such as *Nettlefold*, *Penfold* or *Pinfold* (p. 135). *Sty*, not originally limited to pigs, has given *Hardisty*, the sty of Heardwulf. *Frith*, a park or game preserve, is probably more often the origin of a surname than the other *frith* (p. 116). It is cognate with Ger. *Fried*hof, cemetery. *Chase* is still used of a park and *Game* once meant rabbit-warren. *Warren* is Fr. *garenne*. *Garth*, the Scandinavian doublet of *Yard*, and cognate with *Garden*, has given the compounds *Garside*, *Garfield*, *Hogarth* (from a place in Westmorland), and *Applegarth*, of which *Applegate* is a corruption. We have a compound of *yard* in *Wynyard*, Anglo-Sax. *win*, vine. We have also the name *Close* and its derivative *Clowser*. *Gate*, a barrier or opening, Anglo-Sax. *geat*, is distinct from the Scandinavian *gate*, a street (p. 128), though of course confused with it in surnames. From the northern form we have *Yates*, *Yeats*, and *Yeatman*, and the compounds *Byatt*, by gate, *Hyatt*, high gate. *Agate* is for *atte gate*, and *Lidgate*, whence *Lidgett*, means a swing gate, shutting like a lid. *Fladgate* is for flood-gate. Here also belongs *Barr*. *Hatch*, the gate at the entrance to a chase, survives in Colney Hatch. The apparent dim. *Hatchett* is for *Hatchard* (p. 81); cf. *Everett* for Everard (p. 17). *Hay*, also *Haig*, *Haigh*, *Haw*, *Hey*, is cognate with *Hedge*. Like most monosyllabic local surnames, it is commonly found in the plural, *Hayes*, *Hawes*. The bird nickname *Hedgecock* exists also as *Haycock*. The curious-

[1] I remember reading in some story of a socially ambitious lady who adopted this commonplace name instead of *Gubbins*. The latter name came over, as Gobin, with the Conqueror, and goes back to Old Ger. Godberaht, whence Old Fr. Godibert.

looking patronymics *Orchardson* and *Townson* are of course corrupt. The latter is for *Tomlinson* and the former perhaps from *Achard* (p. 81).

Several places and families in England are named *Hide* or *Hyde*, which meant a certain measure of land. The popular connection between this word and *hide*, a skin, as in the story of the first Jutish settlement, is a fable. It is connected with an Anglo-Saxon word meaning household, which appears also in *Huish*, Anglo-Sax. *hi-wisc*. *Dike*, or *Dyke*, and *Moat*, also *Mott*, both have, or had, a double meaning. We still use *dike*, which belongs to *dig* and *ditch*, both of a trench and a mound, and the latter was the earlier meaning of Fr. *motte*, now a clod. In Anglo-French we find *moat* used of a mound fortress in a marsh. Now it is applied to the surrounding water. From *dike* come the names *Dicker*, *Dickman*, *Grimsdick*, etc. Sometimes the name *Dykes* may imply residence near some historic earthwork, such as Offa's Dyke, just as *Wall*, sometimes pronounced *Waugh* in the north, may show connection with the Roman wall. With these may be mentioned the French name *Fosse*, whence the apparently pleonastic *Fosdyke* and the name of Verdant Green's friend, Mr. Four-in-hand *Fosbrooke*. *Delves* is from Mid. Eng. *delf*, ditch. *Jury* is for Jewry, the quarter allotted to the Jews, but *Jewsbury* is no doubt for Dewsbury; cf. *Jewhurst* for Dewhurst.

Here may be mentioned a few local surnames which are hard to classify. We have the apparently anatomical *Back*, *Foot*, *Head*, and, in compounds, *-side*. *Back* seems to have been used of the region behind a building or dwelling, as it still is at Cambridge. Its plural has given *Bax*. But it was also a personal name (p. 222), sometimes spelt *Batch*. We should expect

Foot to mean the base of a hill, but it always occurs in early rolls as a personal name. It has also given *Foat* and the dim. *Footett*. It appears to be cognate with Ger. Al*fons*. *Lightfoot*, *Barfoot* are of course nicknames. The simple *Head*, found as Mid. Eng. *del heved*, is perhaps generally from a shop or tavern sign. Fr. Tête, one of the origins of *Tait*, *Tate*, and Ger. Haupt and Kopf also occur as surnames. As a local suffix *-head* appears to mean top-end and is generally shortened to *-ett*, e.g. *Birkett*[1] (cf. Birkenhead), *Brockett* (brook), *Bromet* and *Bromhead* (broom), *Hazlitt* (hazel). *Fawcett* is probably an accidental spelling of *Fossett*, from *fosse*, or of *Forcett* from *force*, a waterfall (Scand.). *Broadhead* may be a nickname, like Fr. *Grossetête* and Ger. *Breitkopf*. The face-value of *Evershed* is boar's head. *Morshead* may be the nickname of mine host of the Saracen's Head or may mean the end of the moor. So the names *Aked* (oak), *Blackett*, *Woodhead* may be explained anatomically or geographically according to the choice of the bearer. *Perrett*, usually a dim. of Peter, may sometimes represent the rather effective old nickname "pear-head." *Side* is local in the uncomfortable sounding *Akenside* (oak), *Fearenside* (fern), but *Heaviside* appears to be a nickname. *Handyside* may mean "gracious manner," from Mid. Eng. *side*, cognate with Ger. *Sitte*, custom. See *Hendy* (p. 211). The simple *end* survives as *Ind* or *Nind* (p. 34) and in *Overend* (p. 116), *Townsend*. *Edge*, earlier *Egg* (p. 31), has given *Titheredge*, but the frequency of place-names beginning with *Edge*, e.g. Edgeley, Edgington, Edgworth, etc., suggests that it was also a personal name.

[1] No doubt sometimes, like *Burchett*, *Buckett*, for the personal name Burchard, Anglo-Sax. Burgheard.

Lynch, a boundary, is cognate with golf-*links*. The following sounds modern, but refers to people sitting in a hollow among the sand-ridges—

> "And are ye in the wont of drawing up wi' a' the gangrel bodies that ye find cowering in a sand-*bunker* upon the *links*?"
>
> (*Redgauntlet*, ch. xi.)

Pitt is found in the compound *Bulpitt*, no doubt the place where the town bull was kept. It is also the origin of the Kentish names *Pett* and *Pettman*. *Arch* refers generally to a bridge. Lastly, there are three words for a corner, viz. *Hearne*, *Herne*, *Hurne*, *Wyke*, the same word as *Wick*, a creek (p. 116), and *Wray* (Scand.). The franklin tell us that "yonge clerkes" desirous of knowledge—

> "Seken in every halke and every *herne*
> Particular sciences for to lerne" (F, 1119).

Wray has become confused with *Ray* (p. 29). Its compound *thack-wray*, the corner where the thatch was stored, has given *Thackeray*.

Highways and Byways

We have already noticed the curious fact that, as surnames, we always find the singular *Street* and the plural *Roades*. The meaning of *Street* has changed considerably since the days when Icknield Street and Watling Street were great national roads. It is now used exclusively of town thoroughfares, and has become such a mere suffix that, while we speak of the *Oxford Róad*, we try to suppress the second word in *Óxford Street*. To *street* belong our place-names and surnames in *Strat-*, *Stret-*, etc., e.g. *Stratton*, *Stretton*,

Stredwick. The usual spelling *Rhodes,* for *roads,* is also curious. In some cases the name is borne by descendants of Jewish immigrants who took their name from the island of Rhodes, while in others it is identical with *Royds* (p. 111), the earlier spelling of which was also *rodes.* *Way* has a number of compounds with intrusive *-a-*, e.g. *Chattaway, Dallaway* (dale), *Greenaway, Hathaway* (heath), *Westaway.* But *Hanway* is the name of a country (see p. 100), and *Otway, Ottoway,* is Old Fr. Otouet, a dim. of Odo. *Shipway* is for sheep-way. In the north of England the streets in a town are often called *gates* (Scand.). It is impossible to distinguish the compounds of this *gate* from those of the native *gate,* a barrier (p. 124), e.g. *Norgate* may mean North Street or North Gate.

Alley and *Court* both exist as surnames, but the latter is from *court* in the sense of mansion, country house. The curious spelling *Caught* may be seen over a shop in Chiswick. *Rowe* has various origins (p. 8), but often means a row of houses, and we find the compound *Townroe.* *Cosway, Cossey,* is from causeway, Fr. *chaussée*; and *Twitchen, Twitchell* represent dialect words used of a narrow passage and connected with the Mid. English verb *twiselen,* to fork, or divide; *Twiss* must be of similar origin, for we find Robert *del twysse* in 1367. Cf. *Birtwistle* and *Entwistle.* With the above may be classed the west-country *Shute,* a narrow street; *Vennell,* also found as *Fennell,* a north-country word for alley, Fr. *venelle,* dim. of Lat. *vena,* vein; *Wynd,* a court, also a north-country word, probably from the verb *wind,* to twist, and the cognate *Went,* a passage—

> "Thorugh a goter, by a prive *wente.*"
> (*Troilus and Criseyde,* iii. 788.)

Water

Names derived from artificial watercourses are *Channell*, now replaced as a common noun by the learned form canal, *Condy* or *Cundy*, a well-known name in Yorkshire, for the earlier *Cunditt*, conduit, *Gott*, cognate with *gut*, used in Yorkshire for the channel from a mill-dam and in Lincolnshire for a water-drain on the coast, *Lade*, *Leete*, connected with the verb to *lead*, and sometimes *Shore* (p. 116), which was my grandfather's pronunciation of *sewer*. *Gott* may also be a personal name, corresponding to Fr. Got, which is sometimes aphetic for Margot. From *weir*, lit. a protection, precaution, cognate with be*ware* and Ger. *wehren*, to protect, we have not only *Weir*, but also *Ware*, *Warr*, *Wear*, and the more pretentious *Delawarr*. The latter name passed from an Earl Delawarr to a region in North America, and thus to Fenimore Cooper's noble red men. *Lock* is more often a land name, to be classed with *Hatch* (p. 124), but was also used of a water-gate. *Key* was once the usual spelling of *quay*. We have the two names combined in the curious name *Keylock*. *Port* seldom belongs here, as the Mid. English is almost always *de la porte*, i.e. *Gates*. From *well* we have a very large number of compounds, e.g. *Cauldwell* (cold), *Halliwell*, the variants of which, *Holliwell*, *Hollowell*, probably all represent Mid. Eng. *hali*, holy. Here belongs also *Winch*, from the device used for drawing water from deep wells.

Buildings

The greater number of the words to be dealt with under this heading enter into the composition of specific place-names. A considerable number of surnames are derived from the names of religious buildings, usually from proximity rather than actual habitation. Such names are naturally of Greco-Latin origin, and were either introduced directly into Anglo-Saxon by the missionaries, or were adopted later in a French form after the Conquest. It has already been noted (p. 5) that *Abbey* is not generally what it seems, but in some cases it is local, from Fr. *abbaye*, of which the Provençal form *Abadie* was introduced by the Huguenots. We find much earlier *Abdy*, taken straight from the Greco-Lat. *abbatia*. The famous name *Chantrey* is for chantry, *Armitage* was once the regular pronunciation of *Hermitage*, and *Chappell* a common spelling of *Chapel*—

> "Also if you finde not the word you seeke for presently after one sort of spelling, condemne me not forthwith, but consider how it is used to be spelled, whether with double or single letters, as *Chappell*, or *Chapell*" (Holyoak, *Latin Dict.*, 1612).

We have also the Norman form *Capel*, but this may be a nickname from Mid. Eng. *capel*, nag—

> "Why nadstow (hast thou not) pit the *capul* in the lathe (barn)?"
> (A, 4088.)

A *Galilee* was a chapel or porch devoted to special purposes—

> "Those they pursued had taken refuge in the *galilee* of the church" (*Fair Maid of Perth*, ch. ix.).

The tomb of the Venerable Bede is in the Galilee of Durham Cathedral. I had a schoolfellow with this uncommon name, now generally perverted to *Galley*. In a play now running (Feb. 1913) in London, there is a character named *Sanctuary*, a name found also in Crockford and the London Directory. I have only once come across the contracted form *Sentry*[1] (*Daily Telegraph*, Dec. 26, 1912), and then under circumstances which might make quotation actionable. *Purvis* is Mid. Eng. *parvis*, a porch, Greco-Lat. *paradisus*. It may be the same as *Provis*, the name selected by Mr. Magwitch on his return from the Antipodes (*Great Expectations*, ch. xl.), but this may be for *Provost*. *Porch* and *Portch* both occur as surnames, but *Porcher* is Fr. *porcher*, a swineherd, and *Portal* is a Huguenot name. *Churcher* and *Kirker*, *Churchman* and *Kirkman*, are usually local; cf. *Bridger* and *Bridgman*.

The names *Temple* and *Templeman* were acquired from residence near one of the preceptories of the Knights Templars, and *Spittlehouse* (p. 34) is sometimes to be accounted for in a similar way (Knights of the Hospital). We even find the surname *Tabernacle*. *Musters* is Old Fr. *moustiers* (*moutiers*), common in French place-names, from Lat. *monasterium*. The word *bow*, still used for an arch in some old towns, has given the names *Bow* and *Bowes*. A medieval statute, recently revived to baffle the suffragettes, was originally directed against robbers and "pillers," *i.e.* plunderers, but the name *Piller* is for pillar; cf. the French name Colonne. With these may be mentioned *Buttress* and *Carnell*, the latter from Old Fr. *carnel* (*créneau*), a battlement.

As general terms for larger dwellings we find *Hall*, *House*, also written *Hose*, and *Seal*, the last-named from the Germanic original which has given Fr. *Lasalle*, whence our surname *Sale*. To the same class belong *Place*, *Plaice*, as in Cumnor Place. The

[1] On the development in meaning of this word, first occurring in the phrase "to take sentrie," *i.e.* refuge, see my *Romance of Words*, ch. vii.

possession of such surnames does not imply ancestral possession of Haddon Hall, Stafford House, etc., but merely that the founder of the family lived under the shadow of greatness. In compounds *-house* is generally treated as in "workus," e.g. *Bacchus* (p. 83), *Bellows, Brewis, Duffus* (dove), *Kirkus, Loftus, Malthus, Windus* (wynd, p. 128). In connection with *Woodhouse* it must be remembered that this name was given to the man who played the part of a "wild man of the woods" in processions and festivities. William Power, skinner, called "Wodehous," died in London in 1391. Of similar origin is *Greenman.* The tavern sign of the Green Man is sometimes explained as representing a forester in green, but it was probably at first equivalent to the German sign "Zum wilden Mann." *Cassell* is sometimes for *Castle,* but is more often a local German name of recent introduction. The northern *Peel,* a castle, as in the Isle of Man, was originally applied to a stockade, Old Fr. *pel* (*pieu*), a stake, Lat. *palus.* From it we have *Pillman. Keep* comes from the central tower of the castle, where the baron and his family kept, *i.e.* lived. A moated *Grange* is a poetic figment, for the word comes from Fr. *grange,* a barn (to Lat. *granum*), hence *Granger.*

With *Mill* and the older *Milne* (p. 25) we may compare *Mullins,* Fr. Desmoulins. *Barnes* is sometimes, but not always, what it seems (see p. 194). With it we may put *Leathes,* from an obsolete Scandinavian word for barn (see quot. p. 130), to which we owe also the names *Leatham* and *Latham.* Mr. Oldbuck's "ecstatic description" of the Roman camp with its prætorium was spoilt by Edie Ochiltree's disastrous interruption—

> "Prætorian here, prætorian there, I mind the *bigging* o't."
> (*Antiquary*, ch. iv.).

The obsolete verb to *big*, i.e. build, whence *Biggar*, a builder, has given us *Biggins*, *Biggs* (p. 38), and *Newbigging*, while from to *build* we have *Newbould* and *Newbolt*. *Cazenove*, Ital. *casa nuova*, means exactly the same. Probably related to *build* is the obsolete *Bottle*, a building, whence *Harbottle*. A humble dwelling was called a *Board*—

> "*Borde*, a little house, lodging, or cottage of timber"
> (Cotgrave)—

whence *Boardman*, *Border*. Other names were *Booth*, *Lodge*, and *Folley*, Fr. *feuillée*, a hut made of branches—

> "*Feuillée*, an arbor, or bower, framed of leav'd plants, or branches" (Cotgrave).

Scale, possibly connected with *shealing*, is a Scandinavian word used in the north for a shepherd's hut, hence the surname *Scales*. In *Bower* and *Bere*, *Beer*, we have names related to *byre*, a hut, cow-house, whence *Byers*. Chaucer says of the poor widow—

> "Ful sooty was hir *bour* and eek hire halle."
> (B, 4022.)

Hence the names *Bowerman*, *Boorman*, *Burman*.

But the commonest of names for a humble dwelling was *cot* or *cote*—

> "Born and fed in rudenesse
> As in a *cote* or in an oxe stalle"
> (E, 397)—

the inhabitant of which was a *Cotman*, *Cotter*, or, diminutively, *Cottrell*, *Cotterill*. Hence the frequent occurrence of the name *Coates*. There are also numerous compounds, e.g. *Alcott* (old), *Norcott*, *Kingscote*, and the many variants of *Caldecott, Calcott,* the cold dwelling, especially common as a village name in the vicinity of the Roman roads. It is supposed to have been applied, like Coldharbour, to deserted posts. The name *Cotton* is sometimes from the dative plural of the same word, though, when of French origin, it represents *Coton,* dim. of Cot, aphetic for Jacot.

Names such as *Kitchin, Spence,* a north-country word for pantry (see p. 186), and *Mews,* originally applied to the hawk-coops (see *Mewer,* p. 150), point to domestic employment. The simple *Mew,* common in Hampshire, is a bird nickname. *Scammell* preserves an older form of *shamble*(*s*), originally the benches on which meat was exposed for sale. The name *Currie,* or *Curry,* is too common to be referred entirely to the Scot. *Corrie,* a mountain glen, or to Curry in Somerset, and I conjecture that it sometimes represents Old Fr. and Mid. Eng. *curie,* a kitchen, which is the origin of Petty Cury in Cambridge and of the famous French name Curie. Nor can *Furness* be derived exclusively from the Furness district of Lancashire. It must sometimes correspond to the common French name Dufour, from *four,* oven. We also have the name *Ovens. Stables,* when not identical with *Staples* (p. 123), belongs to the same class as *Mews. Chambers,* found in Scotland as *Chalmers,* is official, the medieval *de la Chambre* often referring to the Exchequer Chamber of the City of London. *Bellchambers* has probably no connection with this word. It appears to be an imitative spelling of Belencombre, a place near Dieppe; for the entry *de Belencumbre* is of frequeut occurrence.

Places of confinement are represented by *Gale,*

gaol (p. 32), *Penn*, whence *Inkpen* (Berkshire), *Pond*, *Pound*, and *Penfold* or *Pinfold*. But *Gales* is for Anglo-Fr. *Galles*, Wales. *Butts* comes from the archery ground, while *Butt* is rather to be referred to the French name Bout (p. 75) or to *Budd* (p. 75). *Cordery*, for *de la corderie*, of the rope-walk, has been confused with the much more picturesque *Corderoy*, i.e. *cœur de roi*.

Shop Signs

As is well known, medieval shops had signs instead of numbers, and traces of this custom are still to be seen in country towns. It is quite obvious that town surnames would readily spring into existence from such signs. The famous name *Rothschild*, always mispronounced in English, goes back to the "red shield" over Nathan Rothschild's shop in the Jewry of Frankfurt; and within the writer's memory two brothers named Grainge in the little town of Uxbridge were familiarly known as Bible Grainge and Gridiron Grainge. Many names of animals are to be referred partly to this source, e.g. *Bull, Hart, Lamb, Lyon, Ram, Roebuck, Stagg; Cock, Falcon, Peacock, Raven, Swann*, etc., all still common as tavern signs. The popinjay, or parrot, is still occasionally found as *Pobgee, Popjoy*. These surnames all have, of course, an alternative explanation (ch. xxiii.). Here also usually belong *Angel* and *Virgin*. But the largest class of such names probably consists of those taken from figures used in heraldry or from objects which indicated the craft practised. This would seem to be the explanation of *Crowninshield*. Other examples are *Arrow, Bell, Buckle, Crosskeys, Crowne, Crozier, Gauntlett, Hatt, Horne, Image*,

Key, *Lilley*, *Meatyard*, measuring wand—

> "Ye shall do no unrighteousness in judgment, in *meteyard*, in weight, or in measure" (Lev. xix. 35)—

Mullett,[1] *Rose*, *Shears*, and perhaps *Blades*, *Shipp*, *Spurr*, *Starr*, *Sword*. Thomas Palle, called "Sheres," died in London, 1376.

But here again we must walk delicately. The Germanic name Hatto, borne by the wicked bishop who perished in the Mäuseturm, gave the French name *Hatt* with the accusative form *Hatton*,[2] *Horn* is an old personal name, as in the medieval romance of King Horn, *Shipp* is a common provincialism for *sheep*.[3] *Starr* has another explanation (p. 219) and *Bell* has several (p. 8). I should guess that *Porteous* was the sign used by some medieval writer of mass-books and breviaries. Its oldest form is the Anglo-Fr. *porte-hors*, corresponding to medieval Lat. *portiforium*, a breviary, lit. what one carries outside, a portable prayer-book—

> "For on my *porthors* here I make an oath."
>
> (B, 1321.)

But as the name is found without prefix in the Hundred Rolls, it may have been a nickname conferred on some *clericus* who was proud of so rare a possession.

[1] A five-pointed star, Old Fr. *molette*, rowel of a spur.

[2] In Old French a certain number of names, mostly of Germanic origin, had an accusative in *-on*, e.g. Guy, Guyon, Hugues, Hugon, From Lat. *Pontius* came Poinz, Poinson, whence our *Poyntz*, less pleasingly *Punch*, and *Punshon*. In the Pipe Rolls these are also spelt Pin-, whence *Pinch*, *Pinchin*, and *Pinches*.

[3] Hence the connection between the ship and the ha'porth of tar.

CHAPTER XIV

NORMAN BLOOD

"Such, however, is the illusion of antiquity and wealth that decent and dignified men now existing boast their descent from these filthy thieves" (EMERSON, *English Traits*, ch. iv.).

NOT every Norman or Old French name need be included in the group described by Emerson when talking down to an uneducated audience. In fact, it is probable that the majority of genuine French names belong to a later period, for, although the baron who accompanied the Conqueror would in many cases keep his old territorial designation, the minor ruffian would, as a rule, drop the name of the obscure hamlet from which he came and assume some surname more convenient in his new surroundings. Local names of Old French origin are usually taken from the provinces and larger towns which had a meaning for English ears. I have given examples of such in chapter xi. Of course it is easy to take a detailed map of Northern France and say, without offering any proof, that "*Avery* (p. 82) is from Evreux, *Belcher* (p. 196) from Bellecourt, *Custance* (p. 95) from Coutances," and so on. But any serious student knows this to be idiotic nonsense. The fact that, except in some noble families, such as *de Vesci*, whence *Vesey*, *Voysey*, and Scottish *Veitch*, the surname was not hereditary till centuries after the Conquest, justifies any bearer of a

Norman name taken from a village or smaller locality in repudiating all connection with the "filthy thieves" and conjecturing descent from some decent artisan belonging to one of the later immigrations.

That a considerable number of aristocratic families, and others, bear an easily recognizable French town or village name is of course well known, but it will usually be found that such names are derived from places which are as plentiful in France as our own Ashleys, Bartons, Burtons, Langleys, Newtons, Suttons, etc., are in England. In some cases a local French name has spread in an exceptional manner. Examples are *Baines* (Bains, 2 [1]), *Gurney* (Gournai, 6), *Vernon* (3). But usually in such cases we find a large number of spots which may have given rise to the surname, e.g. *Beaumont* (46, without counting *Belmont*), *Dampier* (Dampierre, *i.e.* St. Peter's, 28), *Daubeney*, *Dabney* (Aubigné, 4, Aubigny, 17), *Ferrers* (Ferrières, 22), *Nevill* (Neuville, 58), *Nugent* (Nogent, 17), *Villiers* (58). This last name, representing Vulgar Lat. *villarium*, is the origin of Ger. *-weiler*, so common in village names along the old Roman roads, *e.g.* Badenweiler, Froschweiler, etc.

When we come to those surnames of this class which have remained somewhat more exclusive, we generally find that the place-name is also rare. Thus *Hawtrey* is from Hauterive (7), *Pierpoint* from Pierrepont (5), *Furneaux* from Fourneaux (5), *Vipont* and *Vipan* from Vieux-Pont (3), and there are three places called *Percy*. The following have two possible birthplaces

[1] The figures in brackets indicate the number of times that the French local name occurs in the Postal Directory. This is the usual explanation of *Baines*, which is found with *de* in the Hundred Rolls. But I think it was sometimes a nickname, *bones*, applied to a thin man. I find William *Banes* in Lancashire in 1252; cf. *Langbain*.

each—*Bellew* or *Pellew* (Belleau), *Cantelo* (Canteloup[1]), *Mauleverer* (Maulévrier), *Mompesson* (Mont Pinçon or Pinchon), *Montmorency*, *Mortimer* (Morte-mer). The following are unique—*Carteret*, *Doll*[2] (Dol), *Fiennes*, *Furnival* (Fournival), *Greville*, *Harcourt*, *Melville* (Meleville), *Montresor*, *Mowbray* (Monbrai), *Sackville* (Sacquenville), *Venables*. These names are taken at random, but the same line of investigation can be followed up by any reader who thinks it worth while.

Apart from aristocratic questions, it is interesting to notice the contamination which has occurred between English and French surnames of local origin. The very common French suffix *-ville* is regularly confounded with our *-field*. Thus *Summerfield* is the same name as *Somerville*, *Dangerfield* is for d'Angerville, *Belfield* for Belleville, *Blomfield* for Blonville, and *Stutfield* for Estouteville, while *Grenville*, *Granville* have certainly become confused with our *Grenfell*, green fell, and *Greenfield*. Camden notes that *Turberville* became *Troublefield*, and I have found the intermediate *Trubleville* in the twelfth century. The case of Tess *Durbeyfield* will occur to every reader. The suffix *-fort* has been confused with our *-ford* and *-forth*, so that *Rochford* is in some cases for Rochefort and *Beeforth* for Beaufort or Belfort. With the first syllable of *Beeforth* we may compare *Beevor* for Beauvoir, Belvoir, *Beecham* for Beauchamp, and *Beamish* for Beaumais. The name *Beamish* actually occurs as that of a village in Durham, the earlier form of which points to Old French origin, from *beau mes*, Lat. *bellum mansum*, a fair manse, i.e. dwelling. Otherwise it

[1] But the doublet *Chanteloup*, champ de loup, is common.

[2] This may also be a metronymic, from Dorothy.

would be tempting to derive the surname *Beamish* from Ger. *böhmisch,* earlier *behmisch,* Bohemian.

A brief survey of French spot-names which have passed into English will show that they were acquired in exactly the same way as the corresponding English names. Norman ancestry is, however, not always to be assumed in this case. Until the end of the fourteenth century a large proportion of our population was bi-lingual, and names accidentally recorded in Anglo-French may occasionally have stuck. Thus the name *Boyes* or *Boyce* may spring from a man of pure English descent who happened to be described as *du bois* instead of *atte wood.* This is, however, rarely the case. While English spot-names have as a rule shed both the preposition and the article (p. 104), French usually keeps one or both, though these were more often lost when the name passed into England. Thus our *Roach* is not a fish-name, but corresponds to Fr. *Laroche* or *Delaroche* ; and the blind pirate *Pew,* if not a Welshman, ap Hugh, was of the race of *Dupuy,* from Old Fr. *puy,* a hill, Lat. *podium,* a height, gallery, etc., whence also our *pew,* once a raised platform.

In some cases the prefix has passed into English ; e.g. *Diprose* is from *des préaux,* of the meadows, a name assumed by Boileau among others. There are, of course, plenty of places in France called *Les Préaux,* but in the case of such a name we need not go further than possession of, or residence by, a piece of grass-land—

> " Je sais un paysan qu'on appelait Gros-Pierre,
> Qui, n'ayant pour tout bien qu'un seul quartier de terre,
> Y fit tout alentour faire un fossé bourbeux,
> Et de *monsieur de l'Isle* en prit le nom pompeux."
>
> (Molière, *L'École des Femmes,* i. 1.)

The Old French singular *préal* is perhaps the origin of *Prall, Prawle.* Similarly *Preece,* sometimes for *Price,* is earlier found as *Prees,* i.e. *des prés.* With *Boyes* (p. 140) we may compare *Tallis* from Fr. *taillis,* a copse (*tailler,* to cut). *Garrick,* a Huguenot name, is Fr. *garigue,* an old word for heath.

Trees have in all countries a strong influence on topographical names, and hence on surnames. *Frean,* though usually from the Scandinavian name Fræna, is sometimes for Fr. *frêne,* ash, Lat. *fraxinus,* while *Cain* and *Kaines*[1] are Norm. *quêne* (*chêne*), oak. The modern French for beech is *hêtre,* Du. *heester,* but Lat. *fagus* has given a great many dialect forms which have supplied us with the surnames *Fay, Foy,* and the plural dim. *Failes.* Here also I should put the name *Defoe,* assumed by the writer whose father was satisfied with *Foe.* With Quatrefages, four beeches, we may compare such English names as *Fiveash, Twelvetrees,* and *Snooks,* for "seven oaks."

In Latin the suffix *-ētum* was used to designate a grove or plantation. This suffix, or its plural *-ēta,* is very common in France, becoming successively *-ei*(*e*), *-oi*(*e*), *-ai*(*e*). The name *Dobree* is a Guernsey spelling of d'Aubray, Lat. *arboretum,* which was dissimilated (p. 36) into *alboretum. Darblay,* the name of Fanny Burney's husband, is a variant. From *au*(*l*)*ne,* alder, we have *aunai,* whence our *Dawnay.* So also *frênai* has given *Freeney, chênai, Chaney,* and the Norm. *quênai* is one origin of *Kenney,* while the older *chesnai* appears in *Chesney. Houssaie* from *houx,* holly, gives *Hussey* ; *chastenai,* chestnut grove, exists in Nottingham as *Chasteney* ; *coudrai,* hazel copse, gives *Cowdrey* and

[1] There is one family of *Keynes* derived specifically from Chahaignes (Sarthe).

Cowdery; *Verney* and *Varney* are from *vernai*, grove of alders, of Celtic origin, and *Viney* corresponds to the French name *Vinoy*, Lat. *vinetum*. We have also *Chinnery*, *Chenerey* from the extended *chênerai*, and *Pomeroy* from *pommerai*. Here again the name offers no clue as to the exact place of origin. There are in the French postal directory eight places called Épinay, from *épine*, thorn, but these do not exhaust the number of "spinnies" in France. Also connected with tree-names are *Conyers*, Old Fr. *coigniers*, quince-trees, and *Pirie*, *Perry*, Anglo-Fr. *périe*, a collective from *peire* (*poire*).

Among Norman names for a homestead the favourite is *mesnil*, from Vulgar Lat. *mansionile*, which enters into a great number of local names. It has given our *Meynell*, and is also the first element of *Mainwaring*, *Mannering* from *mesnil-Warin*. The simple *mes*, a southern form of which appears in Dumas, has given us *Mees* and *Meese*, which are thus etymological doublets of the word *manse*. With *Beamish* (p. 139) we may compare *Bellasis*, from *bel-assis*, fairly situated. *Poyntz* is sometimes for *des ponts*; cf. *Pierpoint* for *Pierrepont*. *Travers* or *Travis* means a crossing, or a road starting off from the highway.

Even Norman names which were undoubtedly borne by leaders among the Conqueror's companions are now rarely found among the noble, and many a descendant of these once mighty families cobbles the shoes of more recent invaders. Even so the descendants of the Spanish nobles who conquered California are glad to peddle vegetables at the doors of San Francisco magnates whose fathers dealt in old clothes in some German Judengasse.

CHAPTER XV

OF OCCUPATIVE NAMES

"When Adam delved and Eve span,
Who was then the gentleman?"
Chant of Wat Tyler's followers.

THE occupative name would, especially in villages, tend to become the most natural surname. It is not therefore surprising to find so large a number of this class among our commonest surnames, e.g. *Smith, Taylor, Wright, Walker, Turner, Clark, Cooper*, etc. And, as the same craft often persisted in a family for generations, it was probably this type of surname which first became hereditary. On the other hand, such names as *Cook, Gardiner, Carter*, etc., have no doubt in some cases prevailed over another surname lawfully acquired (see p. 5). It is impossible to fix an approximate date for the definite adoption of surnames of this class. It occurred earlier in towns than in the country, and by the middle of the fourteenth century we often find in the names of London citizens a contradiction between the surname and the trade-name; e.g. Walter *Ussher*, tanner, John *Botoner*, girdler, Roger *Carpenter*, pepperer, Richard *le Hunte*, chaundeler, occur 1336–52. The number of surnames belonging to this group is immense, for every medieval trade and craft was highly specialized and its privileges were jealously guarded. The general public, which now, like Issachar, crouches between the trusts and the trades unions, was in the middle ages similarly victimized by the guilds of merchants and craftsmen. Then, as now, it grumblingly recognized that, "Plus ça change, plus ça reste la même chose," and went on enduring.[1]

By dealing with a few essential points at the outset we shall clear the ground for considering the various groups of surnames connected with trade, craft, profession or office. To begin with, it is certain that such names as *Pope*, *Cayzer*, *King*, *Earl*, *Bishop* are nicknames, very often conferred on performers in religious plays or acquired in connection with popular festivals and processions—

> "Names also have been taken of civil honours, dignities and estate, as *King*, *Duke*, *Prince*, *Lord*, *Baron*, *Knight*, *Valvasor* or *Vavasor*, *Squire*, *Castellan*, partly for that their ancestours were such, served such, acted such parts; or were Kings of the Bean, Christmas-Lords, etc." (Camden).

We find corresponding names in other languages, and some of the French names, usually preceded by the definite article, have passed into English, e.g. *Lempriere*, a Huguenot name, and *Levêque*, whence our *Levick*, *Vick*, *Veck* (p. 33). *Baron* generally appears as *Barron*, and *Duke*, used in Mid. English of any leader, is often degraded to *Duck*, whence the dim. *Duckett*. But all three of these names can also be

[1] If a student of philology were allowed to touch on such high matters as legislation, I would moralize on the word *kiddle*, meaning an illegal kind of weir used for fish-poaching, which has given our name *Kiddell*. From investigations made with a view to discovering the origin of the word, I came to the conclusion that all the legislative powers in England spent three centuries in passing enactments against these devices, with the inevitable consequence that they became ever more numerous.

referred to Marmaduke. We have also the imitative *Ducat*. It would be tempting to put *Palsgrave* in this class. Prince Rupert, the *Pfalzgraf*, i.e. Count Palatine, was known as the Palsgrave in his day, but I have not found the title early enough.

With *Lord* we must put the northern *Laird*, and, in my opinion, *Senior*; for, if we notice how much commoner *Young* is than *Old*, and Fr. *Lejeune* than *Levieux*, we must conclude that *Junior*, a very rare surname, ought to be of much more frequent occurrence than *Senior*; *Synyer*, a fairly common name. There can be little doubt that *Senior* is usually a latinization of the medieval *le seigneur*, whence also *Saynor*. *Knight* is not always knightly, for Anglo-Sax. *cniht* means servant; cf. Ger. *Knecht*. The word got on in the world, with the consequence that the name is very popular, while its medieval compeers, knave, varlet, villain, have, even when adorned with the adj. good, dropped out of the surname list. *Bonvalet*, *Bonvarlet*, *Bonvillain* are still common surnames in France. From *Knight* we have the compound *Roadnight*, a mounted servitor. Thus *Knight* is more often a true occupative name, and the same applies to *Dring* or *Dreng*, a Scandinavian name of similar meaning.

Other names from the middle rungs of the social ladder are also to be taken literally, e.g. *Franklin*, a freeholder, Anglo-Fr. *frankelein*—

> "How called you your *franklin*, Prior Aylmer?"
> "Cedric," answered the Prior, "Cedric the Saxon"
> (*Ivanhoe*, ch. i.)—

Burgess, *Freeman*, *Freeborn*, this latter sometimes for *Freebairn* and existing already as the Anglo-Saxon personal name Freobeorn. *Denison* (p. 14) is occasionally an accommodated form of *denizen*, Anglo-Fr. *deinzein*, a burgess enjoying the privileges belonging to those who lived "*deinz* (in) *la cité*." In 1483 a certain Edward Jhonson—

> "Sued to be mayde *Denison* for fer of ye payment of y^s^ subsedy."
> (*Letter to Sir William Stonor*, June 9, 1483.)

Bond is from Anglo-Sax. *bonda*, which means simply agriculturist. The word is of Icelandic origin and related to *Boor*, another word which has deteriorated and is rare as a surname, though the name *Bauer* is common enough in Germany. *Holder* is translated by *Tennant*. For some other names applied to the humbler peasantry see p. 133.

To return to the social summit, we have *Kingson*, often confused with the local *Kingston*, and its Anglo-French equivalent *Fauntleroy*. *Faunt*, aphetic for Anglo-Fr. *enfaunt*, is common in Mid. English. When the mother of Moses had made the ark of bulrushes, or, as Wyclif calls it, the "jonket of resshen," she—

> "Putte the litil *faunt* with ynne"
> (*Exodus* ii. 3).

The Old French accusative (p. 9, *n.*) was also used as a genitive, as in Bourg-le-roi, Bourg-la-reine, corresponding to our Kingsbury and Queensborough. We have a genitive also in *Flowerdew*, found in French as Flourdieu. Lower, in his *Patronymica Britannica* (1860), the first attempt at a dictionary of English surnames,[1] conjectures *Fauntleroy* to be from an

[1] I have quoted this "etymology" because it is too funny to be lost; but a good deal of useful information can be found in Lower, especially with regard to the habitat of well-known names.

ancient French war-cry Défendez le roi! for "in course of time, the meaning of the name being forgotten, the *de* would be dropped, and the remaining syllables would easily glide into *Fauntleroy*."

Names of ecclesiastics must usually be nicknames, because medieval churchmen were not entitled to have descendants. This appears clearly in such an entry as "Johannes *Monacus* et uxor ejus Emma," living in Kent in the twelfth century. But these names are so numerous that I have put them with the Canterbury Pilgrims (ch. xvii.). Three of them may be mentioned here in connection with a small group of occupative surnames of puzzling form. We have noticed (p. 104) that monosyllabic, and some other, surnames of local origin frequently take an *-s*, partly by analogy with names like *Wills*, *Watts*, etc. We rarely find this *-s* in the case of occupative names, but *Parsons*, *Vicars* or *Vickers*, and *Monks* are common, and in fact the first two are scarcely found without the *-s*. To these we may add *Reeves* (p. 164), *Grieves* (p. 181), and the well-known Nottingham name *Mellers* (p. 164). The explanation seems to be that these names are true genitives, and that John *Parsons* was John the Parson's man, while John *Monks* was employed by the monastery. *Vigors* or *Vigers* I guess to be formed in the same way from Fr. *viguier*—

"*Viguier*, the ordinary judge of a country town" (Cotgrave).

Another exceptional group is that of names formed by adding *-son* to the occupative names, the commonest being perhaps *Clarkson*, *Cookson*, *Smithson*, and *Wrightson*. To this class belongs *Grayson*, which Bardsley clearly shows to be equivalent to the grieve's son.

Our occupative names are both English and French,[1] the two languages being represented by those important tradesmen *Baker* and *Butcher*. The former is reinforced by *Bullinger*, Fr. *boulanger*, and *Furner*—

"*Fournier*, a baker, or one that keeps, or governs a common oven" (Cotgrave).

In some other cases the English and French names for the same trade both survive, e.g. *Cheeseman* and *Firminger*, Old Fr. *formagier* (*fromage*).

We have as endings *-er*, *-ier*, the latter often made into *-yer*, *-ger*, as in *Lockyer*, *Sawyer*, *Kidger* (p. 181), *Woodger*,[2] and *-or*, *-our*, as in *Taylor*, *Jenoure* (p. 33). The latter ending, corresponding to Modern Fr. *-eur*, represents Lat. *-or*, *-orem*, but we tack it on to English words as in "sailor," or substitute it for *-er*, *-ier*, as in *Fermor*, for *Farmer*, Fr. *fermier*. In the Privy Purse Expenses of that careful monarch Henry VII. occurs the item—

"To bere drunken at a *fermors* house . . 1s."

In the same way we replace the Fr. *-our*, *-eur* by *-er*, as in *Turner*, Fr. *tourneur*, *Ginner*, *Jenner* for *Jenoure*.

The ending *-er*, *-ier* represents the Lat. *-arius*. It passed not only into French, but also into the Germanic languages, replacing the Teutonic agential suffix which consisted of a single vowel. We have a few traces of this oldest group of occupative names, e.g. *Webb*, Mid. Eng. *webbe*, Anglo-Sax. *webb-a*, and *Hunt*, Mid. Eng. *hunte*, Anglo-Sax. *hunt-a*—

"With *hunte* and horne and houndes hym bisyde"
(A, 1678)—

[1] We have also a few Latinizations. This type of name is much commoner in Germany, *e.g.* Avenarius, oat-man, Fabricius, smith, Textor, weaver, etc. Mercator, of map projection fame, was a German named Kaufmann.

[2] Woodyer, Woodger may also be for wood-hewer. See *Stanier* (p. 21).

which still hold the field easily against *Webber* and *Hunter*. So also, the German name *Beck* represents Old High Ger. *becch-o*, baker. To these must be added *Kemp*, a champion, a very early loan-word connected with Lat. *campus*, field, and *Wright*, originally the worker, Anglo-Sax. *wyrht-a*. *Camp* is sometimes for Kemp, but may be also from the latinized *in campo*, i.e. *Field*. Of similar formation is *Clapp*, from an Anglo-Sax. nickname, the clapper—

"Osgod *Clapa*, King Edward Confessor's staller, was cast upon the pavement of the Church by a demon's hand for his insolent pride in presence of the relics (of St. Edmund, King and Martyr)."
(W. H. Hutton, *Bampton Lectures*, 1903.)

The ending -*ster* was originally feminine, and applied to trades chiefly carried on by women, e.g. *Baxter*, *Bagster*, baker, *Brewster*, *Simister*, sempster, *Webster*, etc., but in process of time the distinction was lost, so that we find *Blaxter* and *Whitster* for *Blacker*, *Blaker*, and *Whiter*, both of which, curiously enough, have the same meaning—

"*Bleykester* or *whytster*, candidarius" (*Prompt. Parv.*)—

for this *black* represents Mid. Eng. *blāc*, related to *bleak* and *bleach*, and meaning pale—

"*Blake*, wan of colour, *blesme* (*blême*)" (Palsgrave).

Occupative names of French origin are apt to vary according to the period and dialect of their adoption. For *Butcher* we find also *Booker*, *Bowker*, and sometimes the later *Bosher*, *Busher*, with the same sound for the *ch* as in *Labouchère*, the lady butcher. But *Busher* is usually wood-monger, Old Fr. *busche* (*bûche*), log, and *Boger* and *Bodger* represent rather an archaic spelling of *Bowyer*. *Butcher*, originally a dealer in goat's flesh, Fr. *bouc*, has ousted *flesher*. German still has half a dozen surnames derived from names for this trade, *e.g.* Fleischer, Fleischmann,[1] Metzger, Schlechter; but our *flesher* has been absorbed by *Fletcher,* a maker of arrows, Fr. *flèche.* Fletcher Gate at Nottingham was formerly Flesher Gate. The undue extension of *Taylor* has already been mentioned (p. 44). Another example is *Barker,* which has swallowed up the Anglo-Fr. *berquier,* a shepherd, Fr. *berger,* with the result that the *Barkers* outnumber the *Tanners* by three to one—

> "'What craftsman are you?' said our King,
> 'I pray you, tell me now.'
> 'I am a *barker,*' quoth the tanner;
> 'What craftsman art thou?'"
> (*Edward IV. and the Tanner of Tamworth.*)

The name seems to have been applied also to the man who barked trees for the tanner.

With *Barker* it seems natural to mention *Mewer,* of which I find one representative in the London Directory. The medieval *le muur* had charge of the mews in which the hawks were kept while moulting (Fr. *muer,* Lat. *mutare*). Hence the phrase "mewed up." The word seems to have been used for any kind of coop. Chaucer tells us of the Franklin—

> "Ful many a fat partrich hadde he in *muw*" (A, 349).

I suspect that some of the *Muirs* (p. 113) spring from this important office. Similarly *Clayer* has been absorbed by the noble *Clare, Kayer,* the man by the quay, by *Care,* and *Blower,* whether of horn or bellows, has paid tribute to the local *Bloor, Blore. Sewer,* an

[1] Hellenized as Sarkander. This was a favourite trick of German scholars at the Renaissance period. Well-known examples are Melancthon (Schwarzerd), Neander (Neumann).

attendant at table, aphetic for Old Fr. *asseour*, a setter, is now a very rare name. As we know that *sewer*, a drain, became *shore*, it is probable that the surname *Shore* sometimes represents this official or servile title. And this same name *Shore*, though not particularly common, and susceptible of a simple local origin, labours under grave suspicion of having also enriched itself at the expense of the medieval *le suur*, the shoemaker, Lat. *sutor-em*, whence Fr. *Lesueur*. This would inevitably become *Sewer* and then *Shore*, as above. Perhaps, in the final reckoning, *Shaw* is not altogether guiltless, and we also find the surname *Sure*.

The medieval *le suur* brings us to another problem, viz. the poor show made by the craftsmen who clothed the upper and lower extremities of our ancestors. The name *hatter*, once frequent enough, appears to be extinct, and *Capper* is not very common. The name *shoemaker* has met with the same fate, though the trade is represented by the Lat. *Sutor*, whence Scot. *Souter*. Here belong also *Cordner*, *Codner*,[1] Old Fr. *cordouanier* (*cordonnier*), a *cordwainer*, a worker in Cordovan leather, and *Corser*, *Cosser*, earlier *corviser*, corresponding to the French name *Courvoisier*, also derived from Cordova. Chaucer, in describing the equipment of Sir Thopas, mentions—

> "His shoon of *cordewane*" (B, 1922).

The scarcity of *Groser*, grocer, is not surprising, for the word, aphetic for *engrosser*, originally meaning a wholesale dealer, one who sold *en gros*, is of comparatively late occurrence. His medieval representative

[1] Confused, of course, with the local *Codnor* (Derbyshire).

was *Spicer*. On the other hand, many occupative names which are now obsolete, or practically so, still survive strongly as surnames. Many examples of these will be found in chapters xvii.–xx.

Some occupative names are rather deceptive. *Kisser*, which is said still to exist, means a maker of *cuishes*, thigh-armour, Fr. *cuisses*—

> "Helm, *cuish*, and breastplate streamed with gore."
> (*Lord of the Isles*, iv. 33.)

Corker is for caulker, *i.e.* one who stopped the chinks of ships and casks, originally with lime (Lat. *calx*)—

> "Sir, we have a chest beneath the hatches, *caulk'd* and bitumed ready" (*Pericles* iii. 1).

Cleaver represents Old Fr. *clavier*, a mace-bearer. Lat. *clava*, a club, or a door-keeper, Lat. *clavis*, a key. Perhaps even *clavus*, a nail, must also be considered, for a Latin vocabulary of the fifteenth century tells us—

> "Claves, -*vos* vel -*vas* qui fert sit *claviger*."

Neither *Bowler* nor *Scorer* are connected with cricket. The former made wooden bowls, and the latter was sometimes a *scourer*, or scout, Mid. Eng. *scurrour*, from the Old Fr. verb *escourre*, Lat. *excurrere*, to run out, but perhaps more frequently a peaceful scullion, Fr. *écurer*, to scour, Lat. *ex-curare*—

> "*Escureur*, a *scourer*, cleanser, feyer[1]" (Cotgrave).

A *Leaper* did not always leap (p. 165). In some cases the name is for *le leper*, a common medieval entry, generally to be regarded as a nickname. In others it may represent a maker of *leaps*, i.e. fish baskets, or perhaps a man who hawked fish in such a basket. A

[1] A sweeper, now swallowed up, as a surname, by *Fair*.

Slayer made *slays,* part of a weaver's loom, and a *Bloomer* worked in a *bloom*-smithy, from Anglo-Sax. *blōma,* a mass of hammered iron. *Weightman* and *Wayman* represent Mid. Eng. *waþeman,* hunter; cf. the common German surname Weidemann, of cognate origin. *Reader* and *Booker* are not usually literary. The former is for *Reeder,* a thatcher—

"*Redare* of howsys, *calamator, arundinarius*" (*Prompt. Parv.*)—

and the latter is a Norman variant of *Butcher.*

The spelling of occupative surnames often differs from that now associated with the trade itself. In *Naylor, Taylor,* and *Tyler*[1] we have the archaic preference for *y.* Our ancestors thought *sope* as good a spelling as *soap,* hence the name *Soper.* A *Plummer,* i.e. a man who worked in lead, Lat. *plumbum,* is now written, by etymological reaction, plumber, though the restored letter is not sounded. A man who dealt in *'arbs* originated the name *Arber,* which we should now replace by herbalist. We have a restored spelling in *clerk,* though educated people pronounce the word as it was once written—

"*Clarke,* or he that readeth distinctly, *clericus.*"
(Holyoak's Lat. Dict., 1612.)

In many cases we are unable to say exactly what is the occupation indicated. We may assume that a *Setter* and a *Tipper* did setting and tipping, and both are said to have been concerned in the arrow industry. If this is true, I should say that *Setter* might represent the Old Fr. *saieteur,* arrow-maker, from *saiete,*

[1] It may be noted here that John Tiler of Dartford, who killed a tax-gatherer for insulting his daughter, was not Wat Tiler, who was killed at Smithfield for insulting the King. The confusion between the two has led to much sympathy being wasted on a ruffian.

an arrow, Lat. *sagitta*. But in a medieval vocabulary we find "*setter* of mes, *dapifer*," which would make it the same as *Sewer* (p. 151). Similarly, when we consider the number of objects that can be tipped, we shall be shy of defining the activity of the Tipper too closely. I conjecture that a *Trinder*, earlier *trender*, was the same as a *Roller*, but I cannot say what they rolled—

"Lat hym *rollen* and *trenden* withynne hymself the lyght of his ynwarde sighte" (*Boece*, 1043).

There are also some names of this class to which we can with certainty attribute two or more origins. *Boulter* means a maker of bolts for crossbows,[1] but also a sifter, from the obsolete verb to *bolt*—

"The fanned snow, that's *bolted*
By the northern blasts twice o'er."
(*Winter's Tale*, iv. 3.)

Corner means horn-blower, Fr. *cor*, horn, and is also a contraction of coroner, but its commonest origin is local, *in angulo*, in the corner. *Currer* and *Curryer* are generally connected with leather, but Henry VII. bestowed £3 on the *currer* that brought tidings of Perkin Warbeck. *Garner* has five possible origins: (i) a contraction of *gardener*, (ii) from the French personal name *Garnier*, Ger. *Werner*, (iii) Old Fr. *grenier*, grain-keeper, (iv) Old Fr. *garennier*, warren keeper, (v) local, from garner, Fr. *grenier*, Lat. *granarium*. In the next chapter will be found, as a specimen problem, an investigation of the name *Rutter*.

Two phonetic phenomena should also be noticed. One is the regular insertion of *n* before the ending *-ger*, as in *Firminger* (p. 148), *Massinger* (p. 185), *Pot-*

[1] How many people who use the expression "*bolt* upright" associate it with "straight as a *dart*"?

tinger (p. 176), and in *Arminger*, *Clavinger*, from the latinized *armiger*, esquire, and *claviger*, mace-bearer, etc. (p. 152). The other is the fact that many occupative names ending in *-rer* lose the *-er* by dissimilation (p. 36). Examples are *Armour* for armourer, *Barter* for barterer, *Buckler* for bucklerer, but also for buckle-maker, *Callender* for calenderer, one who calendered, *i.e.* pressed, cloth—

> "And my good friend the *callender*
> Will lend his horse to go."
>
> (*John Gilpin*, l. 22)—

Coffer, for cofferer, a treasurer, *Cover*, for coverer, *i.e.* tiler, Fr. *couvreur*, when it does not correspond to Fr. *cuvier*, i.e. a maker of *cuves*, vats, *Ginger*, *Grammer*, for grammarer, *Paternoster*, maker of paternosters or rosaries, *Pepper*, *Sellar*, for cellarer (see p. 29), *Tabor*, for *Taberer*, player on the taber. Here also belongs *Treasure*, for treasurer. *Salter* is sometimes for *sautrier*, a player on the psaltery. We have the opposite process in poulterer for *Poulter* (p. 15), and caterer for *Cator* (p. 33).

Such names as *Ginger*, *Pepper*, may however belong to the class of nicknames conferred on dealers in certain commodities; cf. *Pescod*, *Peskett*, from pease-cod. Of this we have several examples which can be confirmed by foreign parallels, e.g. *Garlick*, found in German as Knoblauch,[1] *Straw*, represented in German by the cognate name Stroh, and *Pease*, which is certified by Fr. Despois. We find *Witepease* in the twelfth century.

Especially common are those names which deal with the two staple foods of the country, bread and

[1] The cognate Eng. *clove-leek* occurs as a surname in the Ramsey Cartulary.

beer. In German we find several compounds of *Brot*, bread, and one of the greatest of chess-players bore the amazing name *Zuckertort*, sugar-cake. In French we have such names as Painchaud, Painlevé, Paintendre—

"Eugene Aram was usher, in 1744, to the Rev. Mr. *Painblanc*, in Piccadilly" (Bardsley).

Hence our *Cakebread* and *Whitbread* were probably names given to bakers. *Simnel* is explained in the same way, and Lambert Simnel is understood to have been a baker's lad, but the name could equally well be from Fr. *Simonel*, dim. of Simon. *Wastall* is found in the Hundred Rolls as *wastel*, Old Fr. *gastel* (*gâteau*). Here also belongs *Cracknell*—

"*Craquelin*, a *cracknell*; made of the yolks of egges, water, and flower; and fashioned like a hollow trendle" (Cotgrave).

Goodbeer is explained by Bardsley as a perversion of *Godber* (p. 72), which may be true, but the name is also to be taken literally. We have Ger. *Gutbier*, and the existence of *Sourale* in the Hundred Rolls and *Sowerbutts* at the present day justifies us in accepting both *Goodbeer* and *Goodale* at their face-value. But *Rice* is an imitative form of Welsh *Rhys*, *Reece*, and *Salt*, when not derived from Salt in Stafford, is from Old Fr. *sault*,[1] a wood, Lat. *saltus*. It is doubtful whether the name *Cheese* is to be included here. Jan Kees, for John Cornelius, said to have been a nickname for a Hollander, may easily have reached the Eastern counties. Bardsley's earliest instance for the name is John *Chese*, who was living in Norfolk in 1273. But still I find *Furmage* as a medieval surname. We also

[1] This is common in place-names, and I should suggest, as a guess, that *Sacheverell* is from the village of Sault-Chevreuil-du-Tronchet (Manche).

have the dealer in meat represented by the classical example of *Hogsflesh,* with which we may compare *Mutton* and *Veal,* two names which may be seen fairly near each other in Hammersmith Road (but for these see also p. 223), and I have known a German named Kalbfleisch. Names of this kind would sometimes come into existence through the practice of crying wares; though if Mr. *Rottenherring,* who was a freeman of York in 1332, obtained his in this way, he must have deliberately ignored an ancient piece of wisdom.

CHAPTER XVI

A SPECIMEN PROBLEM

"Howe sayst thou, man? am not I a joly *rutter?*"
(SKELTON, *Magnyfycence*, l. 762.)

THE fairly common name *Rutter* is a good example of the difficulty of explaining a surname derived from a trade or calling no longer practised. Even so careful an authority as Bardsley has gone hopelessly astray over this name. He says, "German *ritter*, a rider, *i.e.* a trooper," and quotes from Halliwell, "*rutter*, a rider, a trooper, from the German; a name given to mercenary soldiers engaged from Brabant, etc." Now this statement is altogether opposed to chronology. The name occurs as *le roter*, *rotour*, *ruter* in the Hundred Rolls of 1273, *i.e.* more than two centuries before any German name for trooper could possibly have become familiar in England. Any stray Mid. High Ger. *Riter* would have been assimilated to the cognate Eng. *Rider*. It is possible that some German Reuters have become English *Rutters* in comparatively modern times, but the German surname Reuter has nothing to do with a trooper. It represents Mid. High Ger. *riutære*, a clearer of land, from the verb *riuten* (*reuten*), corresponding to Low Ger. *roden*, and related to our *royd*, a clearing (p. 111). This word is apparently not connected with our *root*, though it means to root out, but ultimately belongs to a root *ru* which appears in Lat. *rutrum,* a spade, *rutabulum,* a rake, etc.

There is another Ger. *Reuter,* a trooper, which has given the sixteenth-century Eng. *rutter,* but not as a surname. The word appears in German about 1500, *i e.* rather late for the surname period, and comes from Du. *ruiter,* a mercenary trooper. The German for trooper is *Reiter,* really the same word as *Ritter,* a knight, the two forms having been differentiated in meaning ; cf. Fr. *cavalier,* a trooper, and *chevalier,* a knight. In the sixteenth and seventeenth centuries Ger. *Reiter* was confused with, and supplanted by, this borrowed word *Reuter,* which was taken to mean rider, and we find the cavalry called *Reuterei* well into the eighteenth century. As a matter of fact the two words are quite unrelated, though the origin of Du. *ruiter* is disputed.

The New English Dictionary gives, from the year 1506, *rutter* (var. *ruter, ruiter*), a cavalry soldier, especially German, from Du. *ruiter,* whence Ger. *Reuter,* as above. It connects the Dutch word with medieval Lat. *rutarius,* i.e. *ruptarius,* which is also Kluge's [1] view. But Franck [2] sees phonetic difficulties and prefers to regard *ruiter* as belonging rather to *ruiten,* to uproot. The application of the name up-rooter to a lawless mercenary is not unnatural.

But whatever be the ultimate origin of this Dutch and German military word, it is sufficiently obvious that it cannot have given an English surname which is already common in the thirteenth century. There is a much earlier claimant in the field. The New English Dictionary has *roter* (1297), var. *rotour, rotor,* and

[1] Deutsches Etymologisches Wörterbuch.
[2] Etymologisch Woordenboek der Nederlandsche Taal.

router (1379), a lawless person, robber, ruffian, from Old Fr. *rotier* (*routier*), and also the form *rutar*, used by Philemon Holland, who, in his translation of Camden's *Britannia* (1610), says "That age called foraine and willing souldiours *rutars*." The reference is to King John's mercenaries, *c.* 1215. Fr. *routier*, a mercenary, is usually derived from *route*, a band, Lat. *rupta*, a piece broken off, a *detach*ment. References to the *grandes routes*, the great mercenary bands which overran France in the fourteenth century, are common in French history. But the word was popularly, and naturally, connected with *route*, Lat. (*via*) *rupta*, a highway, so that Godefroy [1] separates *routier*, a vagabond, from *routier*, a bandit soldier. Cotgrave has—

> "*Routier*, an old traveller, one that by much trotting up and down is grown acquainted with most waies; and hence, an old beaten souldier; one whom a long practise hath made experienced in, or absolute master of, his profession; and (in evill part) an old crafty fox, notable beguiler, ordinary deceiver, subtill knave; also, a purse-taker, or a robber by the high way side."

It is impossible to determine the relative shares of *route*, a band, and *route*, a highway, in this definition, but there has probably been natural confusion between two words, separate in meaning, though etymologically identical. Fr. *reître*, a German trooper, which represents Ger. *Reiter* or *Reuter*, appears in the sixteenth century with practically the meaning of *routier*. In fact *un vieux reître* and *un vieux routier* are used indifferently for an artful old dodger, an old soldier in the bad sense. Victor Hugo couples the two words—

> "Au-dedans, *routiers*, *reîtres*,
> Vont battant le pays et brûlant la moisson."
> (*Ruy Blas*, iii. 2.)

[1] *Dictionnaire de l'ancien Français.*

Now our thirteenth-century *rotors* and *ruters* may represent Old Fr. *routier*, and have been names applied to a mercenary soldier or a vagabond. But this cannot be considered certain. If we consult du Cange,[1] we find, s.v. *rumpere*, "*ruptarii*, pro *ruptuarii*, quidam prædones sub xi sæculum, ex rusticis . . . collecti ac conflati," which suggests connection with "*ruptuarius*, colonus qui agrum seu terram rumpit, proscindit, colit," *i.e.* that the *ruptarii*, also called *rutarii*, *rutharii*, *rotharii*, *rotarii*, etc., were so named because they were revolting peasants, *i.e.* men connected with the *roture*, or breaking of the soil, from which we get *roturier*, a plebeian. That would still connect our *Rutters* with Lat. *rumpere*, but by a third road.

Finally, Old French has one more word which seems to me quite as good a candidate as any of the others, viz. *roteur*, a player on the *rote*, i.e. the fiddle used by the medieval minstrels, Chaucer says of his Frere—

> "Wel koude he synge and playen on a *rote*."
> (A, 236.)

The word is possibly of Celtic origin (Welsh *crwth*) and a doublet of the archaic *crowd*, or *crowth*, a fiddle. Both *rote* and *crowth* are used by Spenser. *Crowd* is perhaps not yet obsolete in dialect, and the fiddler in Hudibras is called *Crowdero*. Thus *Rutter* may be a doublet of *Crowther*. There may be other possible etymologies for *Rutter*, but those discussed will suffice to show that the origin of occupative names is not always easily guessed.

[1] *Glossarium ad Scriptores mediæ et infimæ Latinitatis.*

CHAPTER XVII

THE CANTERBURY PILGRIMS

"In Southwerk at the Tabard as I lay,
Redy to wenden on my pilgrimage,
To Caunterbury with ful devout corage,
At nyght were come into that hostelrye
Wel nyne and twenty in a compaignye
Of sondry folk, by aventure y-falle
In felaweshipe, and pilgrimes were they alle,
That toward Caunterbury wolden ryde."

(*Prologue*, l. 20.)

THIS famous band of wayfarers includes representatives of all classes, save the highest and the lowest, just at the period when our surnames were becoming fixed. It seems natural to distinguish the following groups. The leisured class is represented by the *Knight* (p. 145) and his son the *Squire*, also found as *Swire* or *Swyer*, Old Fr. *escuyer* (*écuyer*), a shield-bearer (Lat. *scutum*), with their attendant *Yeoman*, a name that originally meant a small landowner and later a trusted attendant of the warlike kind—

"And in his hand he baar a myghty bowe."

(A, 108.)

With these goes the *Franklin* (p. 145), who had been *Sherriff*, i.e. shire-reeve. He is also described as a *Vavasour* (p. 11)—

"Was nowher such a worthy *vavasour*" (A, 360.)

The professions are represented by the *Nunn*, her attendant priests, whence the names *Press*, *Prest*, the *Monk*, the *Frere*, or *Fryer*, " a wantowne and a merye," the *Clark* of Oxenforde, the *Sargent* of the lawe, the *Sumner*, i.e. summoner or apparitor, the doctor of physic, i.e. the *Leech* or *Leach*—

> "Make war breed peace; make peace stint war; make each
> Prescribe to other, as each other's *leech*"[1]
>
> (*Timon of Athens*, v. 4)—

and the poor parson. *Le surgien* and *le fisicien* were once common surnames, but the former has been swallowed up by *Sargent*, and the latter seems to have died out. The name *Leach* has been reinforced by the dialect *lache*, a bog, whence also the compounds *Blackleach*, *Depledge*. Loosely attached to the church is the pardoner, with his wallet—

> " Bret-ful of pardon, comen from Rome al hoot."
>
> (A, 687.)

But he has not left us a surname, for the fairly common *Pardon*, of French origin, is a dim. of Pardolf.

Commerce is represented by the *Marchant*, depicted as a character of weight and dignity, and the humbler trades and crafts by—

> "An haberdasher, and a *Carpenter*,
> A *Webbe*, a deyer (*Dyer*), and a tapiser."
>
> (A, 361.)

To these may be added the Wife of Bath, whose comfortable means were drawn from the cloth trade, then our staple industry.

From rural surroundings come the *Miller* and the *Plowman*, as kindly a man as the poor parson his brother, for—

[1] The same word as the worm *leech*, from an Anglo-Saxon word for healer.

"He wolde threshe, and therto dyke and delve,
For Cristes sake, for every poure wight,
Withouten hire, if it lay in his myght."
(A, 536.)

The *Miller* is the same as the *Meller* or *Mellor*—

"Upon the whiche brook ther stant a *melle*[1];
And this is verray sooth, that I yow tell."
(A, 3923.)

The oldest form of the name is *Milner*, Anglo-Sax. *myln*, Lat. *molina*; cf. *Kilner* from *kiln*, Lat. *culina*, kitchen.

The official or servile class includes the manciple, or buyer for a fraternity of templars, otherwise called an *achatour*, whence *Cator*, *Chaytor*, *Chater*[2] (p. 33), the *Reeve*, an estate steward, so crafty that—

"Ther nas *baillif* (p. 45), ne *herde* (p. 32), nor oother *hyne* (p. 35),
That he ne knew his sleighte and his covyne"
(A, 603);

and finally the *Cook*, or *Coke* (p. 12)—

"To boylle the chicknes and the marybones."
(A, 380.)

In a class by himself stands the grimmest figure of all, the *Shipman*, of whom we are told—

"If that he faught, and hadde the hyer hond,
By water he sente hem hoom to every lond."
(A, 399.)

The same occupation has given the name *Marner*, for mariner, and *Seaman*, but the medieval forms of the rare name *Saylor* show that it is from Fr. *sailleur*,

[1] A Kentish form, used by Chaucer for the rime; cf. *pet* for *pit* (p. 127).

[2] These may be also from *escheatour*, an official who has given us the word *cheat*.

a dancer, an artist who also survives as *Hopper* and *Leaper*—

> "To one that *leped* at Chestre, 6*s*. 8*d*."
> (*Privy Purse Expenses of Henry VII*,[1] 1495.)

The pilgrims were accompanied by the host of the Tabard Inn, whose occupation has given us the names *Inman* and *Hostler*, *Oastler*, Old Fr. *hostelier* (*hôtelier*), now applied to the inn servant who looks after the 'osses. Another form is the modern-looking *Hustler*. Distinct from these is *Osler*, Fr. *oiseleur*, a bird-catcher; cf. *Burder* and *Fowler*.

If we deal here with ecclesiastical names, as being really nicknames (p. 147), that will leave the trader and craftsman, the peasant, and the official or servile class to be treated in separate chapters. Social, as distinguished from occupative, surnames have already been touched on, and the names, not very numerous, connected with warfare have also been mentioned in various connections.

Among ecclesiastical names *Monk* has the largest number of variants. Its Anglo-French form is sometimes represented by *Munn* and *Moon*, while *Money* is the oldest Fr. *monie*; cf. *Vicary* from Old Fr. *vicarie*. But the French names *La Monnaie, de la Monnaie*, are local, from residence near the mint. The canon appears as *Cannon*, *Channen*, and *Shannon*, Fr. *chanoine*—

> "With this *chanoun* I dwelt have seven yere"
> (G, 720);

but *Dean* is generally local (p. 112) and *Deacon* is often an imitative form of *Dakin* or *Deakin*, from David

[1] He was usually more generous to the high arts, *e.g.* "To a Spaynarde that pleyed the fole, £2," "To the young damoysell that daunceth, £30." With which cf. "To Carter for writing of a boke, 7*s*. 4*d*."

(p. 57). *Charter* was used of a monk of the Charterhouse, a popular corruption of Chartreuse—

> "With a company dyde I mete,
> As ermytes, monkes, and freres,
> Chanons, *chartores* . . ."
>
> (*Cock Lorelles Bote.*)

Charter also comes from archaic Fr. *chartier* (*charretier*), a carter, and perhaps sometimes from Old Fr. *chartrier*, "a jaylor; also, a prisoner[1]" (Cotg.), which belongs to Lat. *carcer*, prison. *Charters* may be from the French town Chartres, but is more likely a perversion of Charterhouse, as *Childers* is of the obsolete childer-house, orphanage.

Among lower orders of the church we have *Lister*,[2] a reader, *Bennet*, an exorcist, and *Collet*, aphetic for acolyte. But each of these is susceptible of another origin which is generally to be preferred. *Chaplin* is of course for chaplain, Fr. *chapelain*. The legate appears as *Leggatt*. *Crosier* or *Crozier* means cross-bearer. At the funeral of Anne of Cleves (1557) the mass was executed—

> "By thabbott in pontificalibus wthis *croysyer*, deacon and subdeacon."

The name may sometimes have arisen through the crosier, or bishop's staff, being used as a shop-sign (p. 135). *Canter*, *Caunter* is for chanter, and has an apparent dim. *Cantrell*, but this name may be from Old Fr. *chanterel*, chant-book, and have been acquired in the same way as *Porteous* (p. 136). *Sanger* and *Sangster* were not ecclesiastical *Singers*. *Converse* meant a lay-brother employed as a drudge in a monastery. *Sacristan*, the man in charge of the sacristy, from which

[1] The sense development of these two words is curious.

[2] Found in Late Latin as *legista*, from Lat. *legere*, to read.

we have *Secretan*, is contracted into *Saxton* and *Sexton*, a name now usually associated with grave-digging and bell-ringing, though the latter task once belonged to the *Knowler*—

" *Carilloneur*, a chymer, or *knowler* of bells " (Cotgrave).

It is of course connected with knell, though the only Kneller who has become famous was a German named Kniller.

Marillier, probably a Huguenot name, is an Old Fr. form of *marguillier*, a churchwarden, Lat. *matricularius*. The hermit seems to have survived only in the Huguenot *Lermitte* (*l'hermite*), though the name of his dwelling is common (p. 130); but *Anker*, now anchorite, is still found. Fals-Semblant says—

"Somtyme I am religious,
Now lyk an *anker* in an hous."
(*Romaunt of the Rose*, 6348.)

While a *Pilgrim* acquired his name by a journey to any shrine, a *Palmer* must originally have been to the Holy Land, and a *Romer* to Rome. But the frequent occurrence of *Palmer* suggests that it was often a nickname for a pious fraud. We have a doublet of *Pilgrim* in *Pegram*, though this may come from the name Peregrine, the etymology being the same, viz. Lat. *peregrinus*, a foreigner.

CHAPTER XVIII

TRADES AND CRAFTS

"What d'ye lack, noble sir?—What d'ye lack, beauteous madam?" (*Fortunes of Nigel*, ch. i.)

In the Middle Ages there was no great class of retail dealers distinct from the craftsmen who fashioned objects. The same man made and sold in almost every case. There were of course general dealers, such as the French *Marchant* or his English equivalent the *Chapman* (p. 23), the Dutch form of which has given us the Norfolk name *Copeman*. The *Broker* is now generally absorbed by the local *Brooker*. There were also the itinerant merchants, of whom more anon; but in the great majority of cases the craftsman made and sold one article, and was, in fact, strictly forbidden to wander outside his special line.

Fuller tells us that—

> "England were but a fling,
> Save for the crooked stick and the gray-goose-wing,"

and the importance of the bow and arrow is shown by the number of surnames connected with their manufacture. We find the *Bowyer*,[1] *Bower* or *Bowmaker*, who trimmed and shaped the wand of yew, the *Fletcher*

[1] This is also one source of *Boyer*, but the very common French surname Boyer means ox-herd.

(p. 150), *Arrowsmith*, or *Flower*, who prepared the arrow—

> "His bowe he bente and sette therinne a *flo*[1]" (H, 264)—

and the *Tipper*, *Stringer*, and *Horner*, who attended to smaller details, though the *Tipper* and *Stringer* probably tipped and strung other things, and the *Horner*, though he made the horn nocks of the long-bow, also made horn cups and other objects. The extent to which specialization was carried is shown by the trade description of John Darke, *longbowstringemaker*, who died in 1600. The *Arblaster* may have either made or used the arblast or cross-bow, medieval Lat. *arcubalista*, bow-sling. His name has given the imitative *Alabaster*. We also find the shortened *Ballister* and *Balestier*, from which we have *Bannister* (p. 36). Or, to take an example from comestibles, a *Flanner* limited his activity to the making of flat cakes called *flans* or *flawns*, from Old Fr. *flaon* (*flan*), a word of Germanic origin, ultimately related to *flat*—

> "He that is hanged in May will eat no *flaunes* in Midsummer."
> (*The Abbot*, ch. xxxiii.)

Some names have become strangely restricted in meaning, e.g. *Mercer*, now almost limited to silk, was a name for a dealer in any kind of merchandise (Lat. *merx*); in Old French it meant pedlar—

> "*Mercier*, a good pedler, or meane haberdasher of small wares" (Cotgrave).

On the other hand *Chandler*, properly a candle-maker, is now used in the compounds corn-chandler and ship's chandler. Of all the *-mongers* the only common

[1] The true English word for arrow, Anglo-Sax. *flā*.

survival is *Ironmonger* or *Iremonger*, with the variant *Isemonger*, from Mid. Eng. *isen*, iron.

The wool trade occupied a very large number of workers and has given a good many surnames, including *Laner*, Fr. *laine*, wool. The *Shearer* was distinct from the *Shearman* or *Sherman*, the former operating on the sheep and the latter on the nap of the cloth. For *Comber* we also have the older *Kempster*, and probably *Kimber*, from the Mid. Eng. *kemben*, to comb, which survives in "unkempt." The *Walker*, *Fuller*, and *Tucker* all did very much the same work of trampling the cloth. All three words are used in Wyclif's Bible in variant renderings of Mark ix. 3. *Fuller* is from Fr. *fouler*, to trample, and *Tucker* from *toquer*, to strike, related to "touch." *Fuller* is found in the south and south-east, *Tucker* in the west, and *Walker* in the north. A *Dyer* was also called *Dyter*, *Dyster*, and the same trade is the origin of the Latin-looking *Dexter* (p. 18). From Mid. Eng. *litster*, a dyer, a word of Scandinavian origin, comes *Lister*, as in Lister Gate, Nottingham. With these goes the *Wadman*, who dealt in, or grew, the dye-plant called woad; cf. *Flaxman*. A beater of flax was called *Swingler*—

"Fleyl, *swyngyl*, verga, tribulum" (*Prompt. Parv.*).

A *Tozer* teased the cloth with a teasel. In Mid. English the verb is *tæsen* or *tosen*, so that the names Teaser and Towser, sometimes given to bull-terriers, are doublets. *Secker* means sack-maker.

We have already noticed the predominance of *Taylor*. This is the more remarkable when we consider that the name has as rivals the native *Seamer* and *Shapster* and the imported *Parmenter*, Old Fr. *parmentier*, a maker of *parements*, now used chiefly of facings on clothes. But another, and more usual, origin of *Parmenter*, *Parminter*, *Parmiter*, is *parchmenter*, a very important medieval trade. The word would correspond to a Lat. *pergamentarius*, which has given also the German surname *Berminter*. Several old German cities had a Permentergasse, *i.e.* parchment-makers' street. A *Pilcher* made pilches, *i.e.* fur cloaks, an early loan-word from Vulgar Lat. *pellicia* (*pellis*, skin). Chaucer's version of—

> "Till May is out, ne'er cast a clout"

is—

> "After greet heet cometh colde;
> No man caste his *pilche* away."

Another name connected with clothes is *Chaucer*, Old Fr. *chaussier*, a hosier (Lat. *calceus*, boot), while Admiral *Hozier's* Ghost reminds us of the native word. The oldest meaning of hose seems to have been gaiters. It ascended in Tudor times to the dignity of breeches (cf. trunk-hose), the meaning it has in modern German. Now it has become a tradesman's euphemism for the improper word stocking, a fact which led a friend of the writer's, imperfectly acquainted with German, to ask a gifted lady of that nationality if she were a *Blauhose*. A *Quiller* quilled, *i.e.* gophered, ruffs. A *Chaloner* or *Chawner* dealt in shalloon, Mid. Eng. *chalons*, a material made at Châlons-sur-Marne—

> "And in his owene chambre hem made a bed,
> With sheetes and with *chalons* faire y-spred."
> (A, 4139.)

Ganter or *Gaunter* is Fr. *gantier*, glove-maker.

Some metal-workers have already been mentioned in connection with *Smith* (p. 44), and elsewhere. The French Fèvre is found as *Feaver*. *Fearon* comes from Old Fr. *féron*, smith, from *férir*, to smite. *Face le ferrun*, i.e. Boniface (p. 34) the smith, lived in Northampton in the twelfth century. This is an example of the French use of *-on* as an agential suffix. Another example is Old Fr. *charton*, or *charreton*, a waggoner, from the Norman form of which we have *Carton*. In *Scriven*, from Old Fr. *escrivain* (*écrivain*), we have an isolated agential suffix. The English form is usually lengthened to *Scrivener*. In *Ferrier*, for farrier, the traditional spelling has prevailed over the pronunciation, but we have the latter in *Farrar*. These names (Lat. *ferrum*, iron) are not related to *Fearon* (Lat. *ferire*, to strike). *Aguilar* means needle-maker, Fr. *aiguille*, but *Pinner* is more often official (p. 181). *Cutler*, Fr. *coutelier*, Old Fr. *coutel*, knife, and *Spooner* go together, but the fork is a modern fad. *Poynter* is another good example of the specialization of medieval crafts: the points were the metal tags by which the doublet and hose were connected. Hence the play on words when Falstaff is recounting his adventure with the men in buckram—

> *Fal.* "Their *points* being broken——"
> *Poins.* "Down fell their hose."
>
> (1 *Henry IV*., ii, 4.)

Latimer, *Latner* sometimes means a worker in *latten*, a mixed metal of which the etymological origin is unknown. The Pardoner—

> "Hadde a croys of *latoun* ful of stones" (A, 699).

For the change from *-n* to *-m* we may compare *Lorimer* for *Loriner*, a bridle-maker, belonging ultimately to Lat. *lorum*, "the reyne of a brydle" (Cooper). But *Latimer* comes also from Latiner, a man skilled in Latin, hence an interpreter. Sir John Mandeville tells us that, on the way to Sinai—

> "Men alleweys fynden *Latyneres* to go with hem in the contrees."

The immortal *Bowdler* is usually said to take his name from the art of puddling, or buddling, iron ore. But, as this process is comparatively modern, it is more likely that the name comes from the same verb in its older meaning of making impervious to water by means of clay. *Monier* and *Minter* are both connected with coining, the former through French and the latter from Anglo-Saxon, both going back to Lat. *moneta*,[1] mint. *Conner*, i.e. coiner, is now generally swallowed up by the Irish *Connor*. *Leadbitter* is for *Leadbeater*. The name *Hamper* is a contraction of *hanapier*, a maker of *hanaps, i.e.* goblets. Fr. *hanap* is from Old High Ger. *hnapf* (*Napf*), and shows the inability of French to pronounce initial *hn-* without inserting a vowel: cf. *harangue* from Old High Ger. *hring*. There is also a Mid. Eng. *nap*, cup, representing the cognate Anglo-Sax. *hnæp*, so that the name *Napper* may sometimes be a doublet of *Hamper*, though it is more probably for *Napier* (p. 6) or *Knapper* (p. 107). The common noun *hamper* is from *hanapier* in a sense something like plate-basket. With metal-workers we may also put *Poyser*, scale-maker (poise), and *Furber* or *Frobisher*, i.e. furbisher of armour, etc. Two occupative names of Celtic origin are *Gow*, a smith, as in *The Fair Maid of Perth*, and *Caird*, a tinker—

> "The fellow had been originally a tinker or *caird*."
> (*Heart of Midlothian*, ch. xlix.)

A few more names, which fall into no particular category, may conclude the chapter. *Hillyer* or *Hellier* is an old name for a *Thacker*, or thatcher, of which we have the Dutch form in *Dekker*. It comes from Mid. Eng. *helen*, to cover up. In *Hillard*, *Hill-*

[1] On the curiously accidental history of this word see the *Romance of Words*, ch. x.

yard we sometimes have the same name (cf. the vulgar *scholard*), but these are usually local (p. 124). *Hellier* also meant tiler, for the famous Wat is described as *tiler*, *tegheler*, and *hellier*. An *Ashburner* prepared wood-ash for the *Bloomer* (p. 153), and perhaps also for the *Glaisher*, or glass-maker, and *Asher* is best explained in the same way, for we do not, I think, add *-er* to tree-names. Apparent exceptions can be easily accounted for, e.g. *Elmer* is Anglo-Sax. Ælfmær, and *Beecher* is Anglo-Fr. *bechur*, digger (Fr. *bêche*, spade). Neither *Pitman* nor *Collier* have their modern meaning of coal-miner. *Pitman* is local, of the same class as *Bridgeman*, *Pullman*, etc., and *Collier* meant a charcoal-burner, as in the famous ballad of Rauf Colyear. Not much coal was dug in the Middle Ages. Even in 1610 Camden speaks with disapproval, in his *Britannia*, of the inhabitants of Sherwood Forest who, with plenty of wood around them, persist in digging up "stinking pit-cole."

Croker is for *Crocker*, a maker of crocks or pitchers. The Miller's guests only retired to bed—

> "Whan that dronken al was in the *crowke*" (A, 4158).

The spelling has affected the pronunciation, as in *Sloper* and *Smoker* (p. 41). A *Benner* made hampers, Fr. *benne*. *Tinker* is sometimes found as the frequentative *Tinkler*, the man whose approach is heralded by the clatter of metal utensils—

> "My bonny lass, I work on brass,
> A *tinkler* is my station."
>
> (BURNS, *Jolly Beggars*, Air 6.)

The maker of saddle-trees was called *Fewster*, from Old Fr. *fust* (*fût*), Lat. *fustis*. This has sometimes given *Foster*, but the latter is more often for *Forster*, i.e. *Forester*—

> "An horn he bar, the bawdryk was of grene,
> A *forster* was he soothly as I gesse."
>
> (A, 116.)

The saddler himself was often called by his French name *sellier*, whence *Sellar*, but both this and *Sellars* are also local, at the cellars (p. 29). *Pargeter* means dauber, plasterer, from Old Fr. *parjeter*, to throw over. A *Straker* made the strakes, or tires, of wheels. A *Stanger* made stangs, *i.e.* poles, shafts, etc.

Finally the fine arts are represented by *Limmer*, for limner, a painter, an aphetic form of illuminer, and *Tickner*, a Dutch name, from *tekener*, draughtsman, cognate with Eng. token, while the art of self-defence has given us the name *Scrimgeoure*, with a number of corruptions, including the local-looking *Skrimshire*. It is related to scrimmage and skirmish, and ultimately to Gr. *schirmen*, to fence, lit. to protect. The name was applied to a professional sword-player—

> "Qe nul teigne escole de *eskermerye* ne de bokeler deins la citee."
>
> (*Liber Albus*.)

A particularly idiotic form of snobbishness has sometimes led people to advance strange theories as to the origin of their names. Thus *Turner* has been explained as from *la tour noire*. Dr. Brewer, in his *Dictionary of Phrase and Fable*,[1] apparently desirous of dissociating himself from malt liquor, observes that—

> "Very few ancient names are the names of trades. . . . A few examples of a more scientific derivation will suffice for a hint:—
>
> *Brewer*. This name, which exists in France as Bruhière and Brugère, is not derived from the Saxon *briwan* (to brew), but the French *bruyère* (heath), and is about tantamount to the German

[1] Thirteenth edition, revised and corrected.

Plantagenet (broom plant). *Miller* is the old Norse *melia*, our *mill* and *maul*, and means a mauler or fighter.

Ringer is the Anglo-Saxon *hring-gar* (the mailed warrior).

Tanner, German *Thanger*, Old German *Dane-gaud*, is the Dane-Goth.

This list might easily be extended."

There is of course no reason why such a list should not be indefinitely extended, but it is already quite long enough to make the reader feel dizzy. The fact is that there is no getting away from a surname of this class, and the bearer must try to look on the brighter side of the tragedy. *Brewer* is occasionally an accommodated form of the French name Bruyère or Labruyère, but is usually derived from an occupation which is the high-road to the House of Lords. The ancestor of any modern *Barber* may, like Salvation Yeo's father, have "exercised the mystery of a barber-surgeon," which is getting near the learned professions. A *Pottinger* (see p. 155) looked after the soups, Fr. *potage*, as a *Saucer* did after the sauces, but the name also represents *Pothecary* (apothecary), which gave in early Scottish the aphetic forms *poticar*, *potigar*—

"'Pardon me,' said he, 'I am but a poor *pottingar*. Nevertheless, I have been bred in Paris and learnt my humanities and my *cursus medendi*'" (*Fair Maid of Perth*, ch. vii.).

CHAPTER XIX

HODGE AND HIS FRIENDS

"Jacque, il me faut troubler ton somme ;
Dans le village, un gros huissier
Rôde et court, suivi du messier.
C'est pour l'impôt, las ! mon pauvre homme.
Lève-toi, Jacque, lève-toi :
Voici venir l'huissier du roi."

BÉRANGER.

GENERAL terms for what we now usually call a farmer are preserved in the surnames *Bond* (p. 146), whence the compound *Husband*, used both for the goodman of the house and in the modern sense, and *Tillman*. The labouring man was *Day*, from the same root as Ger. *dienen*, to serve. It persists in "dairy" and in the compound *Faraday*, a travelling, or wayfaring, labourer. A similar meaning is contained in the names *Swain*, *Hind*, for earlier *Hine* (p. 35), *Tasker*, *Wager*, and *Man*. The mower has given us the names *Mather* (cf. after*math*), and *Mawer*, the latter usually swallowed up by *Moore*, while *Fenner* is sometimes for Old Fr. *feneur*, haymaker (Lat. *fœnum*, hay). For mower we also find the latinized *messor*, whence *Messer*. Whether the *Ridler* [1] and the *Sivier* made, or used, riddles and sieves can hardly be decided. With the

[1] *Riddle* is the usual word for sieve in the Midlands. Hence the phrase "riddled with holes, or wounds."

Wenman, who drove the wain, we may mention the *Leader* or *Loader*. The verbs to lead and to load are etymologically the same, and in the Midlands people talk of leading, *i.e.* carting, coal. But these names could also come from residence near an artificial water-course (p. 129). *Beecher* has already been explained (p. 174), and *Showler* is formed in the same way from dialect *showl*, a shovel—

> "'I,' said the owl,
> 'With my spade and *showl*.'"

To the variants of the *Miller* (p. 225) may be added *Mulliner*, from Old French. *Tedder* means a man who *teds*, i.e. spreads, hay, the origin of the word being Scandinavian—

> "I *teede* hey, I tourne it afore it is made in cockes, *je fene*."
> (Palsgrave.)

But the greater number of surnames drawn from rural occupations are connected with the care of animals. We find names of this class in three forms, exemplified by *Coltman, Goater, Shepherd*, and it seems likely that the endings *-er* and *-erd* have sometimes been interchanged, *e.g.* that *Goater* may stand for goat-herd, *Calver* for calf-herd, and *Nutter* for northern *nowt-herd*, representing the otherwise absent neat-herd. The compounds of herd include *Bullard, Calvert, Coltard, Coward*, for cow-herd, not of course to be confused with the common noun *coward*, Fr. *couard*, a derivative of Lat. *cauda*, tail, *Ewart*, ewe-herd, but also a Norman spelling of Edward, *Geldard, Goddard*, sometimes for goat-herd, *Hoggart*, often confused with the local *Hogarth* (p. 124), *Seward*, for sow-herd, or for the historic Siward, *Stobart*, dialect *stob*, a bull, *Stodart*, Mid. Eng. *stot*, meaning both a bullock and a nag. Chaucer tells us that—

> "This reve sat upon a ful good *stot*" (A, 615).

Stoddart is naturally confused with *Studdart*, stud-herd, stud being cognate with Ger. *Stute*, mare. We also have *Swinnert*, and lastly *Weatherhead*, sometimes a perversion of wether-herd, though usually a nickname, sheep's head. The man in charge of the tups, or rams, was called *Tupman* or *Tupper*, the latter standing sometimes for tup-herd, just as we have the imitative *Stutter* for *Stodart* or *Studdart*. We have also *Tripper* from *trip*, a dialect word for flock, probably related to troop. Another general term for a herdsman was *Looker*, whence *Luker*.

I have headed this chapter "Hodge and his Friends," but as a matter of strict truth he had none, except the "poure Persone," the most radiant figure in Chaucer's pageant. But his enemies were innumerable. Béranger's lines impress one less than the uncouth "Song of the Husbandman" (temp. Edward I.), in which we find the woes of poor Hodge incorporated in the persons of the *hayward*, the *bailif*, the *wodeward*, the *budel* and his *cachereles* (catchpoles)—

> "For ever the furthe peni mot (must) to the kynge."

The bailiff has already been mentioned (p. 45). The *budel*, or beadle, has given us several surnames. We have the word in two forms, from Anglo-Sax. *bytel*, belonging to the verb to bid, whence the names *Biddle* and *Buddle*, and from Old Fr. *bedel* (*bédeau*), whence *Beadle* and its variants. The animal is probably extinct under his original name, but modern democracy is doing its best to provide him with an army of successors. We find *le cacherel* strangely perverted into *le catherel*, whence *Catherall, Cattrall.*

Names in *-ward* are rather numerous, and, as they mostly come from the titles of rural officials and are often confused with compounds of *-herd*, they are all put together here. The simple *Ward*, cognate with Fr. *garde*, is one of our commonest surnames. Like its derivative *Warden* it had a very wide range of meanings. The antiquity of the office of church-warden is shown by the existence of the surname *Churchward.* Sometimes the surname comes from the abstract or local sense, *de la warde.* As the original *-weard* occurs very frequently in Anglo-Saxon personal names, it is not always possible to say whether a surname is essentially occupative or not, *e.g.* whether *Durward* is rather door-ward or for Anglo-Sax. Deorweard. It is certain that *Howard* is both for *Harward* (Hereward), later *Haward*, and for the official *Hayward*, the latter source accounting for most of the Howards outside the ducal family.

Owing to the loss of *w-* in the second part of a word (see p. 39), *-ward* and *-herd* often fall together, *e.g.* *Millard* for *Milward*, and *Woodard* found in Mid. Eng. as both *wode-ward* and *wode-hird.* *Hayward* belongs to *hay*, hedge, enclosure (p. 124), from which we also get *Hayman.* The same functionary has given the name *Haybittle*, a compound of beadle. *Burward* and *Burrard* no doubt represent the once familiar office of bear-ward; cf. *Berman.* I had a schoolfellow called *Lateward*, apparently the man in charge of the *lade* or *leet* (p. 129). *Medward* is for mead-ward. The name *Stewart* or *Stuart* became royal with Walter the Steward of Scotland, who married Marjorie Bruce in 1315. It stands for sty-ward, where sty means pen, not necessarily limited to pigs. Like most official titles, it has had its ups and downs, with the result that its present meaning ranges from a high officer of the crown to the sympathetic concomitant of a rough crossing.

The *Reeve*, Anglo-Sax. *ge-refa*, was in Chaucer a kind of land agent, but the name was also applied to local officials, as in port-reeve, shire-reeve. It is the same as *Grieve*, also originally official, but used in Scotland of a land steward—

> "He has got a ploughman from Scotland who acts as *grieve*."
> (Scott, *Diary*, 1814.)

This is one source of the names *Graves* and *Greaves*. The name *Woodruff* or *Woodroffe* is too common to be referred to the plant woodruff, and the fact that the male and female of a species of sand-piper are called the *ruff* and *reeve* suggests that Wood*ruff* may have some relation to wood-*reeve*. It is at any rate a curious coincidence that the German name for the plant is *Waldmeister*, wood-master. Another official surname especially connected with country life is *Pinder*, also found as *Pinner*, *Pender*, *Penner*, *Ponder* and *Poynder*, the man in charge of the pound or pinfold; cf. *Parker*, the custodian of a park, of which the *Palliser* or *Pallister* made the palings.

The itinerant dealer was usually called by a name suggesting the pack which he carried. Thus *Badger*, *Kidder*, *Kiddier*, *Pedder*, now pedlar, are from *bag*, *kid*, related to *kit*, and the obsolete *ped*, basket; cf. *Leaper*, p. 152. The badger, who dealt especially in corn, was unpopular with the rural population, and it is possible that his name was given to the stealthy animal formerly called the *bawson* (p. 8, *n.*), *brock* or *gray* (p. 225). To these may be added *Cremer*, *Cramer*, a huckster with a stall in the market, but this surname is sometimes of modern introduction, from its German cognate *Krämer*, now generally used for a grocer. *Packman*, *Pakeman*, and *Paxman* belong more probably to the font-name *Pack* (p. 89), which also appears in *Paxon*, Pack's son, and the local *Paxton*.

The name *Hawker* does not belong to this group. Nowadays a hawker is a pedlar, and it has been assumed, without sufficient evidence, that the word is of the same origin as huckster. The Mid. Eng. *le haueker* or *haukere* (1273) is quite plainly connected with hawk, and the name may have been applied either to a *Falconer*, *Faulkner*, or to a dealer in hawks. As we know that itinerant vendors of hawks travelled from castle to castle, it is quite possible that our modern hawker is an extended use of the same name. Nor is the name *Coster* to be referred to costermonger, originally a dealer in costards, *i.e.* apples. It is sometimes for Mid. Eng. *costard* (cf. such names as *Cherry* and *Plumb*), but also represents Port. *da Costa* and Ger. *Köster*, both of which are found in early lists of Protestant refugees.

Jagger, whence *Jaggard*, was a north-country name for a man who worked draught-horses for hire. Mr. Hardy's novel *Under the Greenwood Tree* opens with "the *Tranter's* party." A carrier is still a tranter in Wessex. In Medieval Latin he was called *travetarius*, a word apparently connected with Lat. *transvehere*, to transport.

CHAPTER XX

OFFICIAL AND DOMESTIC

> "Big fleas have little fleas
> Upon their backs to bite 'em;
> Little fleas have smaller fleas,
> And so *ad infinitum*."
>
> ANON.

IT is a well-known fact that official nomenclature largely reflects the simple housekeeping of early times, and that many titles, now of great dignity, were originally associated with rather lowly duties. We have seen an example in *Stewart*. Another is *Chamberlain*. Hence surnames drawn from this class are susceptible of very varied interpretation. A *Chancellor* was originally a man in charge of a chancel, or grating, Lat. *cancelli*. In Mid. Eng. it is usually glossed *scriba*, while it is now limited to very high judicial or political office. *Bailey*, as we have seen (p. 45), has also a wide range of meanings, the ground idea being that of care-taker. Cotgrave explains Old Fr. *mareschal* (*maréchal*) as—

> "A *marshall* of a kingdome, or of a camp (an honourable place); also, a blacksmith; also, a farrier, horse-leech, or horse-smith; also, a harbinger," [1]

which gives a considerable choice of origins to any modern *Marshall* or *Maskell*. Another very vague term is sergeant, whence our *Sargent*. Its oldest meaning is

[1] *I.e.* a quartermaster. See *Romance of Words*, ch. vii.

servant, Lat. *serviens, servient-*. Cotgrave defines *sergent* as—

"A *sergeant*, officer, catchpole, pursuyvant, apparitor; also (in Old Fr.) a footman, or souldier that serves on foot."

Probably catchpole was the commonest meaning—

"*Sargeauntes*, katche pollys, and somners" (*Cocke Lorelles Bote*).

The administration of justice occupied a horde of officials, from the *Justice* down to the *Catchpole*. The official title *Judge* is rarely found, and this surname is usually from the female name Judge, which, like Jug, was used for Judith, and later for Jane—

"*Jannette, Judge,* Jennie; a woman's name" (Cotgrave).

The names *Judson* and *Juxon* sometimes belong to these. *Catchpole* has nothing to do with poles or polls. It is a Picard *cache-poule* (*chasse-poule*), collector of poultry in default of money. Another name for judge was *Dempster*, the pronouncer of doom, a title which still exists in the Isle of Man. We also find *Deemer*—

"*Demar*, judicator" (*Prompt. Parv.*).

Mayor is a learned spelling of *Mair*, Fr. *maire*, Lat. *major*, but *Major*, which looks like its latinized form, is imitative for the Old French personal name *Mauger*. Bishop Mauger of Worcester pronounced the interdict in 1208, and the surname still exists. *Gaylor, Galer*, is the Norman pronunciation of gaoler—

"And Palamon, this woful prisoner,
As was his wone, bi leve of his *gayler*,
Was risen" (A, 1064).

Usher is Fr. *huissier*, door-keeper, Fr. *huis*, door, Lat. *ostium*. I conjecture that *Lusher* is the French name *Lhuissier,* and that *Lush* is local, for Old Fr. *le huis*; cf. *Laporte.* *Wait,* corruptly *Weight,* now used only of a Christmas minstrel, was once a watchman. It is a dialect form of Old Fr. *gaite,* cognate with watch. The older sense survives in the expression "to lie in *wait.*" *Gate* is the same name, when not local (p. 124). The *Todhunter,* or fox-hunter (p. 225), was a parish official whose duty was to exterminate the animal now so carefully preserved. *Warner* is for *Warrener.* The *Grosvenor* (*gros veneur*), great hunter, was a royal servant. *Bannerman* is found latinized as *Penninger* (p. 155). *Herald* may be official or from Harold (p. 69), the derivation being in any case the same. *Toller* means a collector of tolls. Cocke Lorelle speaks of these officials as "false *Towlers.*" Connected with administration is the name *Mainprice,* taken by hand, used both for a surety and a man out on bail—

> "*Maynprysyd,* or *memprysyd,* manucaptus, fideijussus"
> (*Prompt. Parv.*);

and *Shurety* also exists.

The individual bigwig had a very large retinue, the members of which appear to have held very strongly to the theory of one man, one job. The *Nurse,* or *Norris,* Fr. *nourrice,* was apparently debarred from rocking the cradle. This was the duty of the rocker—

> "To the *norice* and *rokker* of the same lord, 25*s.* 8*d.*"
> (*Household Accounts of Elizabeth of York,* March, 1503),

from whom Mr. *Roker,* chief turnkey at the Fleet in Mr. Pickwick's time, was descended. The *Cook* was assisted by the *Baster* and *Hasler,* or turnspit. This is from Old Fr. *hastille,* spit, dim. of Lat. *hasta,* spear. The *Chandler* was a servant as well as a manufacturer.

A *Trotter* and a *Massinger*, i.e. messenger, were perhaps much the same thing. *Wardroper* is of course wardrobe keeper, but Chaucer uses *wardrope* (B. 1762) in the sense which Fr. *garde-robe* now usually has. The *Lavender, Launder* or *Lander* saw to the washing. *Napier*, from Fr. *nappe*, cloth, meant the servant who looked after the napery. The martial sound with which this distinguished name strikes a modern ear is due to historical association, assisted, as I have somewhere read, by its riming with *rapier*! The water-supply was in charge of the *Ewer*.

The provisioning of the great house was the work of the *Lardner*, Fr. *lard*, bacon, the *Panter*, or *Pantler*, who was, at least etymologically, responsible for bread, and the *Cator* (p. 33) and *Spencer* (p. 33), whose names, though of opposite meaning, buyer and spender, come to very much the same thing. *Spence* is still the north-country word for pantry, and is used by Tennyson in the sense of refectory—

> "Bluff Harry broke into the *spence*
> And turn'd the cowls adrift."
>
> (*The Talking Oak*, l. 47.)

Purser, now used in connection with ships only, was also a medieval form of bursar, and every castle and monastery had its almoner, now *Amner*. Here also belongs *Carver*. In Iver Church (Bucks) is a tablet to Lady Mary Salter with a poetic tribute to her husband—

> "Full forty years a *carver* to two kings."

As the importance of the horse led to the social elevation of the marshal and constable (p. 45), so the *hengstman*, now henchman, became his master's right-hand man. The first element is Anglo-Sax. *hengest*, stallion, and its most usual surnominal forms are *Hens-*

man and *Hinxman*. Historians now regard Hengist and Horsa, stallion and mare, as nicknames assumed by Jutish braves on the war-path. *Sumpter*, Old Fr. *sommetier*, from *somme*, burden, was used both of a packhorse and its driver, its interpretation in *King Lear* being a matter of dispute—

> "Return with her?
> Persuade me rather to be slave and *sumpter*
> To this detested groom" (*Lear*, ii, 4).

As a surname it probably means the driver, Medieval Lat. *sumetarius*.

Among those who ministered to the great man's pleasures we must probably reckon *Spelman*, *Speller*, *Spillman*, *Spiller*, from Mid. Eng. *spel*, a speech, narrative—

> "Now holde your mouth, par charitee,
> Bothe knyght and lady free,
> And herkneth to my *spelle*" (B, 2081).

The cognate *Spielmann*, lit. *Player*, was used in Medieval German of a wandering minstrel.

The poet is now *Rymer* or *Rimmer*, while *Trover*, Fr. *trouvère*, a poet, minstrel, lit. finder, has been absorbed by *Trower*, for *Thrower*, a name connected with weaving. Even the jester has come down to us as *Patch*, a name given regularly to this member of the household in allusion to his motley attire. Shylock applies it to Launcelot—

> "The *patch* is kind enough; but a huge feeder."
> (*Merchant of Venice*, ii. 5.)

But the name has another origin (p. 89). *Buller* and *Cocker* are names taken from the fine old English sports of bull-baiting and cock-fighting.

Two very humble members of the parasitic class

have given the names *Bidder* and *Maunder*, both meaning beggar. The first comes from Mid. Eng. *bidden*, to ask. Piers Plowman speaks of "bidderes and beggers." *Maunder* is perhaps connected with Old Fr. *quemander*—

"*Quemander*, or *caimander*, to beg; or goe a begging; to beg from doore to doore" (Cotgrave),

but it may mean a maker of maunds, *i.e.* baskets. A *Beadman* spent his time in praying for his benefactor. A medieval underling writing to his superior often signs himself "your servant and *bedesman*."

CHAPTER XXI

OF NICKNAMES IN GENERAL

"Here is Wyll Wyly the myl pecker,
And Patrick Pevysshe heerbeter,
With lusty Hary Hangeman,
Nexte house to Robyn Renawaye;
Also Hycke Crokenec the rope maker,
And Steven Mesyllmouthe muskyll taker."
(*Cocke Lorelles Bote.*[1])

EVERY family name is etymologically a nickname, *i.e.* an eke-name, intended to give that auxiliary information which helps in identification. But writers on surnames have generally made a special class of those epithets which were originally conferred on the bearer in connection with some characteristic feature, physical or moral, or some adjunct, often of the most trifling description, with which his personality was associated. Of nicknames, as of other things, it may be said that there is nothing new under the sun. Ovidius Naso might have received his as a schoolboy, and *Moss cum naso*, whom we find in Suffolk in 1184, lives on as "Nosey Moss" in Whitechapel. Some of our nicknames occur as personal names in Anglo-Saxon times (p. 71), but as surnames they are seldom to be traced back to that period, for the simple reason

[1] This humorous poem, inspired by Sebastian Brandt's *Narrenschiff*, known in England in Barclay's translation, was printed early in the reign of Henry VIII. It contains the fullest list we have of old trade-names.

that such names were not hereditary. An Anglo-Saxon might be named *Wulf*, but his son would bear another name, while our modern *Wolfe* does not usually go farther back than some Ranulf *le wolf* of the thirteenth or fourteenth century. This is of course stating the case broadly, because the personal name Wolf also persisted and became in some cases a surname. In this and the following chapters I do not generally attempt to distinguish between such double origins.

Nicknames are formed in very many ways, but the two largest classes are sobriquets taken from the names of animals, e.g. *Hogg*, or from adjectives, either alone or accompanied by a noun, e.g. *Dear*, *Goodfellow*. Each of these classes requires a chapter to itself, while here we may deal with the smaller groups.

Some writers have attempted to explain all apparent nicknames as popular perversions of surnames belonging to the other three classes. As the reader will already have noticed, such perversions are extremely common, but it is a mistake to try to account for obvious nicknames in this way. Any of us who retain a vivid recollection of early days can call to mind nicknames of the most fantastic kind, and in some cases of the most apparently impossible formation, which stuck to their possessors all through school-life. A very simple test for the genuineness of a nickname is a comparison with other languages. Camden says that *Drinkwater* is a corruption of Derwentwater. The incorrectness of this guess is shown by the existence as surnames of Fr. *Boileau*, It. *Bevilacqua*, and Ger. *Trinkwasser*. It is in fact a perfectly natural nickname for a medieval eccentric, the more normal attitude being represented by Roger *Beyvin* (*boi-vin*), who died in London in 1277.

Corresponding to our *Goodday*, we find Ger. *Gutentag* and Fr. *Bonjour*. The latter has been explained as from a popular form of George, but the English and German names show that the explanation is unnecessary. With *Dry* we may compare Fr. *Lesec* and Ger. *Dürr*, with *Garlick* Ger. *Knoblauch* (p. 155), and with *Shakespeare* Ger. *Schüttespeer*. *Luck* is both for Luke and Luick (Liège, p. 100), but Rosa *Bonheur* and the composer *Glück* certify it also as a nickname. *Merryweather* is Fr. *Bontemps* and *Littleboy* appears in the Paris Directory as *Petitgas*, *gas* being the same as *gars*, the old nominative of *garçon*—

"*Gars*, a lad, boy, stripling, youth, yonker" (Cotgrave).

Bardsley explains *Twentyman* as an imitative corruption of *twinter-man*, the man in charge of the twinters, two-year-old colts. This may be so, but there is a German confectioner in Hampstead called *Zwanziger*, and there are Parisians named *Vingtain*. *Lover* is confirmed by the French surnames *Amant* and *Lamoureux*, and *Wellbeloved* by *Bienaimé*. *Allways* may be the literal equivalent of the French name *Partout*. On the other hand, the name Praisegod *Barebones* has been wrongly fixed on an individual of French descent named *Barbon*, from *barbe*, beard.

It may seem strange that the nickname, conferred essentially on the individual, and often of a very offensive character, should have persisted and become hereditary. But schoolboys know that, in the case of unpleasant nicknames, the more you try to pull it off, the more it sticks the faster. *Malapert* and *Lehideux* are still well represented in the Paris Directory. Many objectionable nicknames have, however, disappeared, or have been so modified as to become inoffensive.

Sometimes such disappearance has resulted from the depreciation in the meaning of a word, e.g. *le lewd*, the layman, the unlettered, was once as common as its opposite *le learned*, whence the name *Larned*. But many uncomplimentary names are no longer objected to because their owners do not know their earlier meanings. A famous hymn-writer of the eighteenth century bore all unconsciously a surname that would almost have made Rabelais blush. Drinkdregs, Drunkard, Sourale, Sparewater, Sweatinbed, etc. have gone, but we still have *Lusk*—

> "*Falourdin*, a *luske*, lowt, lurden, a lubberlie sloven, heavie sot, lumpish hoydon" (Cotgrave)—

and many other names which can hardly have gratified their original possessors.

A very interesting group of surnames consists of those which indicate degrees of kinship or have to do with the relations existing between individuals. We find both *Master* and *Mann*, united in *Masterman*, meaning the man in the service of one locally known as the master. With this we may compare *Ladyman*, *Priestman*, etc. But *Mann* is often local, from Le Mans, the capital of Maine. In some cases such names are usually found with the patronymic *-s*, e.g. *Masters*, *Fellows*, while in others this is regularly absent, e.g. *Guest*, *Friend*. The latter name is sometimes a corruption of Mid. Eng. *fremed*, stranger, cognate with Ger. *fremd*, so that opposite terms, which we find regularly contrasted in Mid. Eng. "*frend* and *fremed*," have become absorbed in one surname. The frequent occurrence of *Fellows* is due to its being sometimes for the local *Fallows*. From Mid. Eng. *fere*, a companion, connected with *faren*, to travel, we get *Littlefair* and

Playfair. In Wyclif's Bible we read that Jephthah's daughter—

"Whanne sche hadde go with hir felowis and *pleiferis*, sche biwept hir maydynhed in the hillis" (Judges xi. 38).

Springett is for *springald*, and *Arlett* is Mid. Eng. *harlot*, fellow, rascal, a word which has changed its gender and meaning—

"He was a gentil *harlot* and a kynde,
A betre felawe sholde men noght fynde."
(A, 647.)

In surnames taken from words indicating family relationship we come across some survivals of terms no longer used, or occurring only in rustic dialect. The Mid. Eng. *eme*, uncle, cognate with Ger. *Oheim*, has given *Eames*. In Chaucer's *Troilus and Criseyde*, the heroine addresses Pandarus as "uncle dere" and "uncle mine," but also uses the older word—

"'In good feith, *em*,' quod she, 'that liketh me'" (ii. 162);

and the word is used more than once by Scott—

"Didna his *eme* die . . . wi' the name of the Bluidy Mackenzie?"
(*Heart of Midlothian*, ch. xii.)

It is also one of the sources of *Empson*, which thus corresponds to *Cousins* or *Cozens*. In *Neame* we have a prosthetic *n-* due to the frequent occurrence of *min eme* (cf. the Shakespearean *nuncle*, *Lear*, i. 4). The names derived from cousin have been reinforced by those from *Cuss*, i.e. Constant or Constance (p. 95). Thus *Cussens* is from the Mid. Eng. dim. *Cussin*. Anglo-Sax. *nefa*, whence Mid. Eng. *neve*,[1] *neave*, is cognate with, but not derived from, Lat. *nepos*. This

[1] In all books on surnames that I have come across this is referred to Old Fr. *le neve*. There is no such word in Old French, which has nom. *niés*, acc. *neveu*.

is now replaced as a common noun by the French word nephew, but it survives in the surname *Neave*. It also meant in Mid. English a prodigal or parasite, as did also Lat. *nepos*—

> "*Neve*, neverthryfte, or wastowre" (*Prompt. Parv.*).

It is likely that *Nevison* and *Nevinson* are sometimes derivatives of this word; cf. *Widdowson* and *Empson*.

Child was sometimes used in the special sense of youth of gentle blood, or young knight; cf. Childe Harold and Childe Rowland (*Lear*, iii. 4). But the more general meaning may be assumed in its compounds, of which the most interesting is *Leifchild*, love-child, but without the unhappy sense which we now give to the term. The corresponding *Faunt* (p. 146) is now rare. Another word, now only used in dialect or by affectation, is bairn, the chief source of the very common surname *Barnes*; cf. *Fairbairn* and *Goodbairn*, often perverted to *Fairburn*, *Goodburn*, *Goodban*. *Barnfather* is about equivalent to Lat. *paterfamilias*, but *Pennefather* is an old nickname for a miser—

> "*Caqueduc*, a niggard, micher, miser, scrape-good, pinch-penny, *penny-father*; a covetous and greedy wretch" (Cotgrave).

The name *Bastard* was once considered no disgrace if the dishonour came from a noble source, and several great medieval warriors bore this sobriquet. With this we may compare *Leman* or *Lemon*, Mid. Eng. *leof-man*, dear man, beloved, and *Paramor*, Fr. *par amour*, an example of an adverbial phrase that has become a noun. This expression, used of lawful love in Old French, in the stock phrase "aimer une belle dame *par amour*," had already an evil meaning by Chaucer's time—

> "My fourthe housbonde was a revelour,
> This is to seyn, he hadde a *paramour*" (D, 453).

With these names we may put *Drewry* or *Drury*, sweetheart, from the Old French abstract *druerie*, of Germanic origin and cognate with *true*—

> "For certeynly no such beeste
> To be loved is not worthy,
> Or bere the name of *druerie*."
> (*Romaunt of the Rose*, 5062.)

Suckling is a nickname applied to a helpless person; cf. *Littlechild* and "milksop," which "still thrives in the United States as *Mellsop*" (Bardsley). The heir survives as *Ayre* and *Eyre*. *Batchelor*, the origin of which is one of the etymological problems yet unsolved, had in Old French and Mid. English also the meaning of young warrior or squire. Chaucer's Squier is described as—

> "A lovyere and a lusty *bacheler*" (A, 80).

May, maiden, whence *Mildmay*, is used by Chaucer for the Holy Virgin—

> "Now, lady bright, to whom alle woful cryen,
> Thow glorie of wommanhede, thow faire *may*,
> Thow haven of refut, brighte sterre of day" (B, 850).

This is the same word as Mid. Eng. *mæi*, relative, cognate with *maid* and Gaelic *Mac*- (p. 66). It survives in the Nottingham name *Watmough* and perhaps in *Hickmott*—

> "*Mow*, housbandys sister or syster in law" (*Prompt. Parv.*).

I imagine that William *echemannesmai*, who owed the Treasury a mark in 1182, was one of the sponging fraternity.

Virgoe, a latinization of *Virgin*, is almost certainly a shop-sign. *Rigmaiden*, explained by Lower as "a romping girl," is local, from a place in Westmorland. Richard *de Riggemayden* was living in Lancashire in

1307. With this group of names we may put *Gossip*, originally a god-parent, lit. related in God, Mid. Eng. *sib*, kin.

With names like *Farebrother*, *Goodfellow*, we may compare some of French origin such as *Bonser* (bon sire), *Bonamy*, and *Bellamy*—

> "Thou *beel amy*, thou pardoner, he sayde,
> Telle us som myrth, or japes, right anon."
>
> (B, 318.)

Beldam (belle dame), originally a complimentary name for grandmother, or grandam, has become uncomplimentary in meaning—

> *First Witch.* "Why, how now, Hecate! you look angerly."
> *Hecate.* "Have I not reason, *beldams* as you are,
> Saucy and overbold?" (*Macbeth*, iii. 5).

From the corresponding Old Fr. *bel-sire*, *beau-sire*, we have *Bewsher*, *Bowser*, and the Picard form *Belcher*—

> "The great *belsire*, the grandsire, sire, and sonne,
> Lie here interred under this grave stone."
>
> (Weever, *Ancient Funeral Monuments*.)

To relationships by marriage belongs sometimes the name *Gander*, corresponding to Fr. *Legendre*, the son-in-law, Lat. *gener*. Its normal forms are *Gender*, *Ginder*. *Fitch*, usually an animal nickname (p. 225), is occasionally for *le fiz*, the son, which also survives as *Fitz*. *Goodson*, from the personal name *Good* (p. 4), sometimes corresponds to the French surname *Lefilleul*, i.e. the godson.

A possible derivative of the name *May* (p. 195) is *Ivimey*. Holly and Ivy were the names of characters in Christmas games, and an old rime says—

> "Holy and his mery men, they dawnsyn and they syng,
> *Ivy* and hur *maydins*, they wepen and they wryng."

If *Ivimey* is from this source, the same origin must

sometimes be allowed to *Holliman* (p. 6). This conjecture[1] has in its favour the fact that many of our surnames are undoubtedly derived from characters assumed in dramatic performances and popular festivities. To this class belong many surnames which have the form of abstract nouns, e.g. *Charity, Verity, Virtue, Vice.* Of similar origin are perhaps *Bliss, Chance, Luck,* and *Goodluck*; cf. *Bonaventure. Love, Luff,* occur generally as a personal name, hence the dim. *Lufkins,* but it is sometimes a nickname. *Lovell, Lovett,* more often mean little wolf. Both *Louvet* and *Louveau* are common French surnames. The name *Lovell,* in the wolf sense, was often applied to a dog, as in the famous couplet—

> "The ratte, the catte, and *Lovell,* our dogge
> Rule all England under the hogge,"

for which William Collingborne was executed in 1484. *Lowell* is a variant of *Lovell.*

But many apparent abstract names are due to folk-etymology, e.g. *Marriage* is local, Old Fr. *marage,* marsh, and *Wedlock* is imitative for the local *Wedlake*; cf. *Mortlock* for Mortlake and perhaps *Diplock* for deep-lake. *Creed* is the Anglo-Saxon personal name Crēda. *Revel,* a common French surname, is a personal name. *Wisdom* is local, from a spot in Devon, and *Want* is the Mid. Eng. *wont,* mole, whence *Wontner,* mole-catcher. It is difficult to see how such names as *Warr, Battle,* and *Conquest* came into existence. The former, found as *de la warre,* is no doubt sometimes for *Weir* (p. 129), and *Battle* is a dim. of Bat (p. 57). But *de la batayle* is also a common entry, and *Laguerre* and *Labataille* are common French surnames.

[1] Ferguson, in his *Surnames as a Science.*

A nickname was often conferred in connection with some external object regularly associated with the individual. Names taken from shop-signs really belong to this class. Corresponding to our *Hood*[1] we have Fr. *Capron* (*chaperon*). *Burdon*, Fr. *bourdon*, meant a staff, especially a pilgrim's staff. Daunger is described as having—

> "In his honde a gret *burdoun*" (*Romaunt of the Rose*, 3401).

But the name *Burdon* is also local. *Bracegirdle*, i.e. breeks-girdle, must have been the nickname of one who wore a gorgeous belt. The Sussex name *Quaife* represents the Norman pronunciation of coif. More usually an adjective enters into such combinations. With the historic Curthose, Longsword, Strongbow we may compare *Shorthouse*, a perversion of short-hose, *Longstaff*, *Horlock* (hoar), *Silverlock*, *Whitlock*, etc. With *Lovelock* I should put *Crockett*, Old Fr. *crochet*, a curled lock, and perhaps *Lovibond*, found earlier as *love-band*. But the pretty name *Lovelace* is a corruption of the depressing *Loveless*; cf. *Lawless* and probably *Bindloss*. *Woollard* may be the Anglo-Saxon personal name Wulfheard, but is more probably from *woolward*, i.e. without linen, a costume assumed as a sign of penitence—

> "*Wolwarde*, without any lynnen nexte ones body, *sans chemyse*."
> (Palsgrave.)

The three names *Medley*, *Medlicott*, and *Motley* go together, though all three of them may be local (the mid-lea, the middle-cot, and the moat-lea). *Medley*, mixed, is the Anglo-French past participle of Old Fr.

[1] *Hood* has another origin (p. 3), but the garment is made into a personal name in Little Red Ridinghood, who is called in French *le petit Chaperon Rouge*.

mesler (*mêler*). *Motley* is of unknown origin, but it was not necessarily a fool's dress—

> "A marchant was ther with a forked berd,
> In *mottelye*, and hye on horse he sat,
> Upon his heed a Flaundryssh bevere hat" (A, 270).

So also the Serjeant of the Law was distinguished by his, for the period, plain dress—

> "He rood but hoomly in a *medlee cote*" (A, 328).

Gildersleeve is now rare in England, though it still flourishes in the United States.[1]

Names like *Beard*, *Chinn*, *Tooth* were conferred because of some prominent feature. In Anglo-French

[1] We have several instances of this phenomenon. A familiar example is *Lippincott*, the original form of which was Luffincott (Devonshire). But Bardsley's inclusion of American statistics is often misleading. It is a well-known fact that the foreign names of immigrants are regularly assimilated to English forms in the United States. In some cases, such as Cook for *Koch*, Cope (p. 107) for *Kopf*, Stout (p. 209) for *Stolz* or *Stultz*, the change is etymologically justified. But in other cases, such as Tallman for *Thalmann*, dale-man, Trout for *Traut*, faithful, the resemblance is accidental. Beam and Chestnut, common in the States but very rare in England, represent an imitative form of *Böhm* or *Behm*, Bohemian, and a translation of *Kestenbaum*, chestnut tree, both Jewish names. The Becks and Bowmans of New York outnumber those of London by about five to one, the first being for *Beck*, baker (p. 149), and the second for *Baumann*, equivalent to *Bauer*, farmer. Bardsley explains the common American name Arrison by the fact that there are Cockneys in America. It comes of course from Arend, a Dutch name related to Arnold.

"A remarkable record in changes of surname was cited some years ago by an American correspondent of *Notes and Queries*. 'The changes which befell a resident of New Orleans were that when he moved from an American quarter to a German neighbourhood his name of Flint became Feuerstein, which for convenience was shortened to Stein. Upon his removal to a French district he was re-christened Pierre. Hence upon his return to an English neighbourhood he was translated into Peters, and his first neighbours were surprised and puzzled to find Flint turned Peters.'"

(*Daily Chronicle*, April 4, 1913.)

we find *gernon*, moustache, now corrupted to *Garnham*, and also *al gernon*, with the moustache, which has become *Algernon*. But we have already seen (p. 125) that some names which appear to belong to this class are of local origin. So also *Tongue* is derived from one of several places named Tong or Tonge, though the ultimate origin is perhaps in some cases the same, a "tongue" of land. *Quartermain* is for *quatre-mains*, perhaps bestowed on a very acquisitive person; Joscius *quatre-buches*, four mouths, and Roger *tunekes*, two necks, were alive in the twelfth century; and there is record of a Saracen champion named *quinze-paumes*, though this is perhaps rather a measure of height. *Cheek* I conjecture to be for *Chick*. The odd-looking *Kidney* is for the local *Gidney*. There is a rare name *Poindexter*, appearing in French as *Poingdestre*, "right fist."[1] I have seen it explained as from the heraldic term *point dexter*, but it is rather to be taken literally. I find Johannes *cum pugno* in 1184, and we can imagine that such a name may have been conferred on a medieval bruiser. There is also the possibility, considering the brutality of many old nicknames, that the bearer of the name had been judicially deprived of his right hand, a very common punishment, especially for striking a feudal superior. Thus Renaut de Montauban, finding that his unknown opponent is Charlemagne, exclaims—

> "J'ai forfait *le poing destre* dont je l'ai adesé (struck)."

We have some nicknames describing gait, e.g. *Ambler* and *Shaylor*—

> "I *shayle*, as a man or horse dothe that gothe croked with his leggs, *je vas eschays*" (Palsgrave)—

[1] President *Poincaré's* name appears to mean "square fist."

and perhaps sometimes *Trotter*. If George Eliot had been a student of surnames she would hardly have named a heroine Nancy *Lammiter*, i.e. cripple—

"Though ye may think him a *lamiter*, yet, grippie for grippie, he'll make the bluid spin frae under your nails" (*Black Dwarf*, ch. xvii.).

It may also be a variant of Chaucer's *limitour*, a friar with authority to beg within certain bounds. *Pettigrew* and *Pettifer* are of French origin, *pied de grue* (crane) and *pied de fer*. The former is the origin of the word pedigree, from a sign used in drawing genealogical trees. The Buckinghamshire name *Puddifoot* and the aristocratic *Pauncefote* are unsolved. I should like to suggest that the former is a corruption of *Pettifer*. This is not so wild as it looks. We find the intermediate form *Puddifer*, and the further corruption to *Puddifoot* is no more impossible than the transformation of Ger. *Sauer-kraut*, sour cabbage, into Fr. *choucroute*, where the "sour" has become the "cabbage." As for *Pauncefote*, I believe it simply means what it appears to, viz. "belly-foot," a curious formation, though not without parallels among obsolete rustic nicknames, and an almost literal equivalent of the Greek Œdipus.

In other languages as well as English we find money nicknames. It is easy to understand how some of these come into existence, *e.g.* that Pierce Pennilesse was the opposite of Thomas Thousandpound, whose name occurs *c.* 1300. With the latter we may compare Fr. *Centlivre*, the name of an English lady dramatist of the eighteenth century. *Moneypenny* is found in 1273 as *manipeni*, and a Londoner named *Manypeny* died in 1348. The *Money-* is partly north country, partly imitative. *Money* itself is usually occupative or local (p. 165), and *Shilling* is the Anglo-Saxon name Scilling. The oldest and commonest of such nicknames is the simple *Penny*, with which we may compare the German surname *Pfennig* and its compounds *Barpfennig, Weisspfennig*, etc. The early adoption of this coin-name as a personal name is due to the fact that the word was taken in the sense of money in general. We still speak of a rich man as "worth a pretty penny." *Hallmark* is folk-etymology for the medieval *half-mark*. Such medieval names as *four-pence, twenty-mark*, etc., probably now obsolete, are paralleled by Fr. *Quatresous* and *Sixdenier*, still to be found in the Paris Directory. It would be easy to form conjectures as to the various ways in which such names may have come into existence. To the same class must belong *Besant*, the name of a coin from Byzantium, its foreign origin giving it a dignity which is absent from the native *Farthing* and *Halfpenny*, though the latter, in one instance, was improved beyond recognition into *MacAlpine*.

There is also a small group of surnames derived from oaths or exclamations which by habitual use became associated with certain individuals. We know that monarchs had a special tendency to indulge in a favourite expletive. To Roger de Collerye we owe some information as to the imprecations preferred by four French kings—

> "Quand la *Pasque-Dieu* (Louis XI.) décéda,
> Le *Bon Jour Dieu* (Charles VIII.) luy succéda ;
> Au *Bon Jour Dieu* deffunct et mort
> Succéda le *Dyable m'emport* (Louis XII.).
> Luy décédé, nous voyons comme
> Nous duist (governs) la *Foy de Gentilhomme* (Francis I.)."

So important was this branch of linguistics once considered that Palsgrave, the French tutor of Princess Mary Tudor, includes in his *Esclarcissement de la Langue francoyse* a section on "The Maners of Cursyng." Among the examples are "Le grant diable luy rompe le col et les deux jambes," "Le diable l'emporte, corps et ame, tripes et boyaux," which were unfortunately too long for surname purposes, but an abridged form of "Le feu Saint Anthoyne [1] l'arde" has given the French name *Feulard*. Such names, usually containing the name of God, *e.g.* Godmefetch, Helpusgod, have mostly disappeared in this country; but *Dieuleveut* and *Dieumegard* are still found in Paris, and *Gottbehüt*, God forbid, and *Gotthelf*, God help, occur in German. *Godbehere* still exists, and there is not the slightest reason why it should not be of the origin which its form indicates. In *Gracedieu*, thanks to God, the second element is an Old French dative. *Pardoe*, *Purdue*, whence *Purdey*, is for *par Dieu*—

> "I have a wyf *pardee*, as wel as thow" (A, 3158).

There is a well-known professional footballer named *Mordue* ('sdeath), and a French composer named *Boieldieu* (God's bowels). The French nickname for an Englishman, *Goddam* [2]—

> "Those syllables intense,
> Nucleus of England's native eloquence"
> (Byron, *The Island*, iii. 5)—

goes back to the fifteenth century, in which invective references to the *godons* are numerous. Such nicknames are still in common use in some parts of France—

[1] Saint Anthony's fire, *i.e.* erysipelas, burn him!

[2] "Les Anglais en vérité ajoutent par-ci, par-là quelques autres mots en conversant; mais il est bien aisé de voir que *goddam* est le fond de la langue" (Beaumarchais, *Mariage de Figaro*, iii. 5).

"Les Berrichons se désignent souvent par le juron qui leur est familier. Ainsi ils diront : '*Diable me brûle* est bien malade. *Nom d'un rat* est à la foire. La femme à *Diable m'estrangouille* est morte. Le garçon à *Bon You* (Dieu) se marie avec la fille à *Dieu me confonde*.'"

(Nyrop, *Grammaire historique de la langue française*, iv. 209).

Perhaps the most interesting group of nicknames is that of which we may take *Shakespeare* as the type. Incidentally we should be thankful that our greatest poet bore a name so much more picturesque than *Corneille*, crow, or *Racine*, root. It is agreed among all competent scholars that in compounds of this formation the verb was originally an imperative. This is shown by the form; cf. *ne'er-do-well*, Fr. *vaurien*, Ger. *Taugenichts*, good-for-naught. Thus *Hasluck* cannot belong to this class, but must be an imitative form of the personal name Aslac, which we find in Aslockton. As Bardsley well says, it is impossible to retail all the nonsense that has been written about the name *Shakespeare*—"never a name in English nomenclature so simple or so certain in its origin; it is exactly what it looks—*shake-spear*." The equivalent *Schüttespeer* is found in German, and we have also in English *Shakeshaft*, *Waghorn*, *Wagstaff*, *Breakspear*, *Winspear*. "*Winship* the mariner" was a freeman of York in the fourteenth century. Cf. *Benbow* (bend-bow), *Hurlbatt*, and the less athletic *Lovejoy*, *Makepeace*. *Gathergood* and its opposite *Scattergood* are of similar origin, *good* having here the sense of goods. *Dogood* is sometimes for *Toogood*, and the latter may be, like *Thoroughgood*, an imitative form of *Thurgod* (p. 73); but both names may also be taken literally, for we find Ger. *Thunichtgut*, do no good, and Fr. *Troplong*. As a pendant to *Dolittle* we find a medieval *hack-little*, no doubt a lazy woodcutter, while virtue is represented by a twelfth-century *tire-little*. *Sherwin* in some cases represents the medieval *schere-wynd*, applied to a swift runner; cf. Ger. *Schneidewind*, cut wind, and Fr. *Tranchevent*. A nurseryman at Highgate has the appropriate name *Cutbush*, the French equivalent of which, *Taillebois*, has given us *Tallboys*; and a famous herbalist was named *Culpepper*. In *Gathercole* the second element may mean cabbage or charcoal. In one case, *Horniblow* for horn-blow, the verb comes after its object.

Names of this formation are very common in Mid. English as in Old French, and often bear witness to a violent or brutal nature. Thus *scorch-beef*, which is found in the Hundred Rolls, has no connection with careless cookery; it is Old Fr. *escorche*(*écorche*)-*buef*, flay ox, a name given to some medieval "Skin-the-goat." *Catchpole* (p. 184) is formed in the same way, and in French we find, applied to law officials, the surnames *Baillehart*, give[1] halter, and *Baillehache*, give axe, the latter still appropriately borne, as *Bailhache*, by an English judge.

It has sometimes been assumed that most names of this class are due to folk-etymology. The frequency of their occurrence in Mid. English and in continental languages makes it certain that the contrary is the case and that many surnames of obscure origin are perversions of this very large and popular class. I have seen it stated somewhere that *Shakespeare* is a corruption of an Old French name *Sacquespée*,[2] the theorist being apparently unable to see that this latter, meaning *draw-sword*, is merely an additional argument,

[1] *Bailler*, the usual Old French for to give, is still used colloquially and in dialect.

[2] Of common occurrence in Mid. English records.

if such were needed, for the literal interpretation of the English name.[1]

Tredgold seems to have been conferred on some medieval stoic, for we find also *spurnegold*. Without pinning our faith to any particular anecdote, we need have no hesitation in accepting *Turnbull* as a sobriquet conferred for some feat of strength and daring on a stalwart Borderer. We find the corresponding *Tornebeuf* in Old French, and *Turnbuck* also occurs. *Trumbull* and *Trumble* are variants due to metathesis followed by assimilation (p. 35), while *Tremble* is a very degenerate form. In *Knatchbull* we have a dialect form of the verb to " snatch " in its oldest sense of to seize. *Crawcour* is Fr. *Crèvecœur*, break-heart, which has also become a local name in France. With *Shacklock*, shake-lock, and *Sherlock*, *Shurlock*, shear-lock, we may compare Robin Hood's comrade *Scathelock*, though the precise interpretation of all three names is difficult. *Rackstraw*, rake-straw, corresponds to Fr. *Grattepaille*. *Golightly* means much the same as *Lightfoot* (p. 126), nor need we hesitate to regard the John *Gotobed*[2] who lived in Cambridgeshire in 1273 as a notorious sluggard compared with whom his neighbour Serl *go-to-kirke* was a shining example. *Telfer* is Fr. *taille-fer*, the iron cleaver, and Henry II.'s yacht captain was Alan *Trenchemer*, the sea cleaver. He had a contemporary named *Ventados*, wind abaft.

[1] In one day's reading I came across the following: *Baillebien* (give good), *Baysedame* (kiss lady), *Esveillechien* (wake dog), *Lievelance* (raise lance), *Metlefrein* (put the bridle), *Tracepurcel* (track hog), *Turnecotel* (turn coat), together with the native *Cachehare* and *Hoppeschort*.

[2] The name is still found in the same county. Undergraduates contemporary with the author occasionally slaked their thirst at a riverside inn kept by Bathsheba Gotobed.

Slocomb has assumed a local aspect, but may very well correspond to Fr. *Tardif* or Ger. *Mühsam,* applied to some Weary Willie of the Middle Ages. *Doubtfire* is a misspelling of *dout-fire,* from the dialect *dout,* to extinguish (do out), formed like *don* and *doff*. *Fullalove,* which does not belong to the same formation, is also found as *plein d'amour*—

"Of Sir Lybeux and *Pleyndamour*" (B, 2090)—

and corresponds to Ger. *Liebevoll. Waddilove* actually occurs in the Hundred Rolls as *wade-in-love,* presumably a nickname conferred on some medieval Don Juan.

There is one curious little group of nicknames which seem to correspond to such Latin names as Piso, from *pisum,* a pea, and Cicero, from *cicer*—

"*Cicer,* a small pulse, lesse than pease" (Cooper).

Such are *Barleycorn* and *Peppercorn,* the former found in French as *Graindorge*. The rather romantic names *Avenel* and *Peverel* seem to mean very much the same, from Lat. *avena,* oats, and *piper,* pepper. In fact *Peverel* is found in *Domesday* as Piperellus, and *Pepperell* still exists. With these may be mentioned *Carbonel,* corresponding to the French surname *Charbonneau,* a little coal.

CHAPTER XXII

ADJECTIVAL NICKNAMES

"The man replied that he did not know the object of the building; and to make it quite manifest that he really did not know, he put an adjective before the word 'object,' and another—that is, the same—before the word 'building.' With that he passed on his way, and Lord Jocelyn was left marvelling at the slender resources of our language, which makes one adjective do duty for so many qualifications."

(BESANT, *All Sorts and Conditions of Men*, ch. xxxviii.)

THE rejection by the British workman of all adjectives but one is due to the same imaginative poverty which makes the adjective "nice" supreme in refined circles, and which limits the schoolgirl to "ripping" and her more self-conscious brother to the tempered "decent." But dozens of useful adjectives, now either obsolete or banished to rustic dialect, are found among our surnames. The tendency to accompany every noun by an adjective seems to belong to some deep-rooted human instinct. To this is partly due the Protean character of this part of speech, for the word, like the coin, becomes dulled and worn in circulation and needs periodically to be withdrawn and replaced. An epithet which is complimentary in one generation is ironical in the next and eventually offensive. *Moody*, with its northern form *Mudie*, which now means morose, was once valiant (p. 5), and pert, surviving in the name *Peart*, meant active, brisk, etc.—

"Awake the *pert* and nimble spirit of mirth."

(*Midsummer Night's Dream*, i. 1.)

To interpret an adjectival nickname we must go to its meaning in Chaucer and his contemporaries. *Silly*, *Seeley*, *Seely*—

> "This *sely*, innocent Custance" (B, 682)—

still means innocent when we speak of the "silly sheep" and happy in the phrase "silly Suffolk." It is cognate with Ger. *selig*, blessed, often used in speaking of the dead. We have a compound in *Sillifant*, simple child (see p. 94), and *Selibarn* has become *Silburn*. *Seely* was also used for Cecil or Cecilia. *Sadd* was once sedate and steadfast—

> "But thogh this mayde tendre were of age,
> Yet in the brest of hire virginitee
> Ther was enclosed rype and *sad* corage"
> (E, 218);

and as late as 1660 we find a book in defence of Charles I. described as—

> "A *sad* and impartial inquiry whether the King or Parliament began the war."

Stout, valiant, now used euphemistically for fat, is cognate with Ger. *stolz*, proud, and possibly with Lat. *stultus*, foolish. The three ideas are not incompatible, for fools are notoriously proud of their folly and are said to be less subject to fear than the angels. *Sturdy*, *Sturdee*, once meant rebellious, pig-headed—

> "*Sturdy*, unbuxum, *rebellis*, *contumax*, *inobediens*."
> (*Prompt. Parv.*)

Cotgrave offers a much wider choice for the French original—

> "*Estourdi* (*étourdi*), dulled, amazed, astonished, dizzie-headed, or whose head seemes very much troubled; (hence) also, heedlesse, inconsiderate, unadvised, witlesse, uncircumspect, rash, retchlesse, or carelesse; and sottish, blockish, lumpish, lusk-like, without life, metall, spirit."

Sly and its variant *Sleigh* have degenerated in the same way as crafty and cunning, both of which once meant skilled. Chaucer calls the wings of Dædalus "his playes *slye*," i.e. his ingenious contrivances. *Quick* meant alert, lively, as in "the *quick* and the dead." *Slight*, cognate with Ger. *schlecht*, bad, once meant plain or simple.

Many adjectives which are quite obsolete in literary English survive as surnames. Mid. English *Lyte* has been supplanted by its derivative *Little*, the opposite pair surviving as *Mutch* and *Mickle*. The poor parson did not fail—

> "In siknesse nor in meschief to visite
> The ferreste in his parisshe, *muche* and *lyte*."
> (A, 493.)

We have for *Lyte* also the imitative *Light*; cf. *Lightwood*. With *Little* may be mentioned *Murch*, an obsolete word for dwarf—

> "*Murch*, lytyl man, *nanus*."
> (*Prompt. Parv.*)

Lenain is a fairly common name in France. *Snell*, swift and valiant, had become a personal name in Anglo-Saxon, but we find *le snel* in the Middle Ages. *Freake*, *Frick*, also meant valiant or warrior—

> "Ther was no *freke* that ther wolde flye"
> (*Chevy Chase*);

but the *Prompt. Parv.* makes it equivalent to *Craske* (p. 212)—

> "*Fryke*, or *craske*, in grete helth, *crassus*."

It is cognate with Ger. *frech*, which now means impudent. *Nott* has already been mentioned (p. 16). Of the Yeoman we are told—

> "A *not* hed hadde he, with a broun visage."
> (A, 109.)

Stark, cognate with starch, now usually means stiff, rather than strong—

> "I feele my lymes *stark* and suffisaunt
> To do al that a man bilongeth to."
>
> (E, 1458.)

But *Stark* is often for an earlier Sterk (cf. Clark and Clerk), which represents Mid. Eng. *stirk*, a heifer. In the cow with the *crumpled* horn we have a derivative of Mid. Eng. *crum*, crooked, whence the names *Crum* and *Crump*. Ludwig's German Dict. (1715) explains *krumm* as "*crump*, crooked, wry." The name *Crook* generally has the same meaning, the Ger. *Krummbein* corresponding to our northern *Cruikshank*. *Glegg* (Scand.), clear-sighted, has been confused with *Clegg* (Welsh), a rock.

There are some adjectival surnames which are not immediately recognizable. *Bolt*, when not local (p. 133), is for bold, *Leaf* is imitative for *lief*, i.e. dear. *Dear* itself is of course hopelessly mixed up with *Deer*. The timorous-looking *Fear* is Fr. *le fier*, the proud or fierce. *Skey* is an old form of shy; *Bligh* is for *Blyth*; *Hendy* and *Henty* are the same word as handy, and had in Mid. English the sense of helpful, courteous—

> "Oure hoost tho spak, 'A, sire, ye sholde be *hende*
> And curteys, as a man of youre estat.'"
>
> (D, 1286.)

For *Savage* we find also the archaic spelling *Salvage* (Lat. *silvaticus*). *Curtis* is Norman Fr. *curteis* (*courtois*). The adjective garish, now only poetical, but once commonly applied to gaudiness in dress, has given *Gerrish*. *Quaint*, which has so many meanings intermediate between its etymological sense of known or familiar (Lat. *cognitus*) and its present sense of unusual or unfamiliar, survives as *Quint*. But *Coy* is local, from Quy (Cambridgeshire). The name *Neish* represents the familiar Midland adjective *nesh*, over-delicate, namby-pamby, *Craske* is an East Anglian word for fat, and *Crouse* is used in the north for sprightly, confident. To these we may add *Ketch, Kedge, Gedge,* from an East Anglian adjective meaning lively—

"*Kygge*, or joly, *jocundus*" (*Prompt. Parv.*)—

and *Spragg*, etymologically akin to *Spry*. *Bragg* was once used for bold or brave, without any uncomplimentary suggestion. The New English Dictionary quotes (*c.* 1310) from a lyric poem—

"That maketh us so *brag* and bolde
And biddeth us ben blythe."

Crease is a West-country word for squeamish, but the East Anglian name *Creasey, Cressy,* is for the local *Kersey* (Suffolk). The only solution of *Pratt* is that it is Anglo-Sax. *prætt*, cunning, adopted early as a personal name, while *Storr*, of Scandinavian origin, means big, strong. It is cognate with *Steer*, a bull. *Devey* and *Dombey* seem to be the diminutive forms of deaf and dumb, which are still used in dialect in reference to persons thus afflicted. We find in French and German surnames corresponding to these very natural nicknames. Cf. *Crombie* from *Crum* (p. 211).

A large proportion of our adjectival nicknames are of French origin. *Le bel* appears not only as *Bell* but also, through Picard, as *Beal*. Other examples are *Boon, Bone, Bunn* (bon), *Grant* (grand), *Bass* (bas) and its derivative *Bassett, Dasent* (décent), *Follett* and *Folliott*, dim. of *fol* (fou), mad, which also appears in the compound *Foljambe*. *Mordaunt* means biting. *Power* is Anglo-Fr. *le poure* (le pauvre) and *Grace* is for *le gras*, the fat. *Joliffe* represents the Old French form of *joli*—

> "This Absolon, that *jolif* was and gay,
> Gooth with a sencer (censer) on the haliday."
> (A, 3339.)

Prynne, now *Pring*, is Anglo-Fr. *le prin*, the first, from the Old French adjective which survives in *prin*temps. Cf. our name *Prime* and the French name *Premier*. The Old French adjective *Gent*, now replaced by *gentil*, generally means slender in Mid. English—

> "Fair was this yonge wyf, and therwithal
> As any wezele hir body *gent* and smal."
> (A, 3233.)

Begg is in some cases *le bègue*, the stammerer. In *Prowse* and *Prout* we have the nominative and objective (see p. 9, *n.*) of an Old French adjective now represented by *preux* and *prude*, generally thought to be related in some way to Lat. *pro* in *prosum*, and perhaps the source of our *Proud*.

Gross is of course Fr. *le gros*, but *Grote* represents Du. *groot*, great, probably unconnected with the French word. The Devonshire name *Coffin*, which is found in that county in the twelfth century, is the same as *Caffyn*, and both are the Fr. *Chauvin*, bald, the name of the theologian whom we know better in the latinized form *Calvin*. Here belongs probably *Shovel*, Fr. *Chauvel*. We also have the simple *Chaffe*, Old Fr. *chauf* (chauve), bald. *Gaylard*, sometimes made into the imitative *Gaylord*, is Fr. *gaillard*, brisk, lively—

> "*Gaillard* he was as goldfynch in the shawe."
> (A, 4367.)

Especially common are colour nicknames, generally due to the complexion, but sometimes to the garb. As we have already seen (p. 149), *Black* and its variant

Blake sometimes mean pale. *Blagg* is the same word; cf. *Blagrave* (see p. 110). *White* has no doubt been reinforced by *wight,* valiant—

> "Oh for one hour of Wallace *wight*
> Or well-skilled Bruce to rule the fight."
> (*Marmion*, vi. 20.)

As an epithet applied to the hair we often find *Hoar*; cf. *Horlock*. *Redd* is rare, the usual forms being the northern *Reid, Reed, Read*; but we also have *Rudd* from Anglo-Sax. *rud,* whence ruddy and the name *Ruddock,* really a bird nickname, the redbreast. To these must be added *Rudge,* Fr. *rouge, Rouse, Rush* and *Russ,* Fr. *roux,* and *Russell* or *Rowsell,* Old Fr. *roussel* (*Rousseau*). The commonest nickname for a fair-haired person was *Blunt, Blount,* Fr. *blond,* with its dim. *Blundell,* but the true English name is *Fairfax,* from Anglo-Sax. *feax,* hair. The New English Dictionary quotes from the fifteenth century—

> "Then they lowsyd hur *feyre faxe,*
> That was yelowe as the waxe."

The adjective dun was once a regular name, like Dobbin or Dapple, for a cart-horse; hence the name of the old rural sport "Dun in the mire"—

> "If thou art *dun* we'll draw thee from the mire."
> (*Romeo and Juliet*, i. 4.)

It is possible that the name *Dunn* is sometimes due to this specific application of the word. The colour blue appears as *Blew*—

> "At last he rose, and twitch'd his mantle *blew*:
> To-morrow to fresh woods and pastures new"
> (*Lycidas*, l. 192)—

and earlier still as *Blow*—

> "Blak, *blo,* grenysh, swartysh, reed."
> (*House of Fame*, iii. 557.)

Other colour names of French origin are *Morel*, swarthy, like a Moor, also found as *Murrell*,[1] and *Burnell*, *Burnett*, dims. of *brun*, brown. Chaucer speaks of—

> "Daun[2] *Burnel* the asse" (B, 4502);
> "Daun *Russel* the fox" (B, 4524.)

But both *Burnell* and *Burnett* may also be local from places ending in *-hill* and *-head* (p. 126), and *Burnett* is sometimes for *Burnard*. The same applies to *Burrell*, usually taken to be from Mid. Eng. *borel*, a rough material, Old Fr. *burel* (bureau), also used metaphorically in the sense of plain, uneducated—

> "And moore we seen of Cristes secree thynges
> Than *burel* folk, al though they weren kynges."
> (D, 1871.)

The name can equally well be the local Burhill or Burwell.

Murray is too common to be referred entirely to the Scottish name and is sometimes for *murrey*, dark red (Fr. *mûre*, mulberry). It may also represent merry, in its variant form *murie*, which is Mid. English, and not, as might appear, Amurrican—

> "His *murie* men comanded he
> To make hym bothe game and glee."
> (B, 2029.)

Pook, of uncertain origin, is supposed to have been a dark russet colour. *Bayard*, a derivative of bay, was the name of several famous war-horses. Cf. *Blank* and *Blanchard*. The name *Soar* is from the Old French adjective *sor*, bright yellow. It is of Germanic origin and cognate with *sear*. The dim. *Sorrel* may be a colour name, but it was applied in

[1] This, like *Merrill*, is sometimes from Muriel.
[2] Lat. *dominus*, the masculine form of *dame* in Old French.

venery to a buck in the third year, of course in reference to colour; and some of our names, e.g. *Brocket* and *Prickett*,[1] both applied to a two-year-old stag, must sometimes be referred to this important department of medieval language. Holofernes uses some of these terms in his idiotic verses—

> "The preyful princess pierc'd and prick'd a pretty pleasing *pricket*;
> Some say a *sore*; but not a *sore*, till now made *sore* with shooting.
> The dogs did yell; put *l* to *sore*, then *sorel* jumps from thicket."
> (*Love's Labour's Lost*, iv. 2.)

A few adjective nicknames of Celtic origin are so common that they may be included here. Such are the Welsh *Gough*, *Goff*, *Gooch*, *Gutch*, red, *Gwynn* and *Wynne*, white, *Lloyd*, grey, *Sayce*, Saxon, foreigner, *Vaughan*, little, and the Gaelic *Bain*, *Bean*, white, *Boyd*, *Bowie*, yellow-haired, *Dow*, *Duff*, black, *Finn*, fair, *Glass*, grey, *Roy*, *Roe*, red. From Cornish come *Coad*, old, and *Couch*, red, while *Bean* is the Cornish for small, and *Tyacke* means a farmer. It is likely that both *Begg* and *Moore* owe something to the Gaelic adjectives for little and big, as in the well-known names of Callum Beg, Edward Waverley's gillie, and McCallum More. The Gaelic *Begg* is cognate with the Welsh *Vaughan*. Two other famous Highland nicknames which are very familiar in England are *Cameron*, crooked nose, and *Campbell*, wry mouth. With these may be mentioned the Irish *Kennedy*, ugly head, the name of the father of Brian Boru.

[1] Both words are connected with the spiky young horns, Fr. *broche*, spit, being applied in venery to the pointed horns of the second year.

CHAPTER XXIII

BIRDS, BEASTS, AND FISHES

"As I think I have already said, one of Umslopogaas' Zulu names was The Woodpecker."

(HAGGARD, *Allan Quatermain*, ch. vii.)

THE great majority of nicknames coming under the headings typified by *Bird* and *Fowell*, *Best*, and *Fish* or *Fisk* (Scand.) are easily identified. But here, as everywhere in the subject, pitfalls abound. The name *Best* itself is an example of a now misleading spelling retained for obvious reasons—

"First, on the wal was peynted a forest,
In which ther dwelleth neither man nor *best*."

(A, 1976.)

We do not find exotic animals, nor even the beasts of heraldry, at all frequently. *Leppard*, leopard, is in some cases for the Ger. *Liebhart;* and *Griffin*, when not Welsh, should no doubt be included among inn-signs. *Oliphant*, i.e. elephant—

"For maystow surmounten thise *olifauntes* in gretnesse or weighte of body" (Boece, 782)—

may be a genuine nickname, but Roland's ivory horn was also called by this name, and the surname may go back to some legendary connection of the same kind. *Bear* is not uncommon, captive bears being familiar to a period in which the title bear-ward is frequently met with. It is possible that *Drake* may sometimes represent Anglo-Sax. *draca*, dragon, rather than the bird, but the latter is unmistakable in *Sheldrick*, for sheldrake. As a rule, animal nicknames were taken rather from the domestic species with which the peasantry were familiar and whose habits would readily suggest comparisons, generally disparaging, with those of their neighbours.

Bird names are especially common, and it does not need much imagination to see how readily and naturally a man might be nicknamed *Hawke* for his fierceness, *Crowe* from a gloomy aspect, or *Nightingale* for the gift of sweet song. Many of these surnames go back to words which are now either obsolete or found only in dialect. The peacock was once the *Poe*, an early loan from Lat. *pavo*, or, more fully, *Pocock*—

> "A sheaf of *pocok* arwes, bright and kene,
> Under his belt he bar ful thriftily."
>
> (A, 104.)

The name *Pay* is another form of the same word. *Coe*, whence *Hedgecoe*, is an old name for the jackdaw—

> "Cadow, or *coo*, or chogh (chough), *monedula*"
>
> (*Prompt. Parv.*)—

but may also stand for cow, as we find, in defiance of gender and sex, such entries as Robert *le cow*, William *le vache*. Those birds which have now assumed a font-name, such as Jack daw, Mag pie, of course occur without it as surnames, e.g. *Daw* and *Pye*—

> "The thief the chough, and eek the jangelyng *pye*"
>
> (*Parliament of Fowls*, 305).

The latter has a dim. *Pyatt*.

Rainbird is a local name for the green woodpecker. As a surname it may also, like *Rainbow*, be an imitative form of Fr. *Rimbaud* or *Raimbaud*, identical with

Anglo-Sax. Regenbeald. *Knott* is the name of a bird which frequents the sea-shore and, mindful of Cnut's wisdom, retreats nimbly before the advancing surf—

> "The *knot* that called was Canutus' bird of old."
> (Drayton, *Polyolbion*, xxv. 368.)

This historical connection is most probably due to folk-etymology. *Titmus* is of course for tit-mouse. Dialect names for the woodpecker survive in *Speight*, *Speke*, and *Spick*, *Pick*. The same bird was also called *woodwall*—

> "In many places were nyghtyngales,
> Alpes, fynches, and *wodewales*"
> (*Romaunt of the Rose*, 567)—

hence, in some cases, the name *Woodall*. The *Alpe*, or bullfinch, mentioned in the above lines, also survives as a surname. *Dunnock* and *Pinnock* are dialect names for the sparrow. It was called in Anglo-Norman *muisson*, whence *Musson*. *Starling* is a dim. of Mid. Eng. *stare*, which has itself given the surname *Starr*—

> "The *stare*, that the counseyl can be-wrye."
> (*Parliament of Fowls*, 348.)

Heron is the French form of the bird-name which was in English *Herne*—

> "I come from haunts of coot and *hern*."
> (Tennyson, *The Brook*, l. 1.)

The Old French dim. *heronceau* also passed into English—

> "I wol nat tellen of hir strange sewes (courses),
> Ne of hir swannes, ne of hire *heronsewes*."
> (F, 67.)

As a surname it has been assimilated to the local, and partly identical, *Hearnshaw* (p. 110). Some commentators go to this word to explain Hamlet's use of *handsaw*—

"I am but mad north-north-west: when the wind is southerly, I know a hawk from a *handsaw*" (*Hamlet*, ii. 2).

When the author's father was a boy in Suffolk seventy years ago, the local name for the bird was pronounced exactly like *answer*. *Grew* is Fr. *grue*, crane, Lat. *grus*, *gru-*. *Butter*, Fr. *butor*, "a bittor" (Cotgrave), is a dialect name for the bittern, called a "butter-bump" by Tennyson's Northern Farmer (l. 31). *Culver* is a very early loan-word from Latin—

"*Columba*, a *culver*, a dove"

(Cooper)—

hence the local *Culverhouse*. *Dove* often becomes *Duff*. *Whichello*, which can be seen both in Cambridge and Hammersmith, is Ital. *uccello*, identical with Fr. *oiseau*, Vulgar Lat. *avicellus*. *Popjoy* may have been applied to the successful archer who became king of the popinjay for the year. The derivation of the word, Old Fr. *papegai*, whence Mid. Eng. *papejay*—

"The briddes synge, it is no nay,
The sparhawk and the *papejay*,
That joye it was to heere"

(B, 1956)—

is obscure, though various forms of it are found in most of the European languages. In English it was applied not only to the parrot, but also to the green woodpecker. The London Directory form is *Pobgee*.

With bird nicknames may be mentioned *Callow*, unfledged, cognate with Lat. *calvus*, bald. Its opposite also survives as *Fleck* and *Flick*—

"*Flygge*, as byrdis, *maturus*, *volabilis*."

(*Prompt. Parv.*)

Margaret Paston, writing (1460) of the revived hopes of Henry VI., says—

"Now he and alle his olde felawship put owt their fynnes, and arn ryght *flygge* and mery."

We have naturally a set of names taken from the various species of falcons. To this class belongs *Haggard*, probably related to Anglo-Sax. *haga*, hedge, and used of a hawk which had acquired incurable habits of wildness by preying for itself. But *Haggard* is also a personal name (p. 81). *Spark*, earlier *Sparhawk*, is the sparrow-hawk. It is found already in Anglo-Saxon as a personal name, which accounts for the patronymic *Sparks*. *Tassell* is a corruption of *tiercel*, a name given to the male goshawk, so termed, according to the legendary lore of venery—

> "Because he is, commonly, a third part lesse than the female."
> (Cotgrave.)

Juliet calls Romeo her "tassell gentle" (ii. 2). *Muskett* was a name given to a very small hawk—

> "*Musket*, a lytell hauke, *mouchet*."
> (Palsgrave.)

Mushet is the same name. It comes from Ital. *moschetto*, a little fly. For its later application to a firearm cf. *falconet*. Other names of the hawk class are *Buzzard* and *Puttock*, i.e. kite—

> "*Milan*, a kite, *puttock*, glead"
> (Cotgrave);

and to the same bird we owe the name *Gleed*, from a Scandinavian name for the bird—

> "And the *glede*, and the kite, and the vulture after his kind."
> (Deut. xiv. 13.)

To this class also belongs *Ramage*—

> "*Ramage*, of, or belonging to, branches; also, *ramage*, hagard, wild, homely, rude" (Cotgrave)—

and sometimes *Lennard*, an imitative form of the inferior hawk called a lanner—

> "Falcunculus, a *leonard*."
> (Holyoak, Lat. Dict., 1612.)

Povey is a dialect name for the owl, and *Howlett* is not always a double dim. of Hugh (p. 59).

Among beast nicknames we find special attention given, as in modern vituperation, to the swine, although we do not find this true English word, unless it be occasionally disguised as *Swain*. *Hogg* does not belong exclusively to this class, as it is used in dialect both of a young sheep and a yearling colt. Anglo-Sax. *sugu*, sow, survives in *Sugg*. *Purcell* is Old Fr. *pourcel* (pourceau), dim. of Lat. *porcus*, and I take *Pockett* to be a disguised form of the obsolete *porket*—

> " *Porculus*, a pygg : a shoote : a *porket*."
>
> (Cooper.)

The word *shoote* in the above gloss is now the dialect *shot*, a young pig, which has given the surname *Shott*. But *Scutt* is from a Mid. English adjective meaning short—

> " *Scute*, or shorte, *curtus*, *brevis* "
>
> (*Prompt. Parv.*)—

and is also an old name for the hare. Two other names for the pig are the northern *Galt* and the Lincolnshire *Grice*—

> " *Marcassin*, a young wild boare ; a shoot or *grice*."
>
> (Cotgrave.)

Grice also represents *le gris*, the grey; cf. *Grace* for *le gras* (p. 212). *Bacon* is occasionally found as *le bacon*, presumably a bacon-hog, but it is generally a personal name. As it is common in French, it would appear to be an Old French accusative to *Back*, going back to Germanic Bacco (see p. 125). *Hinks* is Mid. Eng. *hengst*, a stallion, and is thus identical with Hengist (p. 186). *Stott* means both a bullock and a nag (p. 179).

Everyone remembers Wamba's sage disquisition on the names of animals in the first chapter of *Ivanhoe*.

Like much of Scott's archæology it is a little anachronistic, for the live animals were also called veals and muttons for centuries after Wamba's death—

> "*Mouton*, a *mutton*, a weather"; "*veau*, a calfe, or *veale*." (Cotgrave.)

Calf has become very rare as a surname, though *Kalb* is still common in Germany. Bardsley regards *Duncalf* and *Metcalf* as perverted from *dun-croft* and *meadow-croft*. It seems possible that they may be for *down-calf* and *mead-calf*, from the locality of the pasture, but this is a pure guess on my part. It is curious that *beef* does not appear to have survived, though *Lebœuf* is common in French, and bullocks are still called "beeves" in Scotland. *Tegg* is still used by butchers for a two-year-old sheep. Palsgrave gives it another meaning—

> "*Tegg*, or pricket (p. 216), *saillant*."

Roe is also found in the older forms *Rae* and *Ray*, of course confused with *Wray* (p. 127), as *Roe* itself is with *Rowe* (p. 9). *Doe* often becomes *Dowe*. *Hind* is usually occupative (p. 35), but Fr. *Labiche* shows that it must sometimes be a nickname—

> "*Biche*, a *hind*; the female of a stagge." (Cotgrave.)

Pollard was applied to a beast or stag that had lost its horns—

> "He has no horns, sir, has he?"
> "No, sir, he's a *pollard*."
> (Beaumont and Fletcher, *Philaster*, v. 4.)

Leverett is certified by the French surname *Levrault*. Derivation from *Lever*, Anglo-Sax. *Leofhere*, whence *Levers*, *Leverson*, or *Leveson*, is much less probable, as these Anglo-Saxon names rarely form dims. (see p. 76). *Luttrel* is in French *Loutrel*, perhaps a dim. of *loutre*, otter, Lat. *lutra*. From the medieval *lutrer* or *lutrarius*, otter hunter, we get *Lutterer*, no doubt confused with the musical *Luter*.

While *Katt* is fairly common in the eastern counties, Robertus *le chien* and Willelmus *le curre*, who were living about the end of the twelfth century, are now completely disguised as *Ken* and *Kerr*. Modern French has both *Lechien* and the Norman *Lequien*.[1] We owe a few other surnames to the friend of man. *Kennett*, from a Norman dim. of *chien*, meant greyhound—

> " *Kenette*, hounde, *leporarius*."
>
> (*Prompt. Parv.*)

The origin of the name *Talbot* is unknown, and it is uncertain whether the hound or the family should have precedence; but Chaucer seems to use it as the proper name of a hound—

> "Ran Colle our dogge, and *Talbot*, and Gerland
> And Malkyn, with a dystaf in hir hand."
>
> (B, 4573.)

The great Earl of Shrewsbury is affectionately called " Talbot, our good dogge " in political rhymes of the fifteenth century.

In early dictionaries may be found long lists of the fanciful names, such as Bright, Lightfoot, Ranger, Ringwood, Swift, Tempest, given to hounds. This practice seems to throw some light on such surnames as *Tempest*, with which we may compare the German names *Storm* and *Sturm*. In the Pipe Rolls the name *le esturmi*, the stormy, occurs several times. To the same class belongs *Thunder*, found in the Pipe Rolls as *tonitruus*, and not therefore necessarily a perversion of *Tunder*, i.e. *Sherman* (p. 170)—

[1] *Lekain*, the name of a famous French actor, has the same origin.

"*Tondeur de draps*, a *shearman*, or clothworker."
(Cotgrave.)

Garland, used by Chaucer as a dog's name, was earlier *graland*, and, as *le garlaunde* is also found, it may be referred to Old Fr. *grailler*, to trumpet. It is no doubt also local.

We should expect *Fox* to be strongly represented, and we find the compounds *Colfox* and *Stelfox*. The first means black fox—

"A *colfox* ful of sly iniquitee"
(B, 4405)—

and I conjecture that the first part of *Stelfox* is connected with stealing, as in the medieval name *stele-cat*—

"The two constables made a thorough search and found John *Stelfox* hiding behind some bushes. Some of the jewellery was found upon him" (*Daily Chronicle*, June 3, 1913).

In the north a fox is called *Tod*, whence *Todhunter*. This *Tod* is probably a personal name, like the French *Renard* and the Scottish *Lawrie* or *Lowrie*, applied to the same animal. Allan Ramsay calls him "slee Tod Lowrie." From the badger we have *Brock* and sometimes *Gray*—

"*Blaireau*, a badger, *gray*, boason, *brock*"
(Cotgrave)—

but *Badger* itself is occupative (p. 181). The polecat survives as *Fitch*, *Fitchett*, and *Fitchew*—

"*Fissau*, a *fitch*, or fulmart."
(Cotgrave.)

On fish-names Bardsley remarks, "We may quote the famous chapter on 'Snakes in Iceland': 'There are no snakes in Iceland,' and say there are no fish-names in England." This is almost true. The absence of marked traits of character in the, usually

16

invisible, fish would militate against the adoption of such names. We should not expect to find the shark to be represented, for the word is of too late occurrence. But *Whale* is fairly common. *Whale* the mariner received £2 from Henry VII.'s privy purse in 1498. The story of Jonah, or very generous proportions, may have originated the name *Whalebelly*, "borne by a respectable family in south-east England" (Bardsley).

But there would obviously be no great temptation to go fishing for nicknames when the beasts of the farm-yard and the forest, the birds of the marshes and the air, offered on every side easily understood comparisons. At the same time Bardsley's statement goes a little too far. He explains *Gudgeon* as a corruption of Goodison. But this, true though it may be in some cases, will not explain the very common French surname *Goujon*. The phrase "greedy gudgeon" suggests that in this case a certain amount of character had been noticed in the fish. *Sturgeon* also seems to be a genuine fish-name. We find Fr. *Lesturgeon* and Ger. *Stoer*, both meaning the same. We have also *Smelt* and the synonymous *Spurling*. In French and German we find other surnames which undoubtedly belong to this class, but they are not numerous and probably at first occurred only in regions where fishing or fish-curing were important industries.

A few examples will show that apparent fish-names are usually not genuine. *Chubb* is for Job (p. 32), *Eeles* is one of the numerous derivatives of Elias (p. 85), *Hake* is, like *Hack*, from the Scandinavian Haco, *Haddock* is a perversion of the local Haydock, *Lamprey* I take to be Fr. *long-pré*, long meadow. We find the halfway form in Fr. *Lompré*. *Pike* is local (p. 107), *Pilchard* is for *Pilcher* (p. 171), *Roach* is Fr. *Laroche, Salmon* is for Salomon, and *Turbot* is the Anglo-Sax. Thurbeorht, which has also given *Tarbut*, as Thurgod has given *Targett*. *Dolphin, Herring*, and *Spratt* or *Sprot* are old personal names possibly unconnected with the corresponding fish-names.

We have also many surnames due to physical resemblances not extending beyond one feature. *Birdseye* may be sometimes of local origin, from *ey*, island (p. 117), but as a genuine nickname it is as natural as the sobriquet of Hawkeye which Natty Bumppo received from the Hurons. German has the much less pleasing *Gansauge*, goose-eye; and Alan *oil de larrun*, thief's eye, was fined for very reprehensible conduct in 1183. To explain *Crowfoot* as an imitative variant of Crawford is absurd when we find a dozen German surnames of the same class and formation and as many in Old or Modern French beginning with *pied de*. Cf. *Pettigrew* (p. 201). We find in the Paris Directory not only *Piedeleu* (Old Fr. *leu*, wolf) and *Piedoie*, (*oie*, goose), but even the full *Pied-de-Lièvre*, Professeur à la Faculté de droit. The name *Bulleid* was spelt in the sixteenth century *bul-hed*, i.e. bull-head, a literal rendering of Front de Bœuf. *Weatherhead* (p. 179) is perhaps usually a nickname—

> "For that old *weather-headed* fool, I know how to laugh at him."
> (Congreve, *Love for Love*, ii. 7.)

Coxhead is another obvious nickname. A careful analysis of some of the most important medieval name-lists would furnish hundreds of further examples, some too outspoken to have survived into our degenerate age, and others which are now so corrupted that their original vigour is quite lost.

Puns and jokes upon proper names are, *pace* Gregory the Great and Shakespeare, usually very inept and stupid; but the following lines by James Smith, which may be new to some of my readers, are really clever—

Men once were surnamed from their shape or estate
(You all may from History worm it);
There was Lewis the Bulky, and Henry the Great,
John Lackland, and Peter the Hermit.
But now, when the door-plates of Misters and Dames
Are read, each so constantly varies
From the owner's trade, figure, and calling, Surnames
Seem given by the rule of contraries.

Mr. *Box*, though provoked, never doubles his fist,
Mr. *Burns*, in his grate, has no fuel;
Mr. *Playfair* won't catch me at hazard or whist,
Mr. *Coward* was wing'd in a duel.
Mr. *Wise* is a dunce, Mr. *King* is a whig,
Mr. *Coffin*'s uncommonly sprightly,
And huge Mr. *Little* broke down in a gig,
While driving fat Mrs. *Golightly*.

Mrs. *Drinkwater*'s apt to indulge in a dram,
Mrs. *Angel*'s an absolute fury,
And meek Mr. *Lyon* let fierce Mr. *Lamb*
Tweak his nose in the lobby of Drury.
At Bath, where the feeble go more than the stout,
(A conduct well worthy of Nero),
Over poor Mr. *Lightfoot*, confined with the gout,
Mr. *Heaviside* danced a Bolero.

Miss *Joy*, wretched maid, when she chose Mr. *Love*,
Found nothing but sorrow await her;
She now holds in wedlock, as true as a dove,
That fondest of mates, Mr. *Hayter*.
Mr. *Oldcastle* dwells in a modern-built hut,
Miss *Sage* is of madcaps the archest;
Of all the queer bachelors Cupid e'er cut,
Old Mr. *Younghusband*'s the starchest.

Mr. *Child*, in a passion, knock'd down Mr. *Rock*,
Mr. *Stone* like an aspen-leaf shivers ;
Miss *Poole* used to dance, but she stands like a stock
Ever since she became Mrs. *Rivers* ;
Mr. *Swift* hobbles onward, no mortal knows how,
He moves as though cords had entwin'd him ;
Mr. *Metcalfe* ran off, upon meeting a cow,
With pale Mr. *Turnbull* behind him.

Mr. *Barker*'s as mute as a fish in the sea,
Mr. *Miles* never moves on a journey ;
Mr. *Gotobed* sits up till half-after three,
Mr. *Makepeace* was bred an attorney.
Mr. *Gardiner* can't tell a flower from a root,
Mr. *Wilde* with timidity draws back,
Mr. *Ryder* performs all his journeys on foot,
Mr. *Foote* all his journeys on horseback.

Mr. *Penny*, whose father was rolling in wealth,
Kick'd down all his fortune his dad won ;
Large Mr. *Le Fever*'s the picture of health,
Mr. *Goodenough* is but a bad one.
Mr. *Cruickshank* stept into three thousand a year,
By showing his leg to an heiress :—
Now I hope you'll acknowledge I've made it quite clear
That surnames ever go by contraries.

INDEX

N.B.—Most surnames have more than one form, many have over a score, and some have over a hundred. This index, consisting of about 3,500 names, will contain twice or thrice as many for the reader who has mastered Ch. III, on sound and spelling. It includes only names still in use.

Printed by Hazell, Watson & Viney, Ld., London and Aylesbury.

Popular Editions

Each **2/6** *net.*

ROUND THE HORN BEFORE THE MAST. An Account of a Voyage from San Francisco round Cape Horn to Liverpool in a Fourmasted "Windjammer," with experiences of the life of an Ordinary Seaman. By BASIL LUBBOCK. With Illustrations.

LETTERS FROM HIGH LATITUDES. Being some Account of a Voyage in 1856, in the Schooner Yacht *Foam*, to Iceland, Jan Meyen, and Spitzbergen. By the late MARQUESS OF DUFFERIN. With Portrait and Illustrations.

FIELD PATHS and GREEN LANES in SURREY AND SUSSEX. By LOUIS J. JENNINGS. Illustrated.

THE LION HUNTER OF SOUTH AFRICA. Five Years' Adventure in the Far Interior of South Africa. With Notices of the Native Tribes and Savages. By R. GORDON CUMMING. With 16 Woodcuts.

DOG BREAKING. The most Expeditious, Certain, and Easy Method. With Odds and Ends for those who love the Dog and Gun. By General W. N. HUTCHINSON. With numerous Illustrations.

THE ROB ROY ON THE JORDAN. A Canoe Cruise in Palestine, Egypt, and the Waters of Damascus. By JOHN MACGREGOR, M.A., Captain of the Royal Canoe Club. With Maps and Illustrations.

A HISTORY OF THE SIEGE OF GIBRALTAR, 1779-1783. With a Description and Account of that Garrison from the Earliest Times. By JOHN DRINKWATER, Captain in the Seventy-second Regiment of Royal Manchester Volunteers. With Plans.

THE LIFE OF JOHN NICHOLSON, Soldier and Administrator. By Captain LIONEL J. TROTTER. With Portrait and 3 Maps.

A SMALLER DICTIONARY OF THE BIBLE. By Sir WILLIAM SMITH. With Maps and Illustrations.

A POPULAR HISTORY OF THE CHURCH OF ENGLAND. From the Earliest Times to the Present Day. By WILLIAM BOYD CARPENTER, Bishop of Ripon, Hon. D.C.L., Oxon. With 16 Illustrations.

MORRIS AUTOMATED INFORMATION NETWORK
0 1022 0041029 2